PATIENT POWER

SARAH HARVEY and IAN WYLIE

PATIENT POWER

GETTING THE BEST FROM YOUR HEALTH CARE

SIMON & SCHUSTER
A VIACOM COMPANY

First published in Great Britain by Simon & Schuster UK Ltd, 1999
A Viacom Company

1 3 5 7 9 10 8 6 4 2

Simon & Schuster UK Ltd
Africa House
64–78 Kingsway
London WC2B 6AH

Simon & Schuster Australia
Sydney

A CIP catalogue record for this book is available from the British Library

ISBN 0–684–84026–X

Typeset by Palimpsest Book Production Limited
Polmont, Stirlingshire

Printed and bound in Great Britain by
Butler & Tanner Ltd, Frome and London

To Siân Griffiths, with love and with thanks;
and to the memory of Anne Harvey,
who asked, 'Why hasn't it been done before?'

Acknowledgements

To the US People's Medical Society, particularly Lowell Leven and Charles Inland, who set out to provide the consumer's equivalent to the American Medical Association, for providing the inspiration for snowballing a consumer health movement in the UK. To the Patient's Association, the NHS Executive, and the many voluntary health organisations in the UK whose excellent publications have helped us. To David Gilbert, Mark Duman, the librarians and other staff at the King's Fund for guidance and information. To Dr John Reynolds and his medical colleagues at the John Radcliffe Hospital in Oxford, and to Dr Andy Chivers for specialist advice on the early chapters. Mary O'Leary and Judy Granville for advice on patient complaints and for providing a model of excellence. To John Harvey and Laurie McMahon, both of whom provided helpful comments and moral support. To Siân Griffiths for reading the rough drafts and providing invaluable information, advice and assistance. To our friends and families whose experiences of the health system, both good and bad, have showed so clearly why *PatientPower* is needed.

CONTENTS

INTRODUCTION

The purpose of this book is to put you in control of the most important things in your life – your health and health care.

In the UK we have had a National Health Service (NHS) for over 50 years. It was set up to take the worry out of paying for health care by providing it free for everyone who needed it. The NHS is not, however, a charity. It is paid through national insurance and taxes. And since it currently costs about £40 billion, that's nearly £1000 for everyone in the country every year.

The NHS tries to live up to its name. It is a 'National' service because it provides for everyone and you should be able to get it wherever you live. 'Health' means that it is there to look after your health, not just your sickness. 'Service' means that it is provided as a benefit to which everyone has a right. Service also means it is there to serve your needs.

The people who work in the NHS are paid by everyone who has paid for the NHS. Thus if you use the NHS, you will be treated by professional people who have chosen to work in a service *for which you have paid*. That gives each one of us a right to expect that our health care needs will be met and a right to make our views known about the care we get. Getting the best health care means health care professionals who treat you as an individual, with respect, dignity and with care. But it also means that the people who use the service use it properly – as expertly as they are treated.

To get the best from your health care you need to know what to expect; you need to know how to help the health service provide you with the best possible care; and you need to know how to respond if the health service fails you in any way. If you think you are already getting the best care possible try asking yourself some of these questions:

- when your GP listens to your chest do you know why?

- is it common for doctors to examine you without telling you their name?

- how experienced is the hospital doctor who appears at your bedside? How can you be sure that you will be operated on by a surgeon with sufficient experience?

- would you know what an angioplasty and CXR were if you read them on your notes?

- who owns your medical notes and what rights do you have to see them?

- when you go to an outpatient clinic do you know what to ask?

- if the doctor did nothing for a health problem, do you know what could happen?

- how do you make a complaint if you are not satisfied?

- do you know what type of home care you can get after hospital treatment?

- how can you prepare yourself for the death of someone who is close to you?

These questions are all basic to the care that you, your family and friends will receive. The chances are you will not have thought much about them, nor will you know the answers to them.

However confident we may be, when the time comes to make use of the health services, most of us feel that we know nothing at all. At a time of stress and anxiety, we are only too willing to be led blindly, without any clear idea of what is happening to us, unable or too scared to find out. We are confused about what services we have a right to; how much choice we have; what our rights are; what standards we can expect; what we might be charged for in our 'free' NHS; what we should do if things don't go as we had hoped; who is responsible for the service; and to whom we can turn for information. We get confused by media reports about treatments being rationed even though it is known they work, while treatments which don't work are still being carried out.

PatientPower provides the answer to these and many other questions. It is the book that you should take with you whenever dealing with the health service – from local family doctors and health centres, to the latest high-technology hospitals with lasers, scanners and famous medical experts. *PatientPower* takes the patient's perspective and guides you, step-by-step through the maze of health services available, from how to register with a GP, how to understand what tests are being done, how to understand medical jargon, to how to ask a top specialist about a particular course of treatment. It is a comprehensive guide to the whole health care system, from care in your home, to complementary medicine, hospital care and the private health sector. It aims to ensure that your experience of the health service is as positive and beneficial as possible. That is the end to which everyone, the doctors, nurses, patients and relatives, should aim.

A ROUTE MAP THROUGH THIS BOOK

PatientPower aims to provide a simple, straightforward, authoritative and accessible guide to health care, from the patient's point of view. For easy reference the book is divided into four parts:

I   A guide to health services
II   The body in question – a guide to medical services, specialists and tests
III   Great expectations – an explanation of standards and complaints
IV   A self-help section

Part I takes you step-by-step through the NHS, from the viewpoint of someone who needs to use the service, rather than someone who just wants to learn about it. The first chapter gives you an overview of the NHS – what it is and how it runs. The next chapter takes you through family health services, from choosing a GP to getting referred to a specialist. Chapter three tells you all you need to know about going to outpatients, and chapter four tells you about staying in hospital. Chapter five is about care and services in the community, including your own home. Chapter six looks at services for long-term health problems, known as chronic health problems, and chapter seven tackles the important area of the care of people who are dying, called terminal care or palliative care.

Part II, beginning at chapter eight, is a guide to the medical specialties and which parts of the body they deal with. Chapter nine debunks medical jargon by explaining the common terms and abbreviations used in the medical world. Chapter ten explains the common tests that are performed to investigate problems.

Part III deals with your rights as a citizen. Chapter eleven explains your rights and responsibilities as a citizen, and what standards you should expect from the NHS. Chapter twelve explains the complaints system and what you should do if you feel you are not getting proper care.

Part IV is the self-help section. Taking control of your own health and health care is the topic of chapter thirteen, while chapter fourteen looks at the growing importance of complementary (or alternative) health care. Chapter fifteen helps you to think about whether to use private health care. Chapter sixteen shows both how to record your care and write letters to professional staff. In addition, there is an Appendix listing useful contacts and addresses for further help, and a Glossary of terms commonly used in the health service.

We hope that this book gives you some of the tools you need to develop your own *PatientPower*. It could be the start of a movement!

Sarah Harvey

Ian Wylie

1999

PART I

YOUR GUIDE TO HEALTH SERVICES

CHAPTER 1: AN OVERVIEW OF THE NATIONAL HEALTH SERVICE

The NHS has been changed by every government in its 50-year history. Although subject to numerous re-organisations the NHS remains, in many aspects, the same as when it was set up. This chapter gives a basic explanation of how the NHS works for those who use it and describes the main ways in which health care is provided, before ending with a brief look at the latest health care changes.

Where the NHS came from

The NHS was born on 5 July 1948. From that moment onwards, people throughout the country could receive health care according to need, irrespective of the ability to pay. Centuries of concern about whether a visit to the doctor could be paid for, or the medicines needed could be afforded, became a thing of the past.

With the dawn of 5 July, what the architect of the NHS, Minister of Health, Aneurin (sometimes called Nye) Bevan called 'the biggest social experiment the world has ever seen' had begun. Care, 'from cradle to grave', became available to everyone, and the British health service the envy of the world. Today, more than 50 years later, the NHS is this country's most valued institution, and in spite of the number of changes to the way it is organised, the founding values of the NHS, of welfare, equity and social justice, remain principles which have withstood the pressures of half a century of changing Britain.

The idea of providing free and universal health care came about during the Second World War, the consequence of a desire to build a better Britain. In 1942 William Beveridge published a report which set out measures to tackle what its author called the scourge of the 'Five Giants': want, idleness, ignorance, disease and squalor. The Report proposed that universal health care should be established, allowing care to be administered to whoever was in need, irrespective of wealth, age, gender or race.

How it's paid for

The NHS may be free when you use it, but that does not mean that you do not pay for it. Everyone in work pays a contribution towards their health care through taxes. The money to run the NHS is agreed by the government and it is up to civil servants, NHS managers and senior clinicians (doctors and nurses) to ensure that the NHS spends it effectively. This means trying to provide as much good quality care as possible without overspending the budget. And the budget is huge: it costs over £100 million a day – £1000 a second – to run the health service.

Responsibility for the NHS

Not surprisingly, given the size of its budget, the NHS is one of the biggest and most complex organisations in the world, employing over a million people in tens of thousands of clinics, health centres, hospitals and homes. Despite this, the way it operates remains relatively simple. The NHS is a public body, a part of the state, and is answerable to parliament through a cabinet minister, the Secretary of State for Health. Day-to-day responsibility for running the NHS is taken by civil servants in the Department of Health and the NHS Executive, and health service managers. There is a chain of responsibility back to the Secretary of State and so to parliament. This is why, if there is a problem in the NHS anywhere in the country, MPs may bring the issue to the floor of the House of Commons, for it is to parliament that everyone who works in the NHS is ultimately accountable. Aneurin Bevan explained the system by saying that if a bedpan was dropped in an NHS hospital, the echo should resound in the corridors of Westminster.

Who runs the NHS?

The organisation of the NHS and its various parts can be confusing even to those who work in it. Here is a brief summary of the main elements.

- In charge of the NHS as a whole is the NHS Executive which is based in Leeds. It is part of the Department of Health. The NHS Executive has eight regional offices, which broadly cover the same geographical areas as the Regional Development Agencies.

- There are around 90 health authorities in England and Wales, each of which spends some half a billion pounds every year on the health care of around half a million people. The health authorities are held accountable for their work by the Regional Office of the NHS Executive which covers their area.

- Health authorities are run by senior NHS managers and doctors. Their job is to make sure that the health services in their areas (which might be a county, a town, or part of a major city) are meeting the health needs of local people. To do this they analyse the health and health care needs of the people who live within their areas and make plans for using the money that they have been allocated by the NHS Executive to meet those needs. When you hear about 'rationing' in the NHS it will normally be about the difficult decisions health authorities face in stretching their funds across all the competing demands for care – from people with Alzheimer's disease to premature babies to prevention of drug abuse.

- Health needs across the country vary. Some health authorities will need to provide more of one service than others. But across the country, the *standard* of a particular service and how easy it is for you to get it if you need it should be equal. Well, that's the theory and the aim that this government has set itself. In reality standards and services vary widely in today's NHS. Later in this book we will look at what to do if you feel you are getting a bad deal from the health service because of where you live.

- When a health authority has planned how it will spend its budget it makes a service agreement with the hospitals and community health services provided by NHS trusts (see below). The agreements state how much of what care will be provided at what price and to what standard. The agreements are meant to cover three years but will be altered slightly from one year to the next. Health authorities can also make agreements for services provided by voluntary organisations or the private sector.

- NHS trusts are the bodies that provide health care services. They vary in the type of services they provide – some just provide acute hospital care or mental health services, whereas others provide the full spectrum of care from hospitals to community health services. NHS trusts can enter into service agreements with their local health authority or others that serve populations further away. Great Ormond Street Hospital, for example, which runs specialist services for sick children, has service agreements with health authorities across the country. But a trust providing local community health care may only have one or two service agreements.

- The other significant players in the health care system are general practitioners (GPs). Increasingly, they will play a more central part in planning health care. All GPs are members of primary care groups. These groups will advise the health authority on what type of service agreements they need to make, but will gradually take on some of the health authorities' work themselves. GPs are independent of the NHS but they have a contract with a health authority to provide primary health care.

- Social services provide important services to people in their own homes such as day care or 'meals on wheels' as well as residential care and hostels. But social services are not formally part of the NHS – they are run by local authorities.

So that is the structure of the NHS. Another way of understanding how it works is to look at how patients experience the NHS from the point at which they first use it through to using more specialist care.

GPs and primary care

Although the NHS has been restructured quite a bit the point of entry to health care has remained remarkably constant – the vast majority of people begin their use of the NHS through their family doctor, or general medical practitioner, usually known as their GP. This is primary care, so called because it is the first level of the NHS. Almost everyone in the country is registered with a GP. The GP and the people who make up the primary care team, such as nurses, midwives, health visitors, receptionists, are thus the first people for any issue that needs attention, either at the surgery or health centre or at your home. They also offer preventive health care, such as immunizations. There are about 40,000 GPs in Britain and everyone who is entitled to NHS care can register with a GP.

Most times – 19 in every 20 visits to the surgery – that is the end of the story. Someone in the primary care team treats you and writes up what he or she has done in your records, or, more commonly now, enters the information on your notes which are kept on the surgery's computer. Sometimes the GP will want to find out more about your health by getting some tests done. For this, the GP, or the nurse, may take samples of blood, urine or faeces, which will be sent to a laboratory at the local hospital to be tested. These results should be ready very quickly, and the computer in the surgery may even be linked to the hospital so the results can be entered into your patient records directly. Sometimes you might have to go to the hospital for a test where they need you there in person, such as for X-rays, or mammograms (breast screening), or to put a scope inside you. Each time the results of the test will go back to your GP. Chapter ten looks at all the different tests you might have. Because all care in the NHS is designed to begin and end with the GP – the carer from 'cradle to grave' – the GP should always be your point of reference for NHS care. If you ever get lost in the system, your GP is the person to turn to, which is why it is really important to choose someone who you can trust and can talk to. Chapter two explains how to go about choosing a GP.

Secondary care

If you have an illness which needs more investigation, or a medical condition that requires greater care or expertise than your GP can give, you will be sent ('referred' is the term doctors use) to a specialist doctor (a consultant) either in hospital or in the community. Because this is the second stage of care it is called secondary care. (Confusingly, secondary care may be your first point of contact with the NHS if you have a major accident and end up being taken to casualty.)

There is a vast range of secondary-care consultants. Chapter eight gives you a guide to their names and the parts of the body in which they specialise. Increasingly they are working from places other than hospitals. Some specialists have begun to hold outpatient clinics in health centres or surgeries to make it easier for people to get there rather than travelling to hospital. Chapter three is all about outpatient care.

Ten years ago it was common for patients all to be told to turn up in the outpatient clinic at the same time. The consultant (the most senior doctor in a specialty) then worked through the outpatient list, seeing one patient after another. That was when the clinic was run for the consultant's convenience, an attitude which, fortunately, is fast disappearing. Now there is more chance of being seen within an hour of your appointment time, and you may even be given a choice of appointments convenient to you!

Getting a referral The system is basically the same for all secondary referrals. Your GP is referring you to a specialist to 'consult' them for their opinion on your problem and a solution. The GP writes a letter requesting that you are seen and after being seen the consultant writes back to the GP. The letters are professional and personal and normally you will not see them, although you do have a right to do so, as we explain in chapter eleven. Depending on what the specialist has written, you will see your GP again and should get a chance to discuss with them the next stage of treatment. This can take various forms. The specialist may have advised your GP how to treat you and will not need to see you again. You may need another outpatient appointment with the consultant or one of the consultant's team of doctors. This may be a regular appointment every few weeks or months for treatment or check-ups or a one-off follow-up. Alternatively, the consultant may decide to admit you for some treatment in the hospital. If your treatment is not an emergency then you may have to wait and your name will be put on the waiting list.

Staying in hospital If you are going to be treated in the hospital you will move from being an 'outpatient' to being an 'inpatient'. You are 'admitted' to a hospital bed, and are 'under the care' of a particular specialist consultant doctor. Doctors work in teams (they call them 'firms') headed by one or two consultants, so most of the time you will see a more junior doctor – chapter eight provides a guide to the different grades of doctor. In the past, consultants would have responsibility for all patients in a ward or several wards of beds. However, as more and more health care now takes place outside hospitals and can be done faster, fewer beds are needed – this means that several consultants may be responsible for patients in any one ward.

Waiting times You may have to wait for a long time for your name to get to the top of the waiting list, although there is more and more pressure on the health service to reduce the time you will have to wait for an outpatient appointment or inpatient treatment. If you have something which needs urgent treatment the consultant will make arrangements to admit you immediately, if necessary. The number of people who are admitted for urgent or emergency treatment has been rising over the last few years, which means that those who need less urgent treatment have to wait longer. This is the subject of chapter four.

Community care

After a period in hospital, you will be 'discharged' to your home. Some parts of the country offer hospital 'hotels' – places midway between hospital and home – to people who still need constant nursing care but who may not need the full intensity of medical back-up that the main hospital provides. This is particularly useful if you are recovering from surgery, or a period of serious illness. If you go home, the hospital or your GP may arrange for you to be visited by some professional 'community' staff, for example a district nurse. You may also be offered help from social services, a home help for example. No one should be discharged from a hospital bed without arrangements having been made for follow-up care. It is not uncommon for people to be well enough to leave hospital but unable to go home either because it takes time to arrange the intensive home care support they need, or because they do not want to leave the hospital. In these situations the patient may be kept in hospital for some time until arrangements can be made. Rather unfairly such people are often referred to as 'bed blockers' by health service staff. Chapter five looks at community care, the care you receive after you leave hospital or if you have a condition that can be treated at home. It also provides advice for people looking after relatives at home.

Nowadays, the NHS likes to get you in and out of hospital as quickly as possible. One reason is that a lot of surgery has got much better with new techniques such as 'key-hole' or micro-surgery, which means the doctors can operate without causing a large wound. Secondly, it is often better for patients to get up and about, rather than lie in hospital beds for days on end, as it reduces the risk of infections, bed sores and blood clots, which can be fatal. Thirdly, it is cheaper! It costs the NHS several hundred pounds a day to keep someone in hospital, so the quicker they can get you out and someone else in, the more efficient they will be. The fastest form of inpatient treatment now happens in a day, and hospitals have special day wards to deal with day case patients who are admitted in the morning, operated on and are ready to go home in the evening.

After any treatment by a specialist, your GP should be told by letter or by phone, by the doctor who has treated you, what has happened and what needs to happen next. At the very least, your GP should know how you have been treated by the time he or she next sees you at the surgery, which is often a follow-up appointment to your hospital care. Hospital medical records and the records kept by your GP remain separate, although as new computers are introduced into the health service, it will be possible to hold your entire medical history on a computer file or even record it on a smart card (a plastic card that will record information electronically) that you carry around with you. The importance of your medical history is that it gives the person who is treating you the best possible idea of what your health is like, how you have been treated in the past, and how best to proceed in the future.

Tertiary care

In some cases the specialist doctor will want to send you on to another specialist. This could happen if you have a rare medical problem that only a few people understand, or where you need particular treatment that is not available locally. This is called a tertiary referral, and the doctor will normally need to get permission to do this because of the potential costs to the health service that could be involved. For example, a referral to a specialist with a new technique or drug could cost several hundred thousand pounds for one patient. Health authorities have a limited budget to get health care for all the population, and if they spend a large sum on one individual, they won't have the money to spend on others. When the money runs out, doctors are stopped from treating people, waiting lists rise, hospital beds close and the media start to talk about crisis in the health service again. New arrangements for organising cancer care make it increasingly likely that patients will have to travel from local cancer units to more specialist tertiary cancer centres. The reason for this is not to make it more inconvenient. It is to ensure that the hospitals, doctors and nurses dealing with the most complex cases and symptoms are those who have the most experience and who therefore have the best track record in treating patients successfully.

Long-term care

Most of what has been described so far concerns 'acute' health services. By acute, we mean a period of illness, from a mild problem like a cold or sore throat, to a serious life-threatening illness such as a car accident or heart attack. Acute care also covers natural events in life which need health care but which are not illnesses, like pregnancy and child birth, family planning services, health checks, plastic surgery and services for the dying. The NHS also caters for people with long-term health problems which can only be improved or managed by health care, not cured. Some of these are long-term disabilities, either physical or mental conditions which are caused by a genetic abnormality, such as cystic fibrosis or rheumatoid arthritis. There are also other disabilities which may have been caused by an accident or an event is someone's life (for example cerebral palsy). There are a range of health problems which can come about at any stage of life (such as diabetes, asthma, depression or schizophrenia). There are also degenerative conditions such as AIDS, multiple sclerosis and some forms of cancer. These health problems are frequently called 'chronic' conditions to distinguish them from 'acute' short-term health issues. Often they need managing rather than treating. This will involve the patient, carers, GP and specialist over many years to keep the individual's health as good as possible, particularly for those conditions for which there is no known cure.

The health service treats chronic conditions, providing long-term care with drugs, professional carers, and long-term inpatient care, if necessary. A generation ago, many people with severe long-term physical or mental disabilities were shut away in large institutions, where they often had little opportunity to develop and lead fulfilling lives. Now, even people with severe disability are given support so they can play a full part in the community. Caring for people with long-term conditions is tackled in chapter six. Chapter seven covers care for those who are terminally ill and require specialist nursing and palliative care.

How your health service is changing

Every government that comes into power tinkers with the NHS, and calls it 'reform'. Some governments are more 'pro' the health service than others. It is said that Mrs Thatcher as prime minister would have got rid of it if she had dared; whilst the Labour party regards the NHS as their own great creation of 1948. In reality all governments throughout the history of the NHS have supported it and have increased public spending on it year-on-year. And all governments have claimed their reforms were concerned with preserving the best of the NHS while getting rid of inefficiency and bureaucracy.

It is possible this section will be out of date not long after this book is published but at the time of writing these are some of the changes that you can expect to see in your health care over the coming years:

- If your GP is a fundholder they will cease to be one as from April 1999. Instead they will be a member of a primary care group (see page 11). As a patient you should not notice the difference.

- The government has abolished the 'internal market' in health care which was introduced by the previous administration. Again as a patient you will probably notice little difference. However, hospitals and community services are now expected to work together more closely rather than try to compete with each other. In time this should improve co-ordination in the care that people get as they go into and out of hospital.

- Each primary care group will bring together about 50 GPs providing and planning health services for their local practice population of about 100,000 local people. It is too soon to tell what effect this will have on patient care.

- There is to be more central regulation of the standards of health care to ensure both greater consistency throughout the country, and that care is effective and produces good outcomes. Very public failings in the quality of care, such as in screening services and in the Bristol children's hospital scandal have strengthened the government's willingness to regulate services.

- More information will be released to the public to help them decide which hospital and which procedure is best for them. These will include guidelines on clinical effectiveness (what types of care do or do not work), league tables on hospital performance, including waiting times, and outcomes for different procedures.

- Apart from these organisational changes the trends in the way that health care is provided that we have seen to date look set to continue. We will get more and more of our care outside of hospital or will go there just for a day. Developments in information and communications technology will mean that we can be 'examined' by specialists in another building or another part of the country (tele-medicine). Less invasive surgical techniques mean that we will recover more quickly after surgery with less scarring. New drugs will be more commonly available to tackle some of the more long-standing problems in health care (for example obesity and Alzheimer's disease). And the growing industry in the health service of analysing what is or is not effective may mean some very common treatments such as dilatation and curettage for women with very heavy periods may become things of the past. As important as all this, is the fact that the health service will be increasingly interested in your opinions and ideas. *PatientPower* is about using that opportunity.

CHAPTER 2: PRIMARY CARE

This chapter aims to help you think through 'What makes a good GP?' and 'How can I get one?' It gives you a guide to the other health care professionals in the primary care team and how you can make best use of their skills. In the NHS, primary care is an everyday term – but many members of the public have no idea what it means. In a recent survey the favourite answer to the question 'What is primary care?' was that it was something do with school nurses. 'Primary care' is essentially the first point of contact that most people have with the health care system. Primary care is provided by general practitioners (GPs – or family doctors) and other health care workers such as nurses and health visitors who work closely with GPs. Together these professionals are known as the primary care team.

What is primary care?

There is no standard answer to this question – a lot of energy has been wasted in the health service trying to come up with an acceptable definition. Basically, primary care is the care that is provided by a primary care team and the members of that team may vary from one place to the next.

A primary care team may be all or some of the following:

- general practitioners
- district nurses
- practice nurses
- health visitors
- midwives
- physiotherapists
- dietitians
- speech and language therapists
- podiatrists/chiropodists
- counsellors
- social workers
- receptionists
- practice managers
- occupational therapists
- psychiatric nurses
- psychologists

Few other countries have a primary care system such as ours. Visiting a GP for minor health problems – an expert in making an initial diagnosis or assessing what further tests or treatment may be necessary – is something that we now take for granted. But in France and the United States, for example, this service is virtually non-existent. In these places accessing health care means thinking – or guessing – for yourself what may be wrong and selecting an appropriate specialist in that part of the body or particular condition. Not very satisfactory.

For most people a GP will be the only health care professional they see from one year to the next. The chances are that you have consulted your GP for only minor problems. But having a good or a poor GP can be a matter of life or death, as they can make the difference between early detection of a serious condition and a slow or inaccurate diagnosis which delays treatment until it is too late. Whatever your needs it is important that you find a GP you can trust – someone with whom you feel comfortable; someone in whose professional skills and judgment you have confidence. This all sounds obvious, yet it is surprising how many people who would never put up with indifferent service from the mechanic mending their car will grumble for years about their local GP without taking any action. Who you decide to be your GP is your choice and you have the right to change your GP without giving a reason.

Some facts about GPs

If you want to understand the way a GP thinks and works these basic facts should give you a clue:

GPs are not employed directly by the NHS They are independent contractors and each GP has a contract with the local health authority to provide core primary care services. The contract means they are responsible for providing that care all year round, 24 hours a day. So even when they are sick or on holiday GPs have a responsibility to provide continuous care to their patients. (They handle this in a number of ways which we will discuss later.) A big plus in being independent operators is that they have freedom to determine their own working conditions and hours.

GPs are not paid a salary Their income is made up from a mix of fees for each small item of service (such as contraceptive advice or an immunization) and capitation payments – that is, a standard amount paid for each patient they have on their list.

GPs do not pay all the expenses of running a surgery They get some money towards this from the health authority and towards the salaries of any staff they employ in the practice (such as receptionists and practice nurses).

GPs tend to work in practices in which there are two or more GPs These practices are run as a partnership. Larger practices have the advantage of being more economic units which can pool their money to buy equipment, improve the building or develop new areas of work. To enter into a partnership a GP will usually have to put in quite a bit of money. GPs see their partnership as something that is long term. Sometimes practices split up.

There are no limits on the number of prescriptions that a GP can issue More recently GPs have been encouraged to try to keep prescription costs under control so that NHS money can be used effectively.

GPs cannot prescribe any drug they want to The NHS has a list of approved drugs which can be used and is trying to encourage the use of generally available drugs rather than those produced by just one pharmaceutical company under a brand name. It's a bit like the difference between aspirin bought from your local chemist or supermarket (the generic drug) and the popular brands of painkillers that are widely advertised. The generic drugs tend to be much cheaper and generally as effective as the branded products.

What all this means is that there is an incentive for GPs to *a)* have as many people on their list as possible, particularly healthy ones, and *b)* to do as many procedures as possible for which they can claim fees. For a GP time is in effect money. The extra five minutes they spend in a consultation with you certainly means less time to see the other patients who are waiting, but may also mean less opportunity to earn from items of service they could be providing to those other people.

Who is eligible for primary care?

Everyone who is resident in this country has the right to be registered with a GP and to receive free care from the primary care team. Increasing efforts are being made to provide access to family doctor services to people who are homeless, to refugees and to those who do not tend to register with a GP. In some parts of the country there are specially designed primary care services for people who do not have a permanent address.

A growing trend is the establishment of 'drop-in' primary care services, which are run from several major railway stations and other public places. These are privately run services which, unlike your local GP, will charge a fee per consultation (around £35 for a basic consultation, more for individual treatments). Some people find that these services offer speedy access to health care close to their place of work rather than home, without the need to book an appointment days in advance and at a time which is more convenient than the clinic times offered by their family doctor. On the down side they will not have your personal health records and will be led by the information that you give them in the consultation.

Choosing your GP – what makes a good general practitioner?

What makes a good GP? How do you find the one that's right for you? Not easy questions to answer. To a large extent it is a matter of personal choice – someone who makes you feel comfortable that you are getting good treatment and advice. Primary health care is very much about individual relationships and trust. However, the main problem is that it is difficult to decide whether you are comfortable with a doctor until you have seen one a couple of times. So before you leap to change your GP or if you have recently moved and need to register with a local practice, here are some tips on things to ask or look out for in your search for a 'good' GP.

- Ask your neighbours and friends about their experiences of local doctors, bearing in mind that most will say their doctor is good so you may need to be more searching in your questions – for example, How difficult is it to get an appointment? What is the GP like if you phone in an emergency outside the surgery's opening hours? What are the other GPs in the practice like? Have they seen any other members of the primary care team, for example the practice nurse? Do they give you enough time to discuss your problems?

- Pay a visit to the surgery and take a look at the waiting room. Is it full of happy patients or disgruntled people who have waited for far longer than they anticipated? How do the reception staff deal with people? Are they courteous and understanding or harassed and rude?

- Ask about the range of services that are provided in the practice – the larger clinics and health centres may provide services as diverse as chiropody (podiatry), dietetics, pain management, speech and language therapy, hearing tests, child health and counselling. Some may conduct minor surgery, such as the removal of warts. Larger health centres may arrange to have consultants from the local hospital run outpatients clinics on site. This is not to say that smaller practices give poor service – many are excellent. It is simply a matter of choice. Some people would like as much as possible to be offered under one roof, others may feel that they are unlikely to use more than the basic consultation with a GP or are happy to travel somewhere else for other health care services.

- Ask to see the practice's information leaflet or practice charter. All practices have to produce an annual report on their work and plans. The larger ones may publish their report so that they can keep their patients informed.

- Larger practices may have a patient participation or liaison group. Attending a meeting or asking to see the minutes might give you a feel for the type of issues of concern to existing patients.

- Check out whether the GPs have any specialist interests which might be relevant to your needs and whether there are any services which they do not offer. Some GPs choose not to provide contraceptive advice or child health surveillance, whilst others develop specialist interests which often reflect the make-up of the local population. The practice leaflet should tell you this. Alternatively the local health authority's list of GP practices should record specialist areas.

There will also be more specific things that you require from a doctor, depending on your health and family circumstances. Here are some examples to consider:

- Are the GPs willing to talk to patients on the phone (an increasing number will offer general advice or opinions about care or whether you need to see a doctor face-to-face)?

- Is the practice accessible to disabled people?

- Are there surgeries at weekends, evenings or early mornings which might fit in with your own work schedule or domestic arrangements?

- How long do patients have to wait to get an appointment for non-urgent matters?

- Will the GPs visit patients in their own homes?

- Do the GPs offer care for women in pregnancy (not all GPs are willing or able to do so)?

- What is the practice's policy on home births – do they actively support them?

- Does the practice dispense medicines itself, in other words can you collect medicines from the surgery without the need to go to a chemist? This may be important if you find travelling difficult. Practices in rural areas are more likely to do this than those in towns and cities.

- What other primary care professionals can you see at the practice premises?

- Does the practice run special clinics, for example for people with diabetes or asthma?

If you are lucky you may be able to arrange a pre-registration interview with the doctor with whom you are thinking of registering. If you do get an opportunity to meet him or her here are some further points to consider:

- Are you at ease with the doctor's appearance, manner and way of speaking? Trust your intuition here!

- Does the doctor understand and appreciate your religious and cultural background – if this is important to you?

- Would you be comfortable talking to the doctor about embarrassing topics such as incontinence or contraception?

- How would the doctor feel if you wanted to take a family member with you when you see him/her?

- Would you find the doctor's views on moral, ethical or medical issues a problem? Does he/she have strong views on the subject of abortion which might cause you difficulties?

There are also some things which are not a very good guide to the quality of a GP:

- Don't be overly swayed by the appearance of the building or waiting room – many GP premises are not as well maintained as we would like. A poor building does not necessarily mean a bad doctor. Equally, brand new premises may be no indication that the GP is the right one for you.

- Some doctors work as single-handed practitioners, but most work with at least one other GP. Working as a single-handed doctor does not necessarily make for poor doctoring. Many GPs go into the profession precisely because they can choose to work more independently. But it will mean that you are less likely to be able to see the wider group of primary care professionals in your GP's surgery – you may have to travel to a larger clinic or health centre.

Getting registered

Getting registered with a GP should be a relatively easy exercise, as simple as finding a GP and asking to be put on their list. Just a matter of minutes. But if you have not yet found your GP where do you start? The simplest thing to do is to look for general practices close to where you live and then do your own investigations as to which is best for you (see above). To help you do this you can get a list of GPs who are local to you from your local health authority or the community health council. Libraries and citizens advice bureaux may keep this information.

In some areas you will have a choice of several practices. In more rural areas, there may only be one practice convenient to where you live, although it is more common for these to be larger practices so you may have a choice of several doctors within the practice. Most GP practices will accept only those patients living within a defined geographical area – their catchment. The boundaries tend to be used as a guide rather than hard and fast rules, so it is worth some gentle questioning or pleading if you are told that you live slightly outside the limits. Try bending the ear of the practice manager or write a letter to the GP in question.

As a last resort, if you have tried to register with a couple of GPs and been rejected or if you have been thrown off a GP's list, write to the health authority which covers the area in which you live and ask them to arrange a registration. You will find a sample letter that you can use in chapter fifteen.

If you are accepted on a GP's register you will be asked a number of questions which will help the practice put together as much information as possible on your health and social circumstances. It will also help the health authority to arrange for your medical notes to be transferred to the new practice. The details you will be asked for include:

Details you may need to give your new GP:

1. Your name, address and family circumstances.
2. Your maiden or any previous names.
3. Your old address (if you have moved) or your place of birth.
4. The name and address of your previous GP (this is so the practice can track down your health records). If you cannot remember who your last GP was the health authority which covered the area where you previously lived should be able to provide this information to the GP.
5. Your date of birth.

You may also be asked about any particular health problems or allergies that you have or have had in the past.

Who does what in the primary health care team?

Most people have a good idea what GPs do, but when it comes to the various nurses and therapists it can get a bit confusing. Here are some crib notes:

District nurses look after people who are acutely or chronically ill, including those who are dying. They visit people at home or may run clinics to which patients will travel. Some of the things that they do include pain control, blood tests, looking after people who have had operations by checking that the wounds have healed or removing the stitches, giving medicines through injections or on a drip system. District nurses can also help people get back to normal after a major illness and give general health advice. They also advise patients who have long-standing conditions such as incontinence or diabetes about how to look after themselves. If you are bed bound or have leg ulcers which need dressing it will most likely be a district nurse who looks after you.

Health visitors mostly work with children under five and their families, visiting them in their own homes or seeing them in health centres. All young babies are allocated a health visitor who will advise parents on child development, immunizations, feeding and problems with behaviour such as disruptive sleep patterns or temper tantrums. Health visitors also do most of the routine development checks that all children must have at certain ages – normally 6 weeks, 6 months, 18 months and 3 years, as well as hearing tests. Health visitors also have a broader public health training so they can answer concerns about things such as environment, diet and housing.

Midwives increasingly now work from or are based in health centres. More places now offer midwife-led care for pregnant women or shared care. The former means that if you have a straightforward pregnancy the midwife will be the person who co-ordinates your care from start to finish – not a doctor. Shared care is where you see the midwife and your GP on alternative occasions for pre-natal health checks. This type of arrangement whereby midwives work closely with GPs and health visitors tends to give women and their babies more continuity of care – that is they are more likely to see the same staff from one visit to the next and there will be better communication between the various professionals. Of course if, at any time, you really feel you need a medical opinion then you are entitled to ask to see a doctor.

Occupational therapists have a job title which does not really describe what they do in practice. They are specialists in assessing people who have some form of disability and in designing approaches to help them regain their independence. These approaches might vary from teaching people basic cooking skills to art therapy. They provide advice on ways of minimising the disability by using different aids and equipment or adaptations to the home.

Physiotherapists are specialists in the way that people move. They can treat problems such as stiff joints, arthritis, muscle weakness, posture, balance and walking difficulties, as well as sporting injuries. They will normally give patients a range of exercises or movements that they need to practise – first with the physiotherapist and then on their own at home. Some of their work involves treating people who are in pain or who have breathing difficulties. Physiotherapists may work with all ages from newborn babies through to the very old.

Podiatrists or chiropodists assess and treat foot disorders. Increasingly, the scope of their work is extending to include minor nail and foot surgery. The traditional image of the chiropodist as a corn-cutter is perhaps a little misleading, since problems such as posture and back pain can often stem from something that is wrong with the feet. Podiatrists can advise on adaptations to shoes which can be effective in correcting these problems.

Practice nurses are employed to work in GP practices. Their role varies from one place to another but they may be involved in some or all of the following areas: health checks, care of wounds and dressings, counselling, blood tests and advice on health promotion, provision of some contraceptive services, cervical smear tests, ear syringeing and advice on what jabs you need if you are going abroad. The role of practice nurses can overlap with that of district nurses, but as a general guide practice nurses stay in the GP surgery or health centre, whereas district nurses tend to go out to people's homes.

Social workers are employed by social services which are run by your local council rather than the health services. But they work very closely with health care professionals. Social workers can advise on benefits and housing, they oversee care for children who are at risk of abuse and assess the needs of people who are elderly or who have disabilities and arrange for support to be provided to meet those needs (for example help with cleaning and bathing). Some specialise in care for people with mental health problems.

Speech and language therapists work with people of all ages from babies with feeding and swallowing problems, children with speech and communication problems such as autism, aphasia or stammering, through to adults and older people with speech impairments or voice disorders which they have developed in later life. They also work with people who are deaf and those with learning disabilities or mental health problems. Speech therapists work in a range of settings such as hospitals, schools, health centres and clients' own homes. As their work is quite specialised, and not something that is needed by the general population, speech and language therapists are not normally considered part of a core primary care team, although they will work very closely with these professionals.

Changing doctors

If you are unhappy with the care that you are getting from your GP or just feel that you can get a better service from a different doctor or practice then take some action. You have the right to change your GP without giving a reason. You may want to write to your current GP to explain why you want to change, but strictly speaking all you need to do to get a new GP is walk into their surgery and ask to be registered.

If it is just a different source of contraceptive advice that you are after, you are entitled to receive this service from a family planning clinic run by your local community health service or any other GP – you do not need to change your regular GP to do this. This does not seem to be widely known as it is rarely used in practice.

If you need a GP for a short time – less than three months – if you are working away from home, for example, or staying with friends for a while, you can get a temporary registration. This means you can get free care from the GP but your medical notes will not be transferred to the 'temporary' doctor.

A GP can refuse to put a new patient on his/her list of patients without giving a reason. This does not happen very often and seems fair given that patients have similar rights. But some factors which may lead to such a decision are interesting. A GP may claim that their list is full – on average GPs have between 1,500 and 2,000 patients on their list, although there is no set number that they have to have. When a GP says that the list is 'full' this usually means that he/she is overcommitted, with more patients than they have time for. Bear in mind, too, that GPs do other things apart from see patients. They have work to do in running the practice. Some are members of committees which advise the health authority on planning decisions or local trusts on aspects of the quality of care they provide. Others have teaching and research commitments.

On occasions a GP may refuse admission to their list on the basis that the patient is likely to make very heavy demands on them. A large part of a GP's income is made up of those capitation payments for each patient on their list. This effectively creates an incentive to take on as many patients as possible. There are limits to how many people one GP can look after properly, but generally speaking they will be able to have more patients on their list if those people are healthy and rarely make demands on their doctor. By consciously or unconsciously selecting the fitter and healthier people and refusing the older and sicker patients a GP can potentially increase his/her scope for income. This type of selection is not considered to be good practice.

The General Medical Council – the professional body which registers doctors – has very clear guidelines which state that it is unacceptable for a GP to refuse to register people by discrimination against them on grounds of their age, sex, sexual orientation, race, colour, religious belief, perceived economic worth or state of health. A strong statement perhaps, but since a GP will rarely disclose the reason for refusing access to a list, in most cases it would be extremely difficult to prove that discrimination had taken place. If you are refused, what you are likely to get is a bland letter from your local health authority telling you the bare facts and what will happen next. If you unhappy about what has happened you can send a letter of complaint to the chief executive of the health authority who is obliged to investigate it and give you an explanation (see chapter twelve for details).

The health check

All new patients who register with a GP are encouraged to have a health check. The practice is paid a small amount for doing this. When you first register you will be asked to make an appointment to have this done. If you are not offered a health check and you would like one, ask your GP to arrange it.

The purpose of the health check is to collect information which may not be included in your health records and to give you feedback on your state of health. It will take less than half an hour. The health check will normally be carried out by a nurse.

What the health check covers:

- your smoking and drinking habits

- your immunization record – the date of your last tetanus or polio jab, for example, or in the case of women whether you have been vaccinated for German Measles (Rubella)

- any recent problems that you wish to discuss, such as breathlessness or dizziness

- your family history – people in your family who have died or who have certain medical conditions, such as heart disease or cancer. They are trying to identify potential problems which may be hereditary, so they can be detected at an early stage if you begin to develop them.

- any regular pills or medicines that you may be taking

The nurse will normally take a urine test to test for protein, which is an early indicator of kidney disease. Your blood pressure, height and weight will also be taken. Women will be asked about the date of their last screening tests, for example cervical smear, mammogram (chapter ten gives you details about these tests).

If you are over 75 years of age you should be offered a free health check once a year, although some health care professionals are doubtful about whether this is a good use of NHS money and may not actively encourage it. These check-ups can be done in your own home if that is more appropriate than travelling to a clinic. These routine health checks do not include sight and hearing tests as charges are made for these (see below).

Your NHS number

All babies when their birth is registered are given a unique NHS number. The rest of the population should also have their own NHS number although most would be hard pressed to know what it is. Your NHS number is the code used to identify you as a patient and to enable your medical records to be located and transferred from one GP or hospital to another. If you register with a new practice you may be given a card which will have your number on it. If you move practices this can be helpful in speeding up the transfer of your notes.

It is not strictly true to say that the NHS number you have is unique. Historically, there have been duplications in the numbers allocated which made the system less effective than it could be. Everyone who has a hospital inpatient appointment now has their NHS number checked, and this process is gradually weeding out those duplications.

Your medical notes

The need to have a unique way of identifying individual patients is becoming increasingly important as computerisation takes hold in the

NHS. It may come as a surprise as the new millennium dawns that very few parts of the NHS rely wholly on computerised patient records. Most patient notes are paper based and hand written. If there are computerised ones these will often be copies of the hand-written versions or summaries of what treatment took place.

GPs and the other professionals in the primary care team that we have mentioned keep a range of notes on their patients. Increasingly, GPs have computerised records – they will enter details of your consultation and any medicines given straight onto the computer, which may even print out the prescription for them. It is unlikely that those records will give a complete picture of your medical history. Your early medical history (pre-computer) is still likely to be kept as a paper record.

Some groups of patients – pregnant women and the parents of children under five for instance – are allowed to keep their own records. This sounds as if they are being given more control over their health care, but bear in mind that a) this is only one version of the medical notes, the doctors, nurses and midwives will normally keep their own set as well, and b) unless you can understand what is written down and can make use of that information it contributes nothing towards *PatientPower*! Children's health records tend to be slightly more patient friendly and some even have sections where parents can record their own observations of their child's development or any concerns they want to discuss with the doctor or health visitor. If you want to find out about your rights to see your medical records you will find details in chapter eleven.

Looking further into the next millennium there have been discussions about encoding patients' records on smart cards – these will be a bit like a credit card but will carry all the details about your health and health care, the treatment and medicines that you have received etc. Smart cards sound a little terrifying but may open the door to more and more patients being able to carry their own records with them, and they could give you much greater control over which health care professionals you see and where. On the down side, without the right type of equipment it is unlikely that you will be able to read the details in your health record, in much the same way that you can't see what is encoded in the credit card from your bank.

Types of GP

The previous government introduced a number of initiatives which led to the formation of different forms of general practices. You may still hear the term 'GP fund holder' but these no longer exist. New arrangements introduced in April 1999 make for a much simpler system. As explained earlier, all GPs are now organised into primary care groups. These groups advise their health authority on what health care should be provided for local people. Increasingly, primary care groups will take on responsibility for providing a wider range of health care themselves and will manage the budgets for hospital care as well as for community services. It is too early to say what these arrangements will mean for patients and the quality of health care that they receive – it may make little difference to the practice that you go to or to your consultation with your doctor. At best it may improve your GP's awareness of the quality of the services which are available locally. What we do know is that primary care groups will be expected to make arrangements to consult their patients about their plans and decisions. So watch out for opportunities to make your views known.

Other than primary care groups, the main differences between practices relate to the number of doctors that work there, whether or not they do any teaching and the arrangements that they make for looking after patients out of core hours. Teaching practices are generally large, and may not only be concerned with the education and training of new GPs or undergraduate medical students, but may also be involved in research. If you are registered with such a practice you may find that your GP will ask you if a student can watch and listen to your consultation. You do not have to agree to the person staying in the room if you find it embarrassing.

Getting help from your GP when the surgery is shut

A GP is bound by a strict set of national 'terms and conditions of service' which are laid down in what is known as the 'Red Book' produced by the Department of Health. One of these conditions is that the GP must provide medical care to his/her patients 24 hours a day and for 52 weeks per year. Clearly this would be impossible for any one person, so GPs are allowed to share this work with colleagues who are also registered with the same health authority. GPs can also sub-contract their work to a deputising agency, although if they do so they still remain responsible for the patient. This condition of service has been the subject of considerable dispute amongst GPs in recent years, many of whom feel this continuous duty of care to be too onerous and too poorly rewarded.

GP co-ops versus deputising services

If you call a GP to come out in the middle of the night it is more than likely you will not be seen by your own GP as they will have made special arrangements for their 'out-of hours' work (during holidays and at night) to be covered by another doctor. If you are put off by the idea of being seen by someone other than you are used to, remember that out-of-hours arrangements do offer advantages to both patients and doctors. Your doctor will not be tired during the day if they have been allowed to get a full night's sleep and they will not be trying to fit your care around other commitments in their lives, such as trying to bath the kids.

When you call a GP at night it is very unlikely that you will be thinking about the relative merits of GP co-ops or deputising agencies. But there are differences in the service that you will get which are worth remembering. The locum doctors which provide the deputising service tend to have very limited knowledge of the patients they see. And at the end of the day they do not have responsibility if anything goes wrong – this remains with your GP. With a GP co-op all the members are GPs who work in a local practice and so each will take responsibility for their actions. The co-op means that the out-of-hours work is shared with a larger number of GPs than would be possible within just one practice, thus an individual doctor will find that their turn comes up less frequently. If the odds are in your favour you could find yourself seeing your own GP or one from the same practice that you have met before. However, whether it is a locum doctor or a co-op GP that you see during the night, remember that they will not be as familiar with your medical history as your own GP. Check out what they know and be prepared to put a bit more effort into explaining the background to your condition.

When to call a doctor out-of-hours

On average, GPs now do fewer routine home visits than they did ten years ago, but they make far more out-of-hours calls at night. Many people believe that GPs are obliged to come to their homes if they ask, but this is not strictly true. The GP's contract does not oblige him/her to visit patients at home on demand, simply that they make the right judgement in each case as to whether a home visit is medically appropriate. Many complaints about GPs centre on differences in perception between what the patient and their GP believe to be the appropriate course of action.

If you do need to call for help in the middle of the night you may find that you get put through to someone unfamiliar. Sometimes you may have to call two numbers – first your GP's where you will be given the number of the out-of-hours service to call. Once you get through to a human rather than an answering machine or recorded message, ask a few questions to find out whether you are talking to a health professional – a doctor or a nurse – or a receptionist. This will guide you as to how much you want to disclose to them on the phone. If you describe the problem over the phone it may be that the GP or nurse will be able to tell how serious your problem is and can give you advice on what to do. They may ask if you are able to get to a special primary care centre which stays open all night or if you can attend an emergency surgery run in the evenings, weekends or early mornings.

It is sometimes difficult when you are ill to know whether or not to call the doctor at night. Perhaps because people err on the side of caution demands on GPs have soared. *PatientPower* is as much about responsible use of your health care as it is about making your views known and getting what you want. One of the things that irritates GPs the most are the night calls for very trivial problems that could wait until morning or may not even need a doctor at all. So think twice before you call.

Getting the best from your GP

The average consultation with a GP is less than ten minutes. The doctor has only a limited time to check out what's wrong with you, consider the options for treating you and decide which is best. Think about how you would feel doing this with a patient who is either very vague or uncommunicative. Getting the best from those ten minutes means thinking ahead:

Go prepared Before you go in to see the doctor think about what you will say to describe what is wrong with you. You need to be as specific as possible – don't leave it up to the GP to guess. So don't talk about being unable to sleep if the real problem is that you stay awake worrying about why you are losing a lot of weight or passing blood.

Try to concentrate on the main problem If you introduce a whole range of problems the GP will find it difficult to know which is the most important and which you want to be sorted.

Do ask questions Before you go in, write down some questions that you may want to ask (see below) and stick to them. And if there is something that your GP says that you do not understand then ask for it to be explained.

Think about how you present yourself Although it may be tempting to try to look and sound as ill as possible, you may find that the more confident and informed you are the more likely your GP will be to involve you in decisions about your care.

Don't try to diagnose what is wrong A common complaint of GPs is that patients try to tell them what's the matter – 'You'd better have a look at this, doctor; it must be skin cancer'. By all means describe the symptoms and what is worrying you but leave the doctor to make the right diagnosis.

Do get informed Once you know what is wrong with you do a bit of research on what types of treatment might be available. Helpful sources are medical journals, self-help books and the medical information sites on the internet. You will also find information reported in newspapers or in popular magazines but be aware that these short reports may not give a balanced account. At best they will give you some questions to ask your doctor.

Don't expect your GP to be an expert on everything If you have read an article on different forms of treatment for a particular ailment and want to discuss the pros and cons with your doctor, then take the paper or cutting with you. GPs can't be expected to read everything. But they also can feel threatened if their patient suddenly appears to be more informed than they are. If you take the information with you it will help your GP to know whether the points you are raising are based on scientific research or journalistic speculation.

Dress comfortably If you think that your doctor is likely to examine you, wear clothes that you will find easy to undo or remove. That way you will avoid the embarrassment of fumbling around trying to get your zip down or having to completely remove your dress just for your chest to be listened to.

Some questions to ask your GP

GPs try hard to be approachable, but once you get into that surgery it can be difficult to think about or voice the right questions. The following table gives you some ideas about what to ask or say in different circumstances.

Situation	Some questions to ask
If you are not given a prescription.	• When can I expect these symptoms to go away? • Can I do anything to manage this illness without a prescription? • What can I do to prevent this from happening again?
If you are given a prescription.	• How will this medicine help me – what will it do by the end of the course? • Are there any side effects that I need to look out for? • What is the best time to take this medicine, e.g. before or after meals? • Are there things that I should avoid doing whilst I am taking this medicine, e.g. driving? Drinking alcohol?
If you do not understand what the GP is saying.	• Please could you explain that to me again? • I don't understand some of the terms you are using – could you explain what X means?
If your GP is trying to end the consultation.	• I have some questions that I would like to ask which we have not yet discussed.
If you are referred for a hospital appointment.	• How long can I expect to wait before being seen/admitted? • What will the hospital be able to do for me? • What is the name of the consultant who will be responsible for me in hospital? • How long will I need to stay in hospital – what is the minimum stay likely to be? • What do I need to take to hospital?
If you are not happy with the GP's diagnosis.	• I would like a second opinion on this – could you arrange for me to see another doctor in the practice or a consultant?
If the medicine you are taking does not agree with you.	• My medicine does not appear to be helping – there are some bad side-effects (list them). Are there other medicines which would not have these side-effects or which would be more effective?

Getting contraceptive advice

One area of health care where there is a choice of services available to patients is contraceptive advice. Many people are happy to get this advice and any products they need such as condoms, the pill or spermicidal creams from their GP or the practice nurse. But others feel embarrassed about talking about such matters to health care professionals that they see time and time again. Young people under the age of 16 can find it particularly difficult to talk to a GP they share with the rest of their family for fear that their parents will be told. Women seeking abortions are another group that often look for a more anonymous service. So apart from your own GP the basic choices are these:

Look for another GP As mentioned earlier, you are entitled to get contraceptive advice from any GP without being formally registered as their patient. If the GP agrees to provide this service you will be asked to sign a form. This allows the GP to get paid for this work. This option is rarely taken up but might be worth considering if, for example, you want to see a GP of your own sex.

The local family planning clinic These confusingly named services are run by community health services and are provided by specially trained doctors and nurses in health centres or public facilities. Family planning does not mean that they are restricted to people who have had children or are planning to have a baby – they are open to men and women of any age. Your local health authority should be able to tell you where and when these clinics are held.

Brook Advisory Service The choice of many under 16s, this is not part of the health service but a national charity. It specializes in contraceptive and abortion advice. They do make a charge for consultations. Brook are also widely used by women seeking abortions. In theory it should be no easier to get an abortion from a Brook clinic than from a GP – in both cases two doctors must agree that the case fits a set of nationally defined criteria such as risk of physical or emotional damage to the mother. Not liking children much or having just split up with your boyfriend would be as unacceptable reasons to Brook as to your GP. A few GPs do have personal moral problems with referring patients for abortions, a problem that you would not encounter at a Brook clinic.

Accident and Emergency Departments Really not an appropriate place to go for contraception but some do prescribe the 'morning after' pill, which can be taken up to three days after unprotected sex, or the more complex abortion pill.

Your local chemist You might not consider this an appropriate place for advice, just somewhere to buy the things you need and leave, but pharmacists are trained to advise you and chemists sell contraceptives which are available over the counter without prescription such as condoms. It is likely that a wider range of products will be available without prescription over the next few years – including the 'morning after' pill.

Dentists, pharmacists and opticians and optometrists

Dentists

Despite what you read in the press there are still dentists who are willing to do dental work on the NHS. In some places – mainly the larger cities – it may be difficult to find one and you may find that you have little choice unless you are prepared to pay for private treatment. Part of the problem is that dentists, like GPs, are paid mainly on a fee for service basis, with capitation payments for continuing care of children who are registered with them. Many dentists stopped doing NHS work as they claimed that the fees from individual items were small and the bureaucracy involved in reclaiming their money meant that it was not worth their while. Some dentists do both private and NHS work so if you are registering with a new dentist make sure that you specify at the outset whether you are having private or NHS work. There will be little real difference in the quality of the care you receive. If you go private you will be able to get some materials which are not available on the NHS. If you go as an NHS patient and you need complex work on your teeth the dentist may first need to get approval from the Dental Estimates Board (which pays dentists for the NHS work that they do). Some dentists will let you mix NHS and private treatment.

If you are taken on as an NHS patient your dental treatment will *not* be free like other NHS care. You can expect to pay the full cost of a dental examination or check-up and 80 per cent of the cost of your treatment up to a maximum. Get an estimate from your dentist of how much the work will cost if you are worried about it. You will not have to pay if you are:

- on family credit, income support, or the job seekers' allowance

- receive or are the partner of someone who gets the disability working allowance

- under 18 or 18 and in full-time education

- pregnant or had a baby within the last 12 months

There are no exemptions for pensioners other than those who fall into the low income groups.

Dentists, like GPs, work best when they can provide care to you and your family over a continuous period. You can register with a dentist in exactly the same way as a GP, although some dentists may want to check on the state of your teeth before they will accept you as a patient. If you are accepted as an NHS patient the dentist may insist that you have regular check-ups or they may remove you from their list. If you are having trouble registering, contact your local health authority for advice.

Pharmacists

Outside hospitals, pharmacists are self-employed professionals who mainly work in small chemists or are employed by larger stores such as Boots. They get a set fee per prescription and a contribution towards the cost of the ingredients. Increasingly pharmacists are looking for a wider role advising on over-the-counter medicines and helping patients understand problems such as drug reactions, side-effects and the difficulties of combining certain medicines. Generally a pharmacist will pay more attention than your GP to the side effects of different drugs and on the best way of taking and storing them. More pharmacists are setting up databases of patients on regular medication which can be used to check any bad inter-reactions between medicines. It is well worth trying to use the same pharmacy or chemist each time you collect a prescription as that way they will get to know you and the type of medicines you are taking.

Opticians and optometrists

These terms are often used interchangeably but they are slightly different. An optometrist is an expert in assessing eye problems and conducting sight tests. Opticians are experts in fitting glasses and contact lenses to counteract eye defects and poor sight. If you don't wear glasses or contact lenses you are in a minority – around 65 per cent of the population need them. And amongst people over 45, over 90 per cent need glasses. Like dental care, sight tests are no longer free on the NHS, unless you are exempt from charges or have a test done whilst you are in hospital. You can claim free tests if you are:

- under 16 or under 19 and a full-time student

- on income support or family credit

- registered blind or partially sighted

- suffering from diabetes or glaucoma

- over 40 and the parent, brother, sister or child of a person suffering from diabetes or glaucoma

- in need of very complex lenses

- receiving the Disability Working Allowance and have less than £8,000 in savings. If this applies to you, any of your dependants would also be eligible

If you are eligible for a free sight test and the optometrist finds that you need glasses, you may be pleased to know that there are no longer standard issue NHS specs. What you will be offered is a voucher (effectively a grant) which can be taken to anyone who sells glasses – an optometrist, optician or even an unregistered seller of glasses in the high street. The latter group, however, are not permitted to dispense prescriptions for children, blind or partially sighted people or for contact lenses. The voucher system in theory gives people more choice over the types of frames that they get. But in practice choice will be limited by price.

CHAPTER 3: OUTPATIENT HEALTH CARE

If your GP refers you to a specialist doctor for investigation, advice or treatment, the chances are you will become an 'outpatient'. All this means is that you are going for a consultation with the specialist doctor, in very much the same way as you went for a consultation to your GP. The difference is that you are now meeting someone who has an in-depth and up-to-date knowledge of a particular area. This chapter looks at how to make the best of seeing the specialist doctors.

What is an Outpatient?

The term 'outpatient' comes from the traditional hospital system which still makes a distinction between a doctor's outpatient clinics and 'inpatient' wards where patients spend most of their time in bed and are visited by a doctor on the 'ward rounds'. The difference between these modes of care is becoming far more blurred – some inpatient stays are over within a day and may take as little time as an outpatient appointment. Another thing that is changing is that specialist doctors see patients in settings other than hospitals, such as in GP surgeries, health centres and in specially planned facilities such as minor injury centres and ambulatory care centres. Some of these

facilities have been designed to take the place of Accident &
Emergency departments, where these have closed or merged, and
they often provide more useful health services that the old A&E
department.

Outpatient waiting times

Despite everything you may have read or heard, waiting times for
hospital appointments are not always long, and sometimes, when
there is a long wait, there is a good medical reason for the delay. When
your GP wants to refer you to a specialist, he or she will write a letter
giving the reasons for the request. The surgery may also ring to book
an outpatient appointment if the GP thinks that it is urgent – people
with cancers and serious illnesses should be seen by a specialist
within days. Many other conditions can wait. Here are some reasons
why you may have to wait for your appointment:

- For some conditions it may not be sensible to rush into early treatment. Some things clear up by themselves.

- The NHS sensibly rations its limited care by dealing with the
  urgent things first.

- Waiting times depend on who you are going to see. A specialist
  who is particularly good at your problem may have a longer
  waiting list because GPs know that that person will give the best
  quality care. It may be quicker but not necessarily better to see
  someone who is less well known. Would you rather wait longer to
  see someone who has a reputation as a better doctor or be seen right
  away?

- You may need to wait if you want to see a woman doctor in certain
  specialties. Your GP should try to arrange this, but you may have to
  wait longer as there are fewer women than men consultants in
  some specialties.

- Waiting times may be due to errors or inefficiencies in the way that appointments are made. These are gradually being weeded out as more and more pressure is put on the NHS to reduce waiting times but it may be possible that your GP's letter of referral was never sent or got lost in the system.

- You may need to wait longer if you are not able or willing to travel to a hospital which has shorter waiting times. You may not always be offered a choice but if you are prepared to travel further afield, ask your GP whether you could be referred to another hospital where the wait is shorter.

What all this means is that it is best to think of waiting times as offering options for your care – ask your GP what choices you have and the advantages and disadvantages of these. The NHS is getting better at publishing waiting times and also the results of hospital performance in relation to different quality standards. So hopefully there will soon be better ways of judging the quality of care that you can expect than mere length of waiting times.

Unacceptable waiting times

To some extent, what is an unacceptable waiting time to be seen by a specialist doctor depends on your own personal circumstances. If your problem is urgent – for example you had a growth or some other symptom which could be cancerous – you should be seen within two weeks of being referred by the GP, and if you need treatment that should follow very quickly. For such conditions, any longer wait than this is unacceptable. Your GP should make sure you get an urgent appointment by telephoning the relevant specialist. Consultants do not have daily surgeries like GPs. They tend to run clinics maybe once or twice a week where they will see a mix of new patients and patients who are returning for a follow-up. Special arrangements can always be made to see someone at a different time if the problem is very urgent. Like dealing with any other service, this is a matter of persuasion, and this is a job for the GP, the 'gatekeeper' to health care. Keep your GP up to date with what is happening to you, particularly if you feel a lot worse or are in severe pain.

If the problem is not life-threatening or aggressive (meaning that it is developing quickly) but it is causing pain or discomfort, you should be seen within a few weeks. The NHS standard is that you should be seen by a specialist doctor within thirteen weeks of referral by your GP. If you have waited several weeks before getting an appointment it is worth checking with the surgery that the GP has written and sent the referral letter to the consultant. Until this has gone, nothing else can happen.

Emergencies and Emergency care

Anybody can go to an Accident & Emergency (A&E) department at any time, but that does not mean that everyone has a right to be treated there. A&E is the one hospital service for which you do not need a GP referral, but it is there specifically to deal with accidents and health emergencies – not minor burns, cuts and bruises. These should be treated by your GP or at a minor injuries centre (of which more later). The better A&E departments now have specialist A&E children's departments, to cater for the different medical and emotional needs of children who have accidents or health emergencies. Although these facilities are designed with children in mind do not expect a nursery full of toys. If you are taking your child to A&E, before you dash out of the house in a panic, try to remember to bring a favourite comfort toy and book for your child and a drink, as it is a feature of A&E departments that you cannot predict how long you will have to wait.

Everyone who turns up at A&E has to be assessed to decide the urgency of their medical problem. This is called 'triage' and it is carried out by an A&E nurse. If you have not had an accident that has caused injury and you are not in need of emergency health treatment, A&E staff may refuse to treat you and will refer you back to your GP. If the problem is minor and not urgent, you may be seen, but only after the more urgent problems are dealt with. Remember this could be several hours, so you may be better off seeing your GP. A&E departments are one of the most poorly understood parts of the health service, because there has been little attempt over the years to explain their role to the public. Indeed, in areas of the country where general practice is poor or where you have to book days ahead to see a GP (unfortunately there are still numerous examples), people often see A&E as the only way of getting decent primary care at a time when they most need it.

If you see a GP with a problem that requires immediate attention such as a suspected broken bone, your GP will send you to the hospital's A&E department directly. You will be given a note to take which says what the problem is, or the GP may phone the hospital to let them know you are on your way. If a GP is called out to visit a patient at home he or she suspects of having a serious or urgent problem, such as meningitis or a suspected heart attack, they will arrange for transport to A&E, and will phone ahead to alert the hospital.

If the GP has identified an urgent medical problem such as a perforated ulcer, you may be referred to a GP admission unit within the A&E department. The hospital staff will assess you for treatment and may admit you. Even with a GP referral it may take several hours for you to be seen, as A&E departments can be very busy, overcrowded places. There is more on Accident & Emergency departments in the next chapter.

Your hospital appointment

Being prepared Hospitals are complex, busy places that, sadly, sometimes feel like faceless, bureaucratic and uncaring organisations. After dealing with your GP or the local chemist who you know, a hospital can seem an unfriendly, bewildering place, particularly if you are feeling vulnerable, anxious or worried about your health or the health of a member of your family or a friend. So before you get involved in the hospital system, prepare yourself by thinking and talking about it. Hospitals are big local employers and thousands of people use them each year. So the chances are that you will know someone who either works in your local hospital or has visited it for their own health care. Find out what the place is like for them and ask if they can give you any advice.

The appointment card When you get your appointment card for the outpatient clinic, read it all through. Check that the details are right, as far as you know. Check, too, if there are special instructions about whether you can eat or drink anything on the day of your appointment. If the card contains any wrong information or if you are unclear about anything, ring the clinic and ask the reception staff. They are usually great sources of information and will have dealt with most things in their time. They are usually very ready to help and advise you. It helps them to help you, for if you know what you are doing, the appointments system will run more smoothly. Don't be put off if you are asked to call back when they are less busy. Remember that as different specialist clinics run on different days, you may be asked to call on a day that the clinic you are going to is running.

You may want to bring a partner, family member or friend with you when you attend for your appointment. There should be no problem in doing this, but if you are unsure, check with the receptionist.

Turning up Treat your appointment as you would treat any other commitment, such as catching a train or going to a show – phone ahead to make sure the appointment is on and is running to time. Indeed, hospital doctors are a bit like public transport: they can get cancelled, diverted or delayed by a range of problems, from having to deal with a medical emergency, to less glamorous delays, such as being off sick or stuck in a meeting. It is also important to let the clinic know if you can't make your appointment. This helps them to arrange for another patient to take your place, and helps you by letting them book a new appointment which suits you. Every day, large numbers of people simply fail to attend their outpatient appointment, and do not let the hospital know. This lengthens waiting times for everyone as well as wasting money. It has been suggested that non-attenders who do not let the clinic know that they cannot come should be charged.

Being seen

If you have an appointment card or a hospital letter try to bring it with you to the appointment. More importantly, bring all your medicine with you, both what you have been prescribed by your GP and anything you have bought over the counter and are taking regularly. Also bring something to do to occupy yourself in case you have to wait. The days have mostly gone when patients' treatment was organised for the convenience of hospital doctors; when everyone was required to turn up at 9am and wait all morning. You should be given a specific time for your outpatient appointment and then you should be seen within 30 minutes of your allocated time, but be prepared to wait longer, if need be. 'Hope for the best but plan for the worst', is a reasonable motto for hospital visits generally. There is no point in getting steamed up by having to wait, as this will only mean the time you do spend with the doctor is badly used, when it needs to be as useful as possible. So bring a book, newspapers or journals, some work, or a personal stereo, or use the time to think about what you want to get out of the meeting with the specialist. If you are with children, make sure that they have plenty with them to do. Some outpatient departments have a children's corner or even a crèche. The receptionists should be able to help if you need anything for your children.

One of the first things to establish is who you will be seeing on your outpatient visit. You may have been referred to Dr X's clinic, but all this means is that Dr X is the consultant in charge. If it is your first visit, you should be seen by Dr X or another consultant, but you may be seen by one of the team who work with Dr X and who will be more junior. Get the name and the title of the doctor so you can report back to your GP. Sometimes the specialist may have one or two medical students observing. You should be asked if you mind the medical students staying. If you do mind, say so: you are perfectly entitled to be seen on your own. If a male doctor needs to carry out an intimate examination on a woman patient he may (but probably won't) ask a woman colleague to come into the room as a chaperone. If he doesn't, you can request that he does so.

Finding out what you want to know

More and more people come into the doctor with lists of questions they want answering, or armed with information on their problem gleaned from magazines or the internet. This is all worth doing, and generally the more prepared you are for the appointment, the more you will get out of it. The important thing is that you have thought about what you feel and what you want to happen. Don't think that the doctor knows best and that you should just sit there quietly and do exactly what you are told. Remember it's your body and your life, and only you can decide what is best. But also don't think that your latest page from the Web is the last word on good care. You have no way of telling whether this information is accurate or junk, nor do you know whether the recommendation to treat your condition with Wonderdrug has come from the makers of Wonderdrug, who are just using the media to sell it. The same advice for dealing with GPs applies to specialists. Do tell the doctor about your symptoms and do ask them about new developments that you may have heard about. But don't expect to get the best from your specialist if you try to do their job for them.

Be clear what you want to get out of the outpatient visit and work to make sure that this happens. Try to find out exactly what the problem is and what impact this will have on your life. Say, for example, the tests you have been having show that you have multiple sclerosis. This term does not tell you much except that it sounds serious. You will want to know what the characteristics of that disease are and what it means for your overall health. You may want to be put in touch with other people in a similar position; or know exactly what the treatment options are and how successful these have been. You may what to know what is going to happen to you in the immediate future, then in future months and years. You will want to know, why me? How was the problem caused, what does this mean for my children, my family? *Work out what you want to know and feel at the end of the appointment with the specialist, and don't stop until you have got the answer or answers you need*. If you are worried that you will forget what has been said or if you think you will find it difficult to ask the questions think about taking a friend with you to your appointment.

Old attitudes die hard

Most doctors will be very happy to tell you as much as they can, but some still think that it is the doctor's role not to worry the poor passive patient by telling them things they won't understand. If you meet this attitude, it doesn't necessarily mean you have run up against a poor doctor, but just one who has not been trained to understand the importance of good communication in helping good health. They do exist, and unfortunately they are young as well as old, women as well as men. If all else fails, wave this book at the doctor and suggest that he or she might like to read it!

The consultation

Most consultations follow the same pattern. The doctor, with a certain level of knowledge and experience, is trying to apply this to your particular, unique situation by getting you to tell him or her what you are experiencing.

The parts of the consultation are:

1. history – when you describe what you have been experiencing
2. examination – looking, touching, listening, smelling
3. tests – to investigate what can't be found from history and examination (see chapter four for details on these)
4. diagnosis – deciding the cause of the changes that have occurred
5. prognosis – the outlook, what is likely to happen with or without treatment
6. treatment – of which there may be a number of alternatives

You don't just have to answer all the doctor's questions, or wait until she or he has finished the consultation to put your points across. If you have something to say about your health which the questions haven't brought out, then say so. It will help both you and the doctor, if you can say how you feel about your illness, whether you are worried or relaxed, anxious for something to be done, or willing to see how it goes. Despite what we would hope for, there are few right or wrong answers in medicine. The more we can explain our own attitude towards a problem, the easier it is for the doctors to find a course of action that will suit us.

At the end of the consultation

Make sure that you understand what is going to happen next. This may be immediate, if the specialist wants you to undergo some diagnostic tests which will help in finding out what is happening – blood samples or X-rays, for instance. You may be put on a course of drugs, you may be asked to come back to see the specialist at a later date, you may be asked to visit your GP, you may be put on the list to come into hospital as an inpatient, or you may be just asked to wait and see how your condition progresses.

You also need to be clear whether you agree with what is being proposed. Your treatment should be a joint agreement between you and the specialist. This does not mean that you have to agree with and consent to everything that the specialist suggests. For most conditions there are alternative ways of treating you, and these should be explained so that you have the opportunity to decide what is right for you. Few if any treatments are guaranteed to be 100 per cent successful, most have some risk attached to them or side-effects of some sort. Ask for the evidence that what is being suggested will work for you. A good specialist will be able to give you this without too much technical jargon. And remember that what matters is good research evidence, not a few anecdotes about a friend of a friend who had the treatment last month. Increasingly, doctors and nurses work to protocols and guidelines which are based on research evidence. Another way of being sure about your treatment is to ask whether it is being done under a protocol. If it is, the odds are that the technique has been evaluated to determine whether it is effective.

You may need to take time to think through the alternative treatments that might be available to you, including doing nothing. In fact, asking what would happen if no treatment was given is a reasonable way of ascertaining how serious your illness is. It may be very convenient for everyone that you agree there and then to a course of action, but it may make all the difference to you if you go back and talk the options through with your family and friends. Don't feel you have to decide right away. If you have taken an active part in deciding about your health care and made a decision with your doctor, then you have a partnership over your care. It's through this sort of partnership that the best health care comes.

What happens next?

If you have tests done, the results of these will be given to the doctor who has seen you and may also be sent to your GP. Find out when the results are due and how you will be told about what they show – by letter or at a visit to your GP. Also find out who is due to see you next, and when this will be. If the tests seem to be taking a long time, then ask for an explanation. And make sure that you have all the information that is relevant to you before you leave a consultation. If, for example, you have a medical condition that is likely to be a long-term problem, such as diabetes, then there is likely to be a support or advice group, and the Appendix at the end of this book lists some of the main ones. There is also published material for thousands of medical conditions. Ask the specialist what he or she could recommend as background reading for you.

CHAPTER 4: HOSPITAL CARE

For many years hospital services were by far the most important part of the NHS, getting much of the money and most of the attention. This has been changing over the past few years as more emphasis has been placed on primary care and community care. But hospitals are still hugely important as centres of a vast range of health care. This chapter looks at the way in which hospitals work, and how you can avoid being 'just a number in the system'.

Hospitals

Hospitals are strange things. Some of them are so big that they are more like small towns, with shopping centres, hairdressers, banks, bookshops, pharmacies (of course), florists, solicitors, fast food outlets and gift shops. Some of the people who work in hospitals have spent most of their working lives there – doctors, nurses, porters, drivers, paramedics, even some managers. They are complete communities in themselves. In fact, the local hospital is often the largest employer in a particular area, and so important that they are one of the principal landmarks and institutions that define the town.

Hospital history

The oldest hospitals in the country date back to the time of the crusades and were established by religious orders. London's St Bartholomew's Hospital was founded in 1123. Medieval plagues and diseases such as leprosy led to further institutions, which had the effect of separating the 'incurables' from the rest of the parish. In the same period the first mad houses were established. The Hospital of the Order of Bethlehem (Bethlem or Bedlam) was built outside the walls of the city of London in 1247. The Poor Law, established in the 16th century, gave all parishes the responsibility for looking after the poor of the parish. Gradually infirmaries became attached to the workhouses that were set up for the poor. After the 16th century, voluntary hospitals began to grow in number with the foundation of the great London hospitals, such as Guy's, St Thomas', St George's and the Royal Free in the 18th and early 19th centuries. By the beginning of the 20th century there was a concentration of hospitals in the large metropolitan areas, all of which were dependent on charitable donation, and a network of hospitals and infirmaries run by local authorities.

Hospitals under the NHS

The formation of the NHS in 1948 brought almost all these hospitals under the control of the Ministry of Health. At a stroke, the voluntary hospitals were relieved of their preoccupation with raising money and could get on with the job of hospital care. This was a huge step forward as many hospitals at the time faced huge financial problems. So the NHS inherited a very uneven distribution of hospitals across the country, matched by differences in the quality of care. To an extent that pattern of distribution is still evident today. Within a square mile of central London there are still five major teaching hospitals and several smaller specialist hospitals, whereas in many regions of the country, hospitals with Accident & Emergency departments, capable of providing general health services, may be thirty or forty miles from each other.

Changing that initial pattern of hospital care under the NHS was (and still is) extremely difficult. All the powerful doctors were in the centres of excellence and they were hugely resistant to arguments that money should be taken from their hospitals and redirected to provincial health care. In 1963 Enoch Powell, as Minister of Health, published the Hospital Plan as a blueprint for hospital development in the UK. In the 1970s this was taken up by the then Minister of Health, David Owen, who began to move money from the better funded parts of the NHS to the less well provided areas and continued building new hospitals in towns and cities to get a fairer distribution of hospital care across the country. New hospitals replaced the old workhouse-infirmary hospitals, and the process of redistributing resources continued through the reforms of the 1980s and 1990s, although even today the distribution remains uneven. Recently both Conservative and Labour governments have encouraged, through the Private Finance Initiative, private investors to put money into building hospitals, though it will be some years before the success of this idea can be judged.

Hospitals in today's NHS

In the last few years there has been an effort to get agreement on the standards of care hospitals should provide, to make sure that the medical and nursing care given is of a high quality, and that the hospital is efficiently and effectively run. As demand for services rises and money for the NHS is not unlimited, hospitals have had to make savings to fund this extra work. And increasingly they are having to show that they are working effectively, treating patients according to the latest good practice for each medical problem. There are benefits and problems with the push for efficiency and effectiveness. On the plus side, there has been much more attention paid to giving the most effective health care, so a patient admitted with a heart attack should receive a plan of treatment which has been properly researched and demonstrated to be the best way of tackling that condition. Improving care and cutting out wastage means both that the individual gets the best deal and that more people can be treated for the limited budget available. On the down side, this has sometimes been done at the cost of losing the personal and more caring side of hospitals which many fondly remember. At its worst the system makes patients feel that they are being treated 'on a conveyer belt', in and out as quickly as possible with less concern about their well-being when they go home. Staff can feel that they are working under greater and greater stress, caring for sicker patients with less time to get to know them, for relatively low rates of pay and for an employer that does not care about their careers and development. Hospitals in the NHS are constantly striving to get this balance right.

Types of hospital

The history of hospitals pre and post the setting up of the NHS shows how different types of hospitals were established. Today, as well as the traditional hospitals, new types of facility are being developed. Here are some of examples of the different hosptials you may encounter:

Teaching hospitals These tend to be the most specialised establishments. As well as being places where doctors, nurses and other professionals receive their practical training with patients, their links with universities make them a magnet for consultants and others interested in medical research. Some of the treatments that patients receive will be guided by the research interests of the medical staff.

District general hospitals These are typical hospitals that you will find in most major towns and communities. Their strength is in having the full range of specialties (branches of medicine and surgery). However, not all hospitals provide all services. For instance, your local hospital may not have its own ear, nose and throat department. They would need to refer you to another hospital if you needed this type of treatment. Increasingly, the NHS is beginning to differentiate between services that need to be available at all general hospitals and those that do not. This is partly because there are shortages of medical and nursing staff in some specialties. But also because having a small department with just one or two consultants is not considered to be good practice – they find it difficult to cover holiday periods and sickness and the opportunities for colleagues to learn from and support one another are limited. So expect to see more changes in the distribution of health services between hospitals over the next few years. Although your instincts may be to object to the changes, bear in mind that they will probably lead to better health care.

Cottage hospitals Typically found in rural or suburban areas, these facilities are enjoying a renaissance. There was a period during which many cottage hospitals were closed as they were thought too small to be economically viable, but now they are now being revived, being seen as providing useful intermediate care between GPs and hospitals. They do not have A&E departments. Some cottage hospitals have 'GP beds'. This means it is your GP who will provide medical input rather than a hospital consultant, although the GP may well be working to guidance or guidelines drawn up by a specialist.

Single specialty hospitals There are a number of specialist hospitals that deal with just one disease or condition. Moorfields Eye Hospital in London and the Nuffield Orthopaedic Hospital in Oxford are two examples. There are also a number of hospitals which specialise in women or children. Increasingly these hospitals are linking up with teaching or district general hospitals so that there are the right connections with other medical specialties that modern care requires.

Minor injuries centres Not strictly hospitals these centres offer care for injuries that do not need the intensive support of an A&E department. They are discussed in more detail below.

Who is in hospital?

Old people, mainly. Six in every ten hospital beds are occupied by people over the age of 65. As most health care is given to people in the last two years of their lives, and as the average age of death in the UK is around 77 years, this statistic is not very surprising. If you couple this statistic to the fact that 95 per cent of health care occurs outside hospitals, it also means that hospitals make very little difference to the general health of the population at a whole. Maternity care aside, we can say that hospitals care for a small proportion of the population, and is mainly concentrated on the final years of life. The vast majority of people, for most of their lives, do not need hospital care. Despite this about half of the £40-or-so billion spent on the NHS each year is spent in or on hospitals.

Emergencies

The NHS offers one of the best emergency medical services in the world. But if you are waiting in A&E for a doctor to see your suspected broken finger it may feel like it is the worst. This is because Accident & Emergency departments are very busy. Many of those who come to A&E departments could be treated elsewhere, by their GP or the chemist. The sheer numbers cause long waits in A&E departments, which at times might be up to seven hours. People who are genuine emergencies – those with head injuries, heart attacks or major bleeding – have to be treated immediately. Every time one of these cases comes through the door on a stretcher, the broken finger brigade will go further down the list of priorities. This is clearly not right, and recently the NHS has begun to look at who is using A&E for what reason, and what can be done to get these departments used better. New alternative services are being established for people that really don't need the specialist care and treatment for which A&E departments are designed (see Minor Injuries page 66).

A&E Departments

These have always been the most glamorous parts of the health service, as the popularity of television programmes such as *Casualty* and *ER* have shown. An A&E department is really only as good as the overall range and quality of care in its hospital. A&E must be able to receive 'blue light' ambulances – those that have responded to a 999 call. To do this, it must be able to call on a full range of specialist medical and nursing staff, and have diagnostic and treatment facilities available. Because of this, A&E departments quickly suffer if services are taken away from a hospital and they will be one of the first departments to close when a hospital is being run down or merged, as has happened to several London hospitals over the past few years.

As discussed in the previous chapter, A&E departments operate what is called a 'triage' system. This means that everyone who comes in needing treatment is seen by a casualty nurse and assessed for the urgency of the treatment needed. The nurse will try to tell you how long you are likely to wait for treatment, which may be several hours when they are busy. However waiting times in A&E are difficult to predict, as the nurses cannot guess whether a serious emergency will happen. You can play your part in helping the health service by making sensible use of your A&E department.

You should *not* go to an A&E department for

minor injuries, e.g. bruises, sprains, minor cuts, infections, contraception, including the 'morning after' pill, mild anxiety or depression

999 Calls

Until recently every 999 medical call was answered with a blue light ambulance, and the Patient's Charter said that the ambulance should be at the scene of the emergency within 14 minutes in towns and 19 minutes in the countryside. Ambulance control centres are now starting to train their staff to respond in different ways to calls, as not every 999 call needs an ambulance. The people who answer the phone will try to prioritise those cases that are the most serious. Paramedics, on motorcycles or in cars, and telephone advice are new ways of providing the right response to make sure that ambulances are used where they are most needed. In the past if you called the ambulance service they rushed you to the closest A&E department as quickly as possible, providing just enough help to keep you stable until hospital. Now many crews are trained to provide a high level of care, and may spend some time with the patient, for example fixing up drips, giving drugs or fluids, stabilising breathing, before transferring to hospital, even if it is just around the corner. Emergency care doctors now travel out with crews to the emergency, and new ways of communicating directly with specialists in A&E departments from the emergency, such as transmitting images directly by satellite (an example of 'tele-medicine'), are now being tested.

Minor injuries

As A&E departments have become busier and the technical quality of the care they provide has risen, the NHS has made some of the smaller departments into 'minor injuries units'. Initially unpopular with the public, the idea is now winning more support. Minor Injuries Units (MIU) are actually able to offer a wide range of good quality services for the sorts of emergencies that are not life-threatening or disabling, but they do depend on good support from GPs. MIUs are cheaper to run, can see patients with minor injuries more quickly, and can be provided more locally than A&E departments. If your problem is not obviously a dire emergency, your ambulance control centre will be able to advise you what to do and where to go if you ring 999.

Emergency hospital admission

There are only two ways for people to enter or leave a hospital: upright or lying down. Both for admission and discharge most of us would prefer the former method, but sometimes this will not be possible.

What's happening? An emergency or urgent admission will usually be made through the A&E department. However, despite what you see in TV hospital soaps, most emergency admissions are not life-and-death fights as the trolley is rushed from the ambulance. Most of the time it is possible for A&E staff to explain to patients and relatives what they think the problem is and what they are proposing to do about it. Even though you may be shocked and worried by the emergency, it is important not to lose your critical reasoning. Does what you are being told about the emergency make sense to you? If it doesn't, say so, and particularly don't be led into describing something that hasn't happened ('Your father has probably been acting oddly over the past few days, hasn't he?'). Like all of us, doctors make mistakes. In an emergency they may jump to a conclusion from having heard only half the story and will then make the rest of the patient's history fit the conclusion.

In an emergency, as in the rest of your health care, you will want to know what are the benefits and risks of a proposed treatment; what will happen if they do nothing for a while? The answer may be 'you'll die'! But it might also be 'as there is no change, we don't have to do anything immediately'. What you need to know are the alternatives.

GP admission Many hospitals also operate a GP admission system, which works alongside the A&E department. If your GP thinks that you need to be seen quickly by the hospital, he or she can send you to hospital and phone ahead to the GP unit to let them know why you need to be seen. The medical team at the hospital will then admit you into a holding area until they can assess what is the best way of treating you.

Admissions without consent In some circumstances an urgent admission to hospital can be made against the wishes of the patient or relatives, if a doctor believes that, by not being admitted, a person might cause harm to themselves or to other people. Generally this is used for people who are mentally ill, and the procedure is known as 'sectioning', after the particular section of the Mental Health Act (see chapter twelve) that is being used to enforce admission. However, it is possible to detain someone in hospital who needs treatment for an infectious or dangerous illness, such as cholera or typhoid, if you have a magistrate's order.

Planned Admission

A planned admission to hospital will come following one or more outpatient appointments, after you and the specialist have agreed on treatment. You will then receive a date for coming into hospital. You may also hear it referred to as an 'elective admission'. Unfortunately, it is these admissions that get cancelled when the hospital is full of urgent or emergency cases.

Waiting times for planned admission
Strictly, there are two waiting times: the first occurs when you wait to see a specialist after your GP suggests you should; the second occurs when you wait to be admitted to hospital for the treatment the specialist has suggested. However, most people mean the second wait when they talk about waiting times and waiting lists, and unfortunately this is when you are most likely to experience the longest period between agreeing treatment and receiving it.

For most treatments, the waiting time is less than a year, and for many it is less than six months. How long you wait will depend on how urgent the specialist thinks your need is (will your problem get worse, are you in pain?), and how much it affects you (can you work, how is your problem affecting your mobility or mental state?). It will also depend on whether you and your GP are able to find a specialist who can treat you more quickly. The NHS national health information line – 0800 554433 – holds details on waiting times for all treatments at all hospitals in all areas of the country, so they will be able to help you if you want to find a quicker route. However, it is important to remember that some doctors have long waiting times because they are known to be the best in their field and so they get many referrals.

Preparing for admission

The admissions office at the hospital will send you details of when you will be admitted to hospital, together with information about the hospital. Make sure that they have got your correct details, and that the hospital number is the one on your outpatient appointment card. You should know at what time and on what day to go, where to go and what to bring with you. You will be asked to let the hospital know that you have accepted the admission and will be there. You will also be asked to phone the hospital on the morning of the day you are coming in, to be sure that there is still a bed for you. It is one of the great shames of the NHS that patients are still regularly cancelled from coming in to hospital very close to the day of admission because there is no bed, or no staff available for them.

Get the information!
Hospitals are much better at providing information about themselves, but don't just rely on it. If you know someone who has been in the same hospital recently ask their advice about what they found useful to bring in. You will almost certainly be admitted to a ward, the basic organisational unit of most NHS hospitals. Wards are run by the most senior nurse. Normally this person will be called a ward manager, although they may also known as sister, if it is a woman, or the charge nurse, if a man. Before the day of admission you might like to ring the ward you are going to be on and ask the ward manager what things you should bring in. We have included some suggestions on pages 70–71. If you have never been to the hospital before, and are likely to spend some time there, there is no harm in arranging to visit before-hand. Ring the ward and ask them what would be the best time to come to look round for a few minutes. You can also find where the admissions office is, the League of Friends shop, and what other services the hospital offers. If it is a large hospital, it will also allow

you to get some of the basic layout clear, so you are not panicking about where to go and how to get there on the day of your admission.

Length of stay in hospital

The average time that people spend in hospital has gone down dramatically over the past twenty years, mainly because treatments have improved. For example, surgery which used to be done through major cutting, causing large wounds, can now be done through a key-hole cut in the skin, so the healing time has been greatly reduced. Around ten years ago, day surgery was rare: now many operations can be carried out in the morning, allowing patients to recover from the anaesthetic in the afternoon and go home in the evening. Some tests (see chapter ten) are also carried out by admitting patients just for the day.

The length of time you spend in hospital is also becoming more predictable due to more procedures being defined in clinical guidance or 'protocols'. Historically, the day of discharge would depend on the decision or whim of the consultant. Now the standard treatment for a particular condition will guide the clinical team through a set procedure, suggesting what to do on Day 1 to Day 4 or 5, when the patient can be discharged if they have had a typical recovery period. This revolution in treatment has made hospitals much more like national retail units than one-off shops, more McDonald's than Harrods. This does not mean that there are no variations in quality, nor centres of excellence, nor that individual doctors and nurses don't make a difference. But the days of the hospital consultant reigning all powerful over patients and staff are fast disappearing, and not before time.

Coming into hospital

You can usually buy the basics of anything you have forgotten at the hospital shop, which in larger hospitals these days may be virtually a whole shopping mall.

Here is a checklist of what you might need for a stay of a few days in hospital:

- toiletries – soap, shampoo, toothbrush and toothpaste, shaving brush/kit, deodorant, tampons, etc

- night clothes, dressing gown, slippers

- change of day clothes

- books, magazines

- fruit, juice

- small pots of relish and preserves (which can make hospital food taste a bit better)

- treats

- radio or personal stereo with CD or tapes

- money for newspapers, drinks, etc

- change for telephone/phonecard

- all the drugs, pills and medicines you have been taking. It is not unusual for ward staff to throw these away as you begin the drug regime prescribed by the hospital doctors

Booking in

Some hospitals ask you to go straight to the ward, others ask you to book yourself in at the admissions office and then go to the ward. If you go up to the ward look for the ward 'station', which is usually the central area from which the nurses and doctors work. Ask to see the ward sister or senior charge nurse who has overall responsibility for the ward and introduce yourself. The staff will show you to your bed and introduce to your 'named nurse' (see below). Your bed may be in a long, open-plan 'Nightingale' ward, but the more common layout these days is in smaller bays accommodating four or six beds, or in a separate room. The ward layout varies from hospital to hospital, but your condition, your sex, chance and, sometimes, who you are may also influence what accommodation you end up in. Mixed sex wards have been the curse of patients for the past few years. They were introduced by NHS managers to allow every bed to be used to its maximum capacity, as pressure on beds has grown. But they are rightly very unpopular and hospitals have now been told to get rid of them. What is likely to happen is that wards will be separated into male and female parts, with separate washing and toilet facilities. If you have a particular problem or preference for separate facilities, do ask the ward sister or senior charge nurse.

Named nurse

Every patient in an NHS hospital ward is supposed to have a named nurse. The idea is that you will always have someone personally responsible for your overall care and well-being during the whole of your stay. Nurses – even when they are overworked – do not stay on duty for 24 hours in each day, so there will be times when your named nurse hands over to another nurse, which often defeats the purpose! Generally, nurses are organised in three shifts, day (8am–3pm), evening (3–10pm) and night (10pm–8am). A second problem with the named nurse idea is that there is a national shortage of nurses so most hospitals have to employ large numbers of 'bank' (agency) nurses. This, too, can mean that the idea of a consistent member of staff to look after each individual patient is more true in theory than practice.

Your named nurse will settle you into the ward, explain the procedures and tell you what you can expect to happen. Don't be afraid to ask questions, however trivial or embarrassing they may seem. The chances are the nurse will have heard it hundred times before. Bodies and what happens to them are part of the professional life of nurses, so your nurse is very unlikely to be surprised or embarrassed by your questions or problems, however personal.

The nurse will at some point during this first conversation, 'admit' you to the ward. They will take down your personal details and a contact number for your closest relative, and carry out some routine checks on your state of health, such as temperature, blood pressure and pulse. This is your base line measurement of health which will be monitored at intervals during your stay to give the clinical team an indication of how you are getting on.

Staff who come to see you

Hospitals can sometimes seem insensitive and humiliating places without anyone meaning it to be so. This is partly because of the unavoidable differences between staff and patients. Staff in hospitals are young, and much of the care is provided by relatively junior people, often still in training. A small proportion of junior doctors can be arrogant, sometimes a defence to cover a lack of confidence in what they are doing. Staff are also healthy and fully clothed, while you, the patient, are neither. It is difficult to see this as an equal partnership between staff and patient, and much of the hospital regime seems to emphasise the gulf between the (powerful) staff and (powerless) patient.

Women patients have reported male staff walking unannounced into their rooms, subjecting them to intimate examinations and leaving again without any identification or explanation being offered. These may be exceptions, but these things do happen. What is important is to make sure that this doesn't happen to you.

One small step is to insist that everyone introduces themselves by name, what they do in the hospital and why they have come to see you – some professionals will do this as a matter of course but by no means all. Any member of hospital staff, from the most junior to the grandest, should carry hospital ID, and clinical staff should wear a name badge. Someone coming in with a white coat and a stethoscope around their neck is not necessarily a doctor, merely someone with a couple of medical props, and you must be satisfied that they have legitimate business with you. Having said that, the incidents of abuse of roles or positions in hospitals are very small. A second thing you can do to feel more in control is to decide what you want the staff to call you. If being called by your first name sounds too familiar ask to be called by your title and surname.

Doctors and the other clinical staff

Hospital care is a team effort. Each medical specialty is organised into teams, called 'firms', led by the consultants, who direct the work of a team of junior doctors below, which will include medical students if the hospital is a 'teaching' hospital, linked to a medical school. Various members of the team will visit you during your stay in hospital, as well as other professional staff who are involved in your care, such as anaesthetists, if you are having surgery, and paramedical staff, such as physiotherapists. You should be asked if you mind students being present during visits, and you can always refuse to have students in attendance.

At some point early on in your hospital experience – however you have arrived – you will be 'clerked in' by a junior doctor. This forms the basis of your medical notes. The doctor will go through a list of questions about your present health and medical state, and about your medical history – this may stretch back as far as asking you whether you were a normal birth (which of course you remember!). Clerking you in involves giving you a basic physical examination, as well as checking what medication you are on. Take this opportunity to build up a relationship with a member of the team that is going to be treating you and to find out a little about them. The more you talk to the people who come to see you, the more you will feel an active part of the process. Ask staff where they fit into the system, what they do, who they are doing it for, then ask them what they are wanting to find out in this interview and why this is important to your care. You might also ask a junior doctor how many hours they have worked before visiting you and when they will go off duty! This should be enough to give them the message that you are taking an active interest in what happens to you. And as everyone is keeping notes and charts on you, you might find it interesting to do the same – keep a diary of your hospital care, recording who you saw, when, and what happened during the interview. An outline for a hospital diary is given in chapter 16.

Ward routines

Ward routines can seem to be completely haphazard and bewildering, but there is a pattern to them which you will begin to recognise after a couple of days. They are complicated because most of the staff who you will see on your ward also do other things in other parts of the hospital. Unfortunately, many of the routines are determined by what is managerially efficient rather than what is convenient or comfortable for patients. Staff work shift patterns, and getting through all the procedures, particularly when understaffed and busy, can mean that individual needs and the personal touch gets forgotten. So be clear and firm if you need something, but be reasonable!

Ward rounds

Ward rounds can be intimidating – the stereotypical image portrayed on television and in films of the grand consultant sweeping all before him (always a him!), terrifying junior staff, insulting patients and barking orders to nurses, is an enduring one. The trouble is that nobody actually explains to patients what the ward round is for, so it often seems to be a ritual in which the patient is surrounded by a mob of faces, most of whom will be unfamiliar, while doctors swap intimate details about the patient in their own shorthand jargon before saying a few things to the patient and moving on.

The ward round is actually the point at which the whole medical and nursing team can review the care that each patient is receiving. Remember that you may have been seen by lots of different people, each of whom will have added to the jigsaw of your treatment. The ward round is the moment when the person who has overall responsibility for your health – the consultant doctor – can get the complete picture, which the more junior doctor must have pieced together to present to the consultant. So it is serving as the focus of all the care that you have received to date, a sort of stocktake of the 'where-are-we-and-where-do-we-need-to-be?' variety. The ward round is also the opportunity for the consultant, as the most experienced and most senior doctor, to take a fresh look at you, and to review what has been done, and whether he or she is satisfied that all is as well as it might be. Consultants also use it as an opportunity to teach and advise the junior staff (who are still learning) and medical students (if you are in a teaching hospital). A further function of the ward round, in these days of constant pressure to free up beds for other patients, is to allow the team to see how long you will be in hospital, and to make sure that you are able to leave when you no longer need to be in hospital, which may mean contacting the hospital social care team, or providing you with aids to facilitate your return home.

The jargon that medical and nursing staff use when they talk about you is not done to cut you out of the discussion. It's a shorthand between the staff to get your situation clear. The team may have to see up to 30 patients on a ward round but this should not put you off if you want them to explain something to you. The consultant should tell you what they have concluded. As it can be quite off-putting to have a sea of faces looking down at you, if there is anything that you want to say to the consultant in confidence, ask your named nurse if you can have a private word with the consultant when he/she is next on the ward. They should certainly make time to see you on your own, and the vast majority will be very happy to do so, busy or not!

Food, cleaning and entertainment

These are sometimes known as the 'hotel' services at the hospital because they are the facilities that need to be provided as well as the medical and nursing care. Reading the papers you may think that the food is always awful, cleaning is non-existent and the only entertainment is hospital radio, run by very amateur volunteers. This is certainly not the whole truth.

Hospital food is provided on a strict budget which is very likely to be far less than you spend on your own food. For short stays in hospital, the effect of this may not be so bad, but for those staying longer the fact that the food may have a lower nutritional value than you are used to is quite worrying. You will be given a choice of food in hospital and should be offered a choice of portion size. Hospitals should also provide food to suit dietary and religious needs but make sure you let them know your requirements. One way to improve the food that is served is to bring in small bottles of relishes and preserves – mustard, pickles, spices, honey, jam – to add to your meals. Also bring in (or have a visitor bring in) some fresh fruit and juice or squash. Hospitals tend to be well heated so you may find you get very thirsty. It is unlikely that you will have access to a fridge so bear this in mind if you bring in any other sorts of food.

Visiting times

Hospital visiting times have become much more relaxed in recent years, although you do still find the odd place which has a '1–4pm, but never when there's a doctor in sight' attitude. This should always be challenged. Ask to talk to the ward sister about the visiting times policy. In most places it is normal practice to allow visitors from morning until night-time unless there are very good reasons which are for the health and well-being of patients. When you are in a ward you are in a public space which has to accommodate many people, some very ill or frail. Partying around the patient's bed or letting the kids run riot is not good visiting behaviour!

Privacy

Privacy can seem like something that is just not on offer in busy hospital wards, with constant visits and inquiries. Hospitals deal with matters of great personal importance and should offer the people they care for an opportunity to meet and speak privately and in confidence, when this is needed. If you need to have a private discussion with one of the team who is looking after you, or with a relative or friend, ask your named nurse or the ward sister or charge nurse if there is somewhere private where you could go for a while.

Asking after someone in hospital

It is natural to want to phone to ask about the condition of a friend or relative who you know is in hospital, particularly just after an operation. While ward staff will try to be helpful, they should not give information over the phone unless they are sure who it is that they are talking to, and they have the permission of the patient. To be sure that you will be able to get information, it is best to introduce yourself to the ward staff or to get the patient to make clear to the staff that information about their health can be given to the following named individuals. Some wards are flexible about allowing relatives to speak to patients on the central ward phone, others will ask the patients to call back on a pay phone – most wards have these on trolleys that can be wheeled to the bedside.

Treatment regime or care plan

You may not be aware of it but your treatment in hospital will follow a plan or protocol which has been laid down for your particular problem. While your problem may feel totally unique to you, the chances are that the hospital has dealt with many similar cases before you and will deal with many more after you leave. The plan or protocol will be flexible, as each person is slightly different, but will broadly follow a pattern, with the same things done at the same time and with any luck the same result, which is successful treatment. There is no reason why you shouldn't know what your treatment plan is and then record the care you receive against the care you were expecting to receive.

If you are having a baby in hospital, then you should be actively involved in your maternity care plan, looking at the different options with your midwife or obstetrician, and deciding what type of birth experience you want for yourself and your baby – whether or not you want pain relief, a water birth or to stand up whilst you are in labour, for example. Of course it does not always turn out as you want but at least you will have something to aim for.

Research in hospitals

Many hospitals, particularly the larger hospitals which are linked to medical schools or research institutions, carry out research on patients. This is not as alarming as it sounds. All research that goes on in hospitals has to pass through some very tough tests before the research can get anywhere near humans. However, as there is still a lot more that we don't know about health care than we do know, hundreds of thousands of clinical trials go on throughout the world at any time, and you may be asked if you want to be entered into a trial. A clinical trial is not as simple as it sounds. If you agree to be part of a research trial then you and your doctor are unlikely to know whether you are having the experimental treatment or the conventional treatment. This is known as the double-blind trial, for obvious reasons, and it is the gold standard in clinical research. Only the researchers will ever know and they will use the results to test the efficacy of a new treatment against the old treatment, or no treatment at all. You have the right to say no if you don't want to be part of the experiment.

What happens if you have an operation?

The two most important people who will visit you before an operation are the surgeon and the anaesthetist. Their roles are complementary: the surgeon will be doing things which would normally deliver a large shock to your system, and the anaesthetist is working to minimise the impact to your body while the surgeon is at work and to restore you to consciousness after the operation. They are the two principal players in the operating theatre and – just as in any other theatre – there are favourite couples who like playing opposite each other.

The surgeon will explain what the team has concluded from all the tests they have done, and will describe how he or she plans to tackle the problem. The surgeon will also explain things to your family or close friends. This might be the first time that the reality of what is happening hits you and this can be disturbing. It is really important that you have the chance to get the picture straight in your mind, if necessary by asking the surgeon questions after they have explained what he or she is going to do.

Questions to ask your surgeon:

1. If you did nothing what would happen to me?
2. What is the likelihood of what you propose to do actually working?
3. Are there alternatives to what you propose and how well do they do?
4. Are there any side-effects and how severe could these be?
5. If I agree to go ahead will that be the end of the problem or will I have to come back again?
6. If you had a son/daughter/mother/father with this problem, would you be happy for them to have this treament?
7. How often have you done this operation and what is your success rate?
8. Will you be doing the operation yourself?
9. How long will it take me to recover from the operation?
10. What is the risk of something going wrong and what would be the result if it did?

These questions sound very gloomy but you do need to know where you are. As the old advert said, when the AIDS epidemic was threatening: Don't Die of Ignorance. Don't agree to the operation until you are satisfied that it is going to be in your best interests. Just because you are in hospital, doesn't mean that you have to agree to the operation that is proposed: that only happens when you sign the consent form for treatment. There is more about consent in chapter eleven.

The anaesthetist will discuss the drugs that you will have, to keep you unconscious and pain free during and after the operation. Tell the anaesthetist about any worries you have about pain or reaction to drugs: he or she will also ask you about previous operations or drug reactions. The anaesthetist will be concerned to get the right combination of drugs for you, because this will give the best conditions for a successful operation and a quick recovery period.

Post-operative period

This is a crucial time for the success or failure of an operation or treatment. Although you may be naturally just concerned to get through the operation or treatment, try to envisage what happens next. When can you get out of bed and start moving around? Will you have help from the hospital physiotherapist or others to help you? How long should it be before you can leave hospital? What drugs will you be on and what will they do to you? You might be surprised by the answer. New techniques, new drugs and new post-operative regimes mean that you will be up and about much more quickly than you think possible. Even people who have had hip replacements are encouraged to get up and move around after a couple of days.

Children in hospital

The care of a parent or a carer is terribly important to a child during a stay in hospital, and all hospital staff should allow family members to support a child by being there at all times, except where this is clearly against the child's interests. As a parent or carer you should feel able to be fully involved in all parts of your child's stay in hospital, by carrying out all the usual roles as if you were at home, such as dressing and washing, to being able to give support and comfort during stressful moments, such as during investigations, anaesthetics and treatment. Hospitals should enable you to stay overnight with your child, either in a folding bed in your child's room, or in a parents' room nearby. Hospitals should offer you washing facilities, sitting room, kitchen and toilets and use of a telephone. As with any admissions, it is advisable to phone ahead to discuss your needs with the ward that your child will be going to, before you arrive.

Leaving hospital and follow-up

Hospital stays are much shorter than they were even five years ago, and it will often not be very long after treatment that you are preparing to go home. This is one of the benefits of new medical practices, better operating techniques, better drugs and advances in nursing practice. Before you are 'discharged' you should have a plan of your home care worked out with you. This may involve the hospital social workers, if you need support at home from social services. You may also need home visits from your GP or the community nursing team. All this may take time to arrange, because of the different organisations and agencies involved. Make sure as well, that your GP will be notified by the hospital as to what has been done while you've been in hospital, and that you have a follow-up appointment with the consultant to check your progress.

Your discharge checklist

1. You know what care you need after hospital and how to get it.
2. You know what drugs you need and who will prescribe them.
3. You know what you should do to speed your recovery.
4. You know that your GP will be notified about your hospital care and discharge.
5. You have a follow-up appointment, if needed.
6. You have discussed arrangements with the ward sister or your named nurse.
7. You have all your personal belongings, including any kept safe for you.
8. You know the transport arrangements to get you home.
9. The consultant is happy that you are ready to leave.
10. You have the numbers and names of the ward and staff if you need to contact them.

CHAPTER 5: COMMUNITY AND HOME HEALTH CARE

'Community' and 'home' sound nice, familiar, friendly places to get your health care, and, as discussed earlier in the book, a lot more health care can now be provided in health centres, GP surgeries and clinics. But although medical technology allows you to go in and out of hospital quicker than ever before, it does not necessarily mean that your recovery after an illness will be quicker – just that the pattern of health care has changed. Increasingly, people who are poorly are being looked after in their own homes by skilled professionals as well as their family and friends. This is what many of us would choose. But how well prepared would you be if it were to happen in the next week or so? Would you know how to get ready for a spell of care at home, even if you were given time to prepare? This chapter helps you think both about what you and your family can expect when you come home from hospital or need short-term care at home. Chapter six covers care that might be needed on a more long-term basis.

THE GOOD AND BAD NEWS OF HOME HEALTH CARE

Some people who are ill would choose automatically to be cared for at home if it were possible, others would want to avoid it all costs. It is easy to make these judgments instinctively without having much idea about what home care would involve – most of us would not even think about it until the event decended on us either as a patient or as the carer for a friend or relative. So what are the positive and negative aspects of home care to consider when deciding what is best for you, your friends or relatives?

The positive aspects of home care

- The patients and their family can feel more in control than in a hospital. Being in your own environment may make it easier to make decisions about what you want and need.

- You can choose your own routine and do not have to fit in with the rhythms of nursing shifts and consultant ward rounds.

- Familiar surroundings and food can help sick people to relax – this in itself can help the healing process.

- Social support from neighbours, family and friends is easier to organise.

- Children tend to be more reassured by a parent who is physically at home, even if their mother or father is ill.

- Being at home can encourage patients to do more things for themselves, putting them back on the road to independence and recovery.

- The risk of catching an infection from another patient is lower than it would be in hospital. A good deal of time and effort in hospitals is devoted to looking after people who have got sicker because of infections they have caught whilst in hospital.

The negative aspects of home care

- Even with good community health and social services support, family and friends will still be called on to do a considerable amount of care. This may be hard work, particularly if the carer does not really have the physical or emotional strength to do it. The carer may also have health problems of their own – it is very common for carers to fail to recognise or admit that they need help until they are at breaking point

- There may be a financial cost to looking after a sick person at home. This is difficult to quantify as it will vary from one person to the next. There may be extra costs from keeping the house warmer, making small changes to your home or room layout, taking unpaid leave to look after someone, prescription charges if you have to pay them (drugs prescribed in hospital are provided free of charge whereas those which are prescribed by GPs may not be).

- Some parts of the country may not have the appropriate equipment or treatment resources to allow home-based care – availability and policies on home care vary across the country. For example, the distribution of home dialysis machines is uneven due to their high cost and because it is not very efficient to lend them out to individual homes.

- Family doctors and community health workers will need to give the patient and carer additional time and effort. If the person's needs are very demanding you may find that the professionals are reluctant to provide that level of support due to other calls on their time. The professionals may prefer the patient to go into or stay in hospital.

Preparing your home

The thought of turning your home into a mini hospital may be a daunting prospect. But if home care conjures images of an iron lung the size of your lounge or turning your bedroom into the set for *Casualty* think again. For short-term care at home such major change is unlikely to be necessary – the patient will be back on their feet in no time. But there are small inexpensive changes that can make life easier for the patient and their carers that are worth considering. If you do need special aids to help with, say, getting into the bath or bed, these will normally be provided free by social services or the local Trust which provides community health services (more on this later).

Here are some basic guidelines to help prepare for caring for a sick person at home. The first rule is to think ahead, and to try to find out as much as possible from the doctors, nurses and other health care professionals about what the patient will or will not be able to do. This applies, too, if you are the patient. It will help you imagine what will happen so that you can begin to make plans for your care at home.

Preparing the room

Where will the patient be spending most of their time? Sitting down or lying down in bed? If you live in a two-storey house try to find a room on the ground floor, ideally next to a bathroom or toilet and fairly near the kitchen. If it is convenient a dining room can be a good location as it will be close to where the care giver will be and will be easier for any nurses or therapists that need to visit. More importantly being closer to the hustle and bustle of family life can often be better than being isolated in a bedroom. This is very much a matter of choice and will depend on how long the person will take to recuperate. A downstairs room will be more appropriate for, say, someone making a slow recovery after a stroke than a person who has just had an appendix removed. If possible choose a room with a window so you can let in some fresh air and to let the patient look out at the world outside.

Making bed-rest easier

If the patient has to spend long spells of time in bed there are some small things that you can do to make it easier for both them and you.

- Have a small table which can be easily reached from the bed to carry essentials such as drinks, tissues or medicines.

- A bell or whistle of some kind can be handy if the patient needs to get your attention without shouting. A radio, television or even a video can also help relieve the tedium. The patient may or may not want a clock to see the time passing.

- Make sure there are extra pillows or a wedge of foam rubber that can be used to provide additional support so that the patient can sit upright in bed.

- Get a bin or bucket with a lid for getting rid of dirty or used dressings and tissues. In some cases these may need to be collected for disposal in a safe container – the district nurses or other people providing health care will be able to advise you on this.

- If the patient has to take a lot of different pills a small box with different compartments can be helpful in avoiding confusion about what has and hasn't been taken. Simply measure out all the pills at the start of the day using one compartment for each time interval. If you cannot find such a box in one of the larger chemists, containers sold for storing hardware such as small nails and screws can do equally well.

- A plug-in nightlight that provides enough glow in the dark to see by – this helps people to look in on the patient to check they are comfortable without putting on a bright light.

- People who are ill or stressed often get dry or cracked lips and a tube of lip salve or a tub of Vaseline can help keep them moist.

- A baby alarm – a useful device which will enable you to hear anything untoward, such as the patient falling out of bed. Most have a relatively long range so you can move from room to room or even into the garden.

If it looks as if the patient will need care at home for several weeks you can ask your GP to arrange for a district nurse or occupational therapist to visit and offer their suggestions about how you can prepare for this. They will also help you to get any equipment you might need, such as a mattress specially designed to prevent pressure sores from developing (these are very common in people who need a long period of bed rest). If your GP is unable to help you in getting the equipment you need there are three places that you can go to direct. First, there is the Home Loans department of the NHS trust that runs community health services; second, the aids and adaptations department in social services and third, in some parts of the country the local branch of the Red Cross may have equipment that you can borrow. For historical reasons, there is a quite a bit of overlap in the things that social services and community health services provide so in some parts of the country the two suppliers provide a combined service.

What equipment can you get on loan?

People with disabilities or who are convalescing at home can get a range of equipment on loan which may help minimise their problems. Some examples of the things that are provided by social services and community health services are:

- hoists for lifting people into and out of bed or the bath

- special mattresses that prevent pressure sores

- wheelchairs of various types

- adaptations to your bath that can lift a person in and out of the water

- tools to help you grip or carry

- commodes and other toilet adaptations

- foot rests

- bed rails

- walking sticks

- zimmer frames which provide support to help people walk

- rubber sheets

Hoists tend to be bulky and require instruction in how to use them properly. It is good practice for the nurse or other primary care professional to teach carers how to use this equipment – ask if they don't offer to do this. Both community nurses and informal carers have an alarming track record of back injuries caused by trying to move or lift patients into position. As a guide, however strong you are, you should never try to lift an adult and take particular care if you need to help them to move. You should use a hoist if the person cannot move themselves into or out of bed or a chair.

If you do borrow some equipment make sure you take it back. A huge amount of equipment each year goes missing or is never returned.

If the person being cared for has difficulty in getting to the toilet or onto a commode or is incontinent, community health services should also be able to provide a supply of incontinence pads. They may limit the number of pads they will issue per person per week. People's needs vary quite a lot so if you find that this is not enough ask for a nurse to do a reassessment of need. If this tactic fails write a letter of complaint to the trust chief executive (see chapter 16 for how to do it).

Care and support at home

The NHS and local authority social services provide a range of services to people in their own homes to keep them independent. There are also many voluntary and private sector bodies which do similar work in this field. Trying to find out what is around and how you can get these community services, however, can be daunting – particularly since health and social services tend to work to different rules and regulations. Moreover, as both bodies set their budgets and plans on an annual basis you may find that there are small changes from one year to the next as to how much of a certain service will be provided and who can get it.

To make your life easier you should, as far as possible, use the GP as the 'gatekeeper' to these other services. Your GP should have the right contacts and know the system well enough to ensure that you get everything you need. If you feel that you are not getting the help you need or that there are things that the GP may have overlooked, your community health council (CHC) or citizens advice bureau will have a wide range of information on what services are available in your area. Look up your local branch in the phone book. If it is voluntary sector services in which you are interested you can try umbrella groups such as Age Concern or your local branch of the Council for Voluntary Services. If you want to find out more about future developments in community care in your area ask to see a copy of the latest Community Care Plan – your CHC or public library should have a copy or you can get one directly from the social services department. These plans are normally a collaborative effort between the local authority, health authority and NHS trusts.

The list below describes some of the more common statutory services that should be available across the country. These are in addition to the care and support that you can get from your GP.

Adaptations to the home If the person's state of health or disability is likely to be longer term or permanent, the local council may be able to provide help in getting the home altered to allow the person to remain at home. For example, someone who is unable to get upstairs to a toilet may need a second bathroom added to the house or a ramp might be needed to enable wheelchair access to the front door. The support you get may be in cash (a grant or loan which you can use to pay a builder to do the work) or direct help (where the council actually makes the adaptations for you).

Care assistants/attendants These are people who have general care skills. Although most are not qualified nurses they are trained to help with some basic care tasks, such as bathing or changing dressings and shopping. Care attendants may either work for a voluntary organisation (Crossroads is one of the largest) or will be employees of social or community health services.

Chiropodists/Podiatrists Both can do home visits if you need them. As well as providing foot treatment they can advise on adaptations to shoes to help with walking problems. This is an NHS service, although there are also a large number of private operators.

Community nursing support District nurses and health visitors will visit patients in their own home offering treatment and advice. Health visitors tend to concentrate on young children and their parents, although in some places they may have a specific role in caring for older people. It's very unusual for the NHS to provide 24-hour nursing to a patient in their own home. Normally nurses will visit for a few minutes to a couple of hours at a time, preferring to visit several times in one day rather than provide continuous support.

Dental care Some private dentists will do home visits. If you have difficulty in getting someone to give dental treatment at home, or if you cannot afford to pay, the dental services run by community health services should be able to help.

Home helps If you have mobility problems you may be able to get assistance in cleaning your home or in tasks such as laundry and shopping. This service is provided by local authorities.

Meals at home These come in two forms – ready heated meals and frozen ones which the person or carer can reheat when they want them. These are mainly provided by social services or by a voluntary sector organization which is funded by social services. The services should make sure that if the meals are frozen the content and use-by-date are clearly labelled. They should also offer a choice of meals.

Pain relief and dressings An increasingly wide range of care can now be provided in people's own homes. Many forms of chemotherapy for cancer patients can be given in the patient's home. And much of the recuperation after fairly major surgery is now expected to take place at home. In both of these cases fairly intensive support from community nurses and GPs will be provided. Macmillan nurses and Marie Curie nurses (they have similar training) are specialists who are trained to provide palliative care for people with a terminal illness, particularly those with cancer. Like community nurses they provide support in people's homes. In the last stages of life, where necessary, this may be more or less continuous care.

Respite care The daily pressures of caring for a friend or relative at home can be physically, emotionally and mentally draining. Some voluntary sector bodies and the NHS offer carers a respite or rest. This may be in the carer's or patient's home in the form of short-term 'patient-sitting' to allow the carer time off to go out. Or it can involve taking the patient into a hospital or residential home for a short period of time. In some parts of the country these services are in short supply. But there are places where people are not aware of what is on offer and, as a result, these valuable services are under-utilised. If you are feeling the strain from providing intensive support to a spouse, relative or friend, talk to your GP to see if some respite can be arranged. It is not an admission of failure if you need to use these services – it is about recognising and doing something about your own health needs. If you look after yourself you will be able to continue caring for far longer than if you struggle along without help.

Social workers Social workers can provide invaluable advice on the benefits to which carers and patients may be entitled and may help people in applying for them. They also co-ordinate 'care packages' for people who need a mix of things to help them manage at home. A bed-bound elderly lady with a daughter who can visit two or three times a week may need a combination of community nursing support – some home care, meals on wheels, a special mattress to prevent pressure sores, plus a care attendant to help her feeding and some small adaptations to her home.

Day hospitals and day centres

These are not, strictly speaking, provided in the home, but are often offered to people who would be otherwise housebound or who do not get out very often. Day hospitals are meant to have a more therapeutic focus with things such as health advice, chiropody, pain relief or physiotherapy laid on. Day centres are intended to have more social activities, for example there may be hairdresser, some art therapy or music sessions. In practice both sets of services have a social role in allowing people who are quite frail to get out of their homes and meet other people. They are very variable in quality. Many centres offer their clients transport to and from day centres or day hospitals by ambulance, taxi or minibus. A big criticism is that these communal transport arrangements often mean quite frail old people spending several hours in a vehicle as it picks up and drops off.

Voluntary services

The services offered by voluntary bodies are diverse but here are some of the services which might be available in your area:

- lunch clubs and social centres

- volunteer visiting or befriending schemes

- toy libraries

- care attendants to provide respite care at home

- loan of disablement equipment

- counselling

- self-help advice

- advocacy and interpreting

If you want to access these services you can contact them directly or ask your GP to put you in touch.

What to ask if you need health care at home

If you are offered the choice of care at home or if you are considering the implications of looking after a friend or relative at home,

the advice of those who have been there before you is simple –
Ask, ask, ask for information! Prepare yourself for being given much
less information than you will feel that you need. Set yourself the task
of getting fully prepared before you start the care at home so that you
know what to expect, and you'll find it much easier to cope:

- *Ask* the GP and the rest of the health team about the patient's
  condition and what is likely to happen next. Doctors can be very
  vague, even reticent about giving such information, not least
  because they don't actually know the answer. This does not necessarily indicate that the doctor is no good, just that it can be difficult
  to predict how a particular patient might react to treatment.

- If your doctor refuses to be clear about the likely progression of the
  illness *ask* them to spell out the various possible outcomes.

- *Ask* for the information that you need to be provided in a written
  form – that way you will be able to refer to it time and again.

- *Ask* about the limitations that the patient will face and how these
  might change over time.

- *Ask* about what type of diet or any exercises that can be done to
  improve the patient's health.

- *Ask* and make sure you understand what medicine needs to be
  taken at what time and how – some pills are best taken on an empty
  stomach whilst others are better when swallowed with food. Also
  ask about any adverse side-effects that you should look out for.

- *Ask* about what professional support will be available in times of
  crisis – if you feel you cannot cope any longer or if the patient takes
  a turn for the worse – and keep the names, addresses and telephone
  numbers in a place that you can easily find.

- *Ask* what support is available to you as a carer. Can you, for
  example, get respite care if you need it and how can you access it?

- *Ask* what signals you need to watch out for which might indicate a
  worsening of the condition or a relapse and agree with the patient's
  GP or consultant what will happen in these circumstances.

- *Ask* if there are any support organisations locally or nationally that specialise in the type of illness or disease with which you are dealing.

- *Ask* what types of aids or adaptations to your home you might be eligible for and what else might be available if you are able to pay for things yourself.

- *Ask* about the benefits for which you or the patient may be eligible to claim.

- *Ask* if the local trust can provide you with training in some basic care skills – for example, help in understanding how to move someone with limited mobility could be just what you need to prevent back strain or other muscular problems.

- *Ask* about which organisation is responsible for what service and the roles of the different professionals you may need to see. If something goes wrong or you need to make a complaint, you will need to know whether the care was provided by an NHS trust or social services and who to contact.

- *Ask* if the patient can be allocated a care manager or co-ordinator – a named person who will act as the main point of contact for all the services that are provided. That way you will not have to waste precious time chasing people who may spend half their working lives in meetings; the care manager should do it for you.

If it looks as if the patient is going to need very long-term or indefinite care the next chapter will give you some ideas about the options and how they are funded.

What should you expect from those providing services?

Before you agree to any service, whether provided by social services or bought from a private care agency, try to discuss things with the care provider to establish the standards that you can expect. Although these vary from one service to the next there are some basics which you should be told about:

- the time and type of service being provided

- how often you can expect the service (is it daily or weekly)

- the name of the person providing the care and what type of identification they will have

- the length of time you can expect the care worker to be with you

- the cost of the service and the arrangements for payment

- how often the service and your need for it will be reviewed

- what happens if the care worker is late or cannot attend (you should be informed)

Similarly, if you need day care you have a right to expect the following:

- to be told the opening times of the centre, the type of patients that it serves and how many can attend

- the centre should provide a range of activities and you should be able to choose what you do there

- to get help with going to the toilet or washing if you need it

- an agreement about the transport arrangements, such as the time you will be picked up and taken home

These basics should apply whether you need short-term care in the home or more complex care on an ongoing basis. Long-term care is the subject of the following chapter.

CHAPTER 6: LONG-TERM CARE IN THE COMMUNITY

To a large extent, the type of care that you may need on a long-term basis may be similar to that outlined in the previous chapter – though perhaps there will be more of it and for a longer period of time. This chapter covers some of the more complicated aspects of 'care in the community', what is available to patients and carers, how that care is funded, what you can do to insure yourself against future costs. People with mental health problems often need care on a long-term basis and this chapter offers a guide to the services they can expect and the legal rights associated with mental health care.

CARE IN THE COMMUNITY – WHAT IT MEANS

There are many groups of people who may need care on a long-term basis. Older people who are physically or mentally frail, people with learning or physical disabilities who cannot manage independently, those with degenerative diseases (i.e. get worse over time), such as multiple sclerosis. Some people with mental health problems may also need help for a considerable period of time. Ten or more years ago the easiest way for these groups to get their care secured was to arrange for a long stay in a hostel or hospital or to get a place in a residential or nursing home. That way social security paid for their care needs.

Subsequently, successive governments have had a policy of trying to ensure that as much care as possible is given 'in the community'. You have probably heard this phrase quite a lot. In simple terms it means that people get the care they need as close to their own home as possible and in the way which is least restrictive on their personal freedom. Under this policy, hospital or nursing home care is meant to be reserved for people who really cannot manage independently – those who would require a level of support at home that would not make economic sense. Increasingly, frail people are being kept independent through complex arrangements of day care, home nursing, support from friends and the occasional episode of respite in hospital or in a nursing home. The type of services they get may be no different to those described in the previous chapter, but they will need more of them and possibly for an indefinite period until their needs change or they die. The task of co-ordinating the various services and making sure that they are appropriate to the individual's needs and family circumstances is also more complex – almost a job in its own right.

The arguments for community care are not economic ones. Effective community-based care for frail and dependent people, whatever their age, health and social circumstances is not a cheap option. An optimistic way of seeing the policy is that it aims to give people more choice about whether they stay in their own homes. But choices do not come without a price tag and there is the rub. There are limited funds for health and social care which can mean that the care and support that an individual gets may be less than ideal and possibly less than adequate for their needs. But care that is provided by the state is not the only option. Historically the care of people with long-term health needs has always relied heavily on support from family, friends and volunteers. Patterns of family and work life have changed dramatically over the last few years and the indications are that fewer people (typically women) may be willing or able to provide such support in the future, either as informal carers or as volunteers. This is something that the government will have to tackle.

There have been changes in the rules around welfare benefits which enable more people to get the support they need in their own homes. However, the funding system remains very complicated for three reasons:

- *Complex needs* People requiring long-term care have a mix of health and social care needs. They may need to be given medicines but they may also need help to find suitable housing or advice in getting the right benefits. Health and social care tasks are the responsibility of different statutory agencies. To complicate matters further the NHS and social services run by local government work to very different rules and cultures. The main difference to worry about is that patients do not have to pay for care given directly by the NHS (other than for certain tests and prescriptions), whereas social services are allowed to make a charge for the things they provide. To calculate how much you can afford to pay or contribute, they assess your income and outgoings (this is called means testing) and check out the seriousness of your need for the service in question (this is called needs assessment). Shortage of resources can leave the patient stuck in the middle whilst health and social service argue about who is allocated what.

- *Complex services* In most places there is a wide range of social care available – provided both by the statutory bodies but also by voluntary and private sector providers. Not all social services departments provide services themselves. An increasing trend is for them to pay private companies or voluntary bodies to provide social services rather than to do it directly themselves. The social services department should still keep an eye on the quality of the services that these organisations provide. This diverse pattern of care provision should work to the benefit of patients as it ought to offer more choice in the type and cost of services. That is the theory, but it will only be true in practice if patients have an opportunity to find out about what is available and a way of influencing what they get.

- *Complex funding* If you need social care services of some sort you will soon find that the rules around benefits, services and what is or is not funded by the state virtually require a PhD in form filling or welfare economics. Benefits and who is or is not eligible for them are changed relatively frequently, which is a further complication.

Both long-term care and care for people with mental health problems are, as we write, the subject of detailed policy reviews by the Government, so there may be further changes afoot. The basic premise of community care is unlikely to be challenged, however. What is expected is some streamlining and simplification of the current arrangements whereby people who do need spells of hospital treatment can get into and out of that system as speedily as possible.

So what does *PatientPower* mean for the more vulnerable people in the community?

- It means understanding what support is available, how to get it and how to pay for it.

- It means making the best use of those whose job it is to make sense of the complex minefield of community care.

- It means knowing what you have a right to expect and how to make sure those rights are recognised by others – this applies as much to carers as to those who are being cared for.

What you can expect as an informal carer

There are around 6 million people in Britain who look after friends and relatives as carers. Britain's informal carers range from people who are themselves quite old and frail to the very young, who look after parents with terminal illnesses or disabilities. The majority are women. In 1995 the Carer's Act was passed to give carers the right to an assessment of their ability to care. The intention was to support those who were finding the care task too much and or who had their own health needs which, if ignored, would prevent them from continuing in their care role. In reality the health service has been slow to respond and there is still too little recognition of the enormous contribution that carers make.

The Government is implementing a national strategy for carers, but until this takes shape here are some things that carers have a right to expect from the statutory services:

- To have their contribution as a carer recognised and acknowledged by health and social services professionals.

- To be are consulted when the person they care for is admitted to or discharged from hospital.

- To have their views taken into account in the way that the discharge is handled and in arranging any follow-up care.

- To be given a copy of an agreed plan when that person is discharged.

- For their GP to understand what support they are giving as a carer and to keep a watchful eye on how they are managing.

- To have their own health and social care needs to be assessed (if appropriate).

- To receive information and advice on how best to carry out their caring duties – some trusts open a number of their training sessions to carers, for example lessons in how to correctly move patients so as to avoid back injury.

The carer's movement is well established and can be a useful source of support and advice. The Carers' National Association should be able to put you in touch with a group which is active in your area (see the Appendix for details).

Who pays for what: your rights if you need long-term care

The days when the NHS looked after wards full of older people who would spend their last months and years in hospital are virtually gone. Often this was due to lack of alternative places for these patients to be looked after – they did not require medical care but could not manage alone at home. All they needed was some support to help them manage the tasks they found physically difficult. The practice of routinely putting older people in residential homes where it was assumed that they would all get on with one another because they were of a similar age are also thankfully over.

Today the NHS provides very little long-term hospital care for frail older people. Those that need medical or nursing care on a long-term basis are now more likely to have this provided at home or in a nursing home that may be run by the independent sector. There are now more than half a million people living in nursing and residential homes. In terms of odds, approximately 1 in 4 women and 1 in 6 men will need long-term care in their later life. Not surprisingly, the changes have caused some confusion. Much has been made of the NHS's founding principle of providing care from cradle to grave. Gradually, however, as we will see below and later in chapter seven, the NHS is sharing this responsibility with other agencies – with social services, with voluntary bodies, with the private sector and with hospices. It's impossible to give a definitive guide about which agency is responsible for what as circumstances do vary around the country. But here are some general answers to the typical questions asked by those needing long-term care:

Will the NHS pay for my care? If you need health care, however long term, the NHS has a duty to provide that care for you, even if it is very expensive. But if your needs are mainly social (shopping, bathing or cleaning fall into this category) then it should be social services who make arrangements for your care. As a guide the NHS should pay for the following:

- an assessment of your needs
- rehabilitation and recovery
- palliative health care (for people in acute pain or with a terminal illness)
- inpatient care
- respite healthcare

- specialist or intensive medical and nursing support to people in nursing homes
- community nursing and primary care services for people at home or in residential care
- specialist transport such as ambulances

Who decides whether my needs are to be met by health or social services? Usually your GP will refer you for an assessment. At this point a 'care manager' will be appointed who will make the decision using a set of local guidelines and looking at how dependent you are on health and social care support. At the heart of these guidelines are a set of 'eligibility criteria'. These will be drawn up by the health authority in discussion with local authorities. They attempt to draw some boundaries between what is counted as health care (which is free) and what is counted as social care (funded by the council and subject to charges and means testing). If you are unclear about how this works locally or want to see if a decision has been made fairly ask to see a copy of the criteria. They are normally phrased in a relatively open and loose way, and are subject to a degree of interpretation, so don't expect a categorical answer of yes or no. The criteria may also use an unwieldy amount of jargon so you may need to ask someone in the health authority or your community health council to guide you through it.

What does the assessment involve? The care manager will look at your medical, nursing and social care needs. They will concentrate on what everyday things you can manage on your own, for example washing, cooking, getting dressed, and those which you will need help with. The care manager will get an opinion from other professionals who are either looking after you or who are specialists, for example occupational therapists. The care manager should discuss the outcome with you and your carers, family or friends. You should be given a written statement which summarises which aspects of your care will be organised and paid for by the NHS. It may also list what help social services will provide.

Who will pay for my social care needs? This depends on your personal and local circumstances. You may get the services free, your social security benefits may be adjusted to pay for social care, or you may need to make a contribution from your own pocket. Social services will assess your income and outgoings and form a view about how much you can afford to pay.

What happens if going home is not possible? If it really is not possible for you to live at home even with regular care and support, then a residential or nursing home or sheltered housing are the main options to consider.

How much does a nursing home cost? Prices vary but the average cost per year is around £17,000 or £336 per week.

In what circumstances will I have to pay for my care? If you have enough income to pay for your care or savings of more than £16,000 then social services will give you no financial help towards the fees. If you currently live in a house that you own the value will be counted as capital. You will be expected to sell your property to pay for your residential care. If you have between £10,000 and £16,000 in savings or capital you will be expected to contribute a proportion of the cost of the fees and if you have less than £10,000 then social services should pay for your care. If you are assessed as needing NHS continuing care the NHS will make all the arrangements and meet all the costs. If you are concerned that you are likely to have to pay for long-term care in the future it may make sense to think ahead about how you would fund it. There are an increasing number of insurance products on the market which offer options for funding long-term care out of regular income.

Should I consider taking out long-term care insurance? There are several incentives to do so. First you may want to top up the services which you have been allocated, say with additional home help or nursing support. You will need some way of paying for these and it may prove expensive if you need them for a period of several years. Second, if you have resources of your own you will have greater choice over the types of services or accommodation available to you. Looking ahead this is an area where the government are keen to see policy changes encouraging people to take greater responsibility for their care needs in later life. The Government is considering introducing a form of matched funding. The way this works is that if you invest say £100 in a fund for your long-term care, the state will pay another £100 into your fund. Further details on funding long-term care are given below.

Can I refuse to go into a residential or nursing home? Yes, although if you are being cared for in a hospital you do not have the right to stay there indefinitely. You should be offered alternative types of services that allow you to stay in your own home.

What happens if I am not happy with my assessment? You can ask for it to be reviewed if you feel that the eligibility criteria have not been followed. This should be done within one week of the assessment – talk to your care manager, social worker or doctor and they will ensure that this is done. If you continue to be dissatisfied then ask for the name of the person who deals with continuing care at the hospital or community trust and write to them explaining the reasons why. The Trust should set up an independent panel comprising health and local authority representatives to review the decision within the next couple of weeks. If you are in hospital, you will not be discharged whilst this review is being carried out. If you are still dissatisfied after all of this you can use the hospitals complaints process, see chapter thirteen for details.

What standards of care can I expect from a residential or nursing home? This is one of the few parts of the health care system where the standards are routinely monitored by independent inspectors. You can get a copy of the standards that the inspectors use in their work from the relevant body if you need them. Health authorities currently have responsibility for registering and inspecting nursing homes. Local authorities have similar schemes for registering residential care homes. Regional commissions are now being set up to take over the regulation of care standards. Some suggestions on the things to look for in a residential or nursing home are given later in this chapter.

What benefits are available?

As we noted in the previous chapter, being cared for or caring for someone at home may cost money, particularly if the carer has had to give up work. There are, however, welfare benefits available to carers and the person they look after. It is beyond the scope of this book to describe in detail the packages available and how they may affect you. But the table on pages 108–9 gives a brief description of the main types of benefit – these can be a critical factor in deciding whether or not people can manage independently or need to rely totally on support from the statutory services.

Funding long-term care

Private health care and medical insurance are covered in detail in chapter fifteen. But most of these products exclude long-term care in a nursing home or residential home and many do not cover payment of intensive nursing support at home. So where do you start if you think that you are likely to need some form of long-term care in the future or you just want to make provision in case you or your relatives need it? The first thing to consider are the various ways of paying for long-term care. As well as the insurance-based products other options include enhancing your pension, taking out some form of life or sickness insurance or taking out a specific investment which you hope will provide a secure income or lump sum. The best advice is to go to a professional who can tailor the solution to your personal financial situation. Some of these options have off-putting names such as pre-funded plans, immediate care annuities and home income plans. If you do look to professional advice bear in mind that long-term care plans are relative newcomers in the insurance market and most are not yet covered by the financial services regulatory system. Make sure the advice you get is independent rather than from someone paid commission just to sell the company's products.

Long-term care policies As a basic guide you will find that there are two payment types for long-term care policies, those where you pay a lump sum up front and those where you pay a regular sum each month. The policies are taken out before you actually need care, and indeed insurance companies may refuse your application if they think you are likely to need care in the immediate future. Irrespective of how you pay, the way in which payouts from policies are triggered tends to be the same. The person's needs will be assessed (using a similar method to that employed by social services when assessing for services or claims for attendance allowance), i.e. the number of activities of daily living (for example washing and getting out of bed) that the person can manage on their own will be checked. The payouts are determined by the degree of restriction that the person has in these tasks, which is an indicator of how much care they will need. Many long-term care policies exclude conditions associated with mental illness, self-inflicted injuries and possibly AIDS-related illnesses – if you want protection against these check the small print.

The cost of long-term care premiums The main problem with long-term care insurance is that it is not cheap and if you are lucky enough not to need care then you will not really get the value from your premiums (other than peace of mind that you were covered). It is difficult to give a reliable figure on costs of premiums as prices vary considerably. But as a rough guide a 60-year-old man could expect to pay around £45 per month and a 60-year-old woman £5 more. Alternatively, a one-off premium can be paid, which would cost around £6,000. A recent innovation is the long-term care bond which refunds most of the premium if health care turns out not to be needed. The ones on the market at present typically require a big cash lump sum. Bonds may be suitable if you have a life policy that matures or have spare capital to invest and are looking for maximum flexibility

Claimant	Benefit	Criteria/target group	Value	Other notes
Carer	Invalid Care Allowance	• Caring for someone >35hrs per week • Earning less than £50 per week • Between 16 and 65 • Not getting other benefits at higher rate, e.g. Maternity Allowance	£38.70 per week	This benefit is unaffected by any savings. You can claim even if your partner works You can still get ICA if you go into hospital for up to 12 weeks
Carer	Income Support	• For people on low income who do not have to sign on for work • People with <£8k in savings	Dependent on whether you are a single/a couple/ renting or a home owner and how many children you may have	There are also carer premiums
Carer	National Insurance Contributions	You will be credited with NI contributions for every week that you claim Invalid Care Allowance		
Carer	Other benefits such as income support, job seekers' allowance or housing benefits	People who cannot work	To be able to claim these benefits you need to show that you are caring either as a volunteer (i.e. you get no pay) or as a close relative	The volunteer and relative definitions are important. If they do not apply to you the Benefits Agency may decide that you are capable of work as a paid carer which will limit the benefits that you can claim

Claimant	Benefit	Criteria/Target Group	Value	Other notes
Person being cared for	Attendance Allowance	• Disabled people over 65 • People needing help with personal care or watching • People who have had this level of need for at least 6 months (unless terminally ill)	There are two elements: • Personal care • Watching over There are two rates depending on degree of care or watching required. Lower rate is £34.30 per week and higher rate is £51.30	This benefit is not taxable and does not reduce the amount of other benefits that the person gets Payment is stopped if disabled person is in hospital for more than 4 weeks
Person being cared for	Disability Living Allowance	• Disabled people under 65 • People needing help with personal care or who have problems walking outside • People who have had the disability for at least three months and are likely to fit the criteria for a further 6 months	There are two elements: Care: three levels depending on the degree of disability (£13.60 / £34.30 / £51.30 per week) Mobility: there are two rates: higher rate of £35.85 and lower rate of £13.60	This benefit is not taxable and does not reduce the amount of other benefit that the person gets This benefit can be paid for children over 3 months if their needs are greater than children of a similar age who are not disabled. Payment is stopped if the person is in hospital for more than 4 weeks

from your investments. Again an insurance broker will be best placed to advise you on the pros and cons of the options available.

Things to consider in choosing a residential or nursing home

The vast majority of the population will never need a place in a residential or nursing home. They will manage independently, perhaps with informal support from friends and relations or care from health or social services. But those who do need some form of sheltered care face some very difficult decisions, typically at a time in their lives when they are least able to make them. There are choices about which place is best for them, decisions about what they can afford and possibly choices about how to pay. But even if a residential or nursing home place is to be funded by the health or local authority there should be a choice of accommodation.

The residential and nursing home market has grown significantly over the past decade or so. Those that can afford to pay themselves may find a wide range of places to choose from, although the distribution of homes across the country is very variable. There are very few, for instance, in London, but a large concentration in the Home Counties. The terms nursing home and residential home are a little misleading. The reality is that more and more residential homes provide nursing care, although legally they are not required to have a qualified nurse on duty 24 hours a day. Some homes are run as a combined residential and nursing home which should allow the residents some transition in the intensity of care they need if their health deteriorates.

Choosing somewhere that may be your (or your relative's) home for the foreseeable future is always a challenge, but even more so for residential care. A big difference between choosing a place in a care home compared with a new flat or house is that people moving into residential care surrender some of their independence. So apart from checking whether the bedrooms are nice and if there is a garden to sit in, one of the most important things to look into is how big a step the transition will be. How does the home help its residents to retain some control over their lives on a day-to-day basis?

The choice you make has to be a personal one – somewhere that feels comfortable and has the right atmosphere. The chances are that you will have had little or no experience of residential and nursing homes until the point at which you or your relative needs one. To narrow down the search start with the local health authority or social services department – the registering bodies – as they can provide information on the homes that are available in the area and the basic facilities that each offers. But this is only a rough guide to what those homes will be like. A list of questions to think about in assessing the pros and cons of each home is given below. If the length of the list seems daunting pick out the questions that you think are critical to whether a home is right or wrong and focus your attention on these.

How are future residents prepared for moving into the home?
- Does the home do an assessment of prospective residents' needs so they can be sure they are able to meet them?

- Do they offer a meeting with other residents?

- Is there a brochure or video that people who are too frail to visit can watch?

- Does the home manager visit the resident at home or in hospital before they move in?

- Can self-funding residents try out the home for a trial period to see if they like it?

- Are residents given a handbook or contract of care which describes what the home offers and its policies and procedures?

What choices are residents able to make in the home?
- Are there opportunities for residents to contribute to the running of the home, is there a residents committee for example, and can residents make menu suggestions?

- Is there any choice about mealtimes?

- Can residents control the heat and light in their own rooms?

- Can residents choose when they go to bed, when they get up and how they spend their day?

- Can they choose things such as books, magazines and which TV programmes to watch?

- Is there a process by which residents can make their views known, for example, a suggestion scheme?

- Can residents choose whether or not they share a room?

- Are residents addressed by their preferred name or title?

- Can residents wear their own clothes?

- Can residents choose to receive their care from a male or female member of staff?

- Are residents encouraged to bring in personal possessions?

- Are residents given help to shop for personal things?

How is privacy maintained?
- What arrangements are made for the residents' post?

- Do residents have the use of a phone where their conversations will not be overheard?

- Is there a private place for residents to meet visitors?

- Is the furniture in communal areas arranged to allow some relatively private space?

- Can residents lock bathroom doors from the inside?

What checks are made by the home to make sure they are meeting residents' needs?
- Does each resident have a care plan?

- Is there a procedure for making, recording and investigating complaints – do relatives and residents know about it and how it works?

- Is the home proactive in getting the views of residents and relatives?

- How do current relatives feel about making suggestions or complaints – would they be worried about the consequences?

As mentioned earlier there are formal registration and inspection bodies who take an overall perspective on the quality of residential and nursing homes. These inspections are time consuming and will be done on a rolling basis over a period of years. If you find anything untoward or undesirable point it out to the home or bring it to the attention of the registering body.

GETTING CARE IF YOU HAVE A MENTAL ILLNESS

Mental illness is far more common than we might believe. Around a quarter of the population will have a mental illness at some stage in their lives – about the same proportion as will have heart disease. A large percentage of those will be looked after by their GP and the primary care team. Only about one in ten of those diagnosed with mental health problems will ever need specialist psychiatric services. There will also be people whose problems are never properly identified, for example only about half the people who eventually commit suicide are likely to have had any contact with psychiatric services. Despite these figures, for those who newly encounter mental illness, either personally or as a friend or carer of someone who develops it, the very label 'mental illness' can be almost as traumatic as the condition itself. There is still a huge social stigma attached to these conditions.

If you need an operation to remove your appendix the chances are that you will get to the operating table in one of two ways, either by referral from your GP or by direct admission through an A&E department. If you have a mental health problem there are many possible ways in which your condition might be first identified or in which you seek the help you need. It's difficult to describe a typical sequence of events which describes how you will be looked after and where. This depends on the nature of your illness, its severity and the pattern and philosophy of mental health care that is available locally. People with mental health problems rarely progress in a straight line from the less intensive forms of help available to the more intensive. Having said that, the following is a description of the different levels of intensity of care available.

Primary and community based mental health care

GPs are experienced in dealing with the milder forms of mental health. An increasing number now employ counsellors to provide psychological help to patients. The practice may also have a community psychiatric nurse or social worker who is part of the primary care team (or will have named contacts for this).

Specialist mental health care

If the GP thinks you need intensive support he or she will refer you either for an outpatient appointment with a psychiatrist or possibly, as a first step, with the community psychiatric nurse. They will decide whether the help you need can be provided in the community or if you need a stay in hospital. If you do need to go into hospital you may go in as an informal patient or on a formal basis. The latter means that your needs are severe enough to warrant some protection under the Mental Health Act. What this means is covered in more detail later, but basically, if you have a formal admission to hospital, it means that you will have restricted choice as to when you leave. As an informal patient you can choose to discharge yourself at any point if you feel fit enough.

Although specialist mental health care covers a wide range of services relating to a broad spectrum of conditions and needs, there are two elements of care which should be standard. The first is that all patients needing specialist mental health care should be given a key worker who will co-ordinate their care and the second is that they should be offered the care programme approach and help with arranging the social aspects of their care such as work, housing and benefits.

The care programme approach

There have been many tragic cases of people with mental health problems failing to get proper support. This sometimes occurs because their care falls between the health and social care agencies or because there is poor communication between these two agencies. But it also happens because the professionals have a very complex task keeping track of people with mental health problems who are not in hospital – particularly if those people resist help from the formal service providers (often with good reason based on previous experience). The care programme approach (CPA) was developed to help mental health professionals reach an agreement (called a care plan) with each other and with the service user about the care and support that person needs within the community. The care programme approach is for people who have never needed an inpatient stay as well as those who are about to be discharged home.

The care plan is a written record of what services you need, what the different agencies will provide and how those services are expected to help you. The process starts with an assessment of your needs, which is normally done by a community psychiatric nurse or a specially qualified social worker. You should be given the opportunity to contribute to putting the care plan together. Before you have a CPA meeting it is a good idea to try to write down what sort of support you think might help you and the things that you do and don't like. That way you will have something to show your key worker that you can discuss together. Don't worry if you are not sure what services are available or what you can expect, that is for the key worker to sort out. Concentrate on the general type of help you think will help you. The formal service system can be rather rigid and tied to core day-time hours, and it can still be difficult for people with mental health problems to get help at weekends and at night. But if this is really what you need, write it down, as there may be some voluntary organisations that can offer just what you are looking for. If you find it difficult to think about what support you need it may help to talk it through with a friend or member of your family. Some health services and voluntary groups provide 'advocates' – people who are specially trained to help those who are unable to voice their views themselves. Often advocates are people who have previous experience of using mental health services themselves.

There are different levels of the care programme approach which relate to the complexity of your condition and needs:

- Level 1 (simple CPA) means that you will have contact with just one mental health care worker – an outpatient appointment with a community psychiatric nurse, for example.

- Level 2 (complex CPA) means that more than one type of mental health worker will be looking after you – this might be a social worker to help you find housing and look after your benefits and a community psychiatric nurse who might be providing regular medication or health checks.

- Level 3 (the highest level of the CPA) means that you are put on a Supervision Register. This is reserved for people who are likely to be at risk to themselves (if they have had a recent suicide attempt, for example) or are a risk to others (if they have a history of violence, for example). The Supervision Register is also reserved for people whose care is governed by certain sections of the Mental Health Act (see below).

Care plans are meant to be reviewed regularly as people's health and social care needs change over time. At a minimum on Level 1 your plan should be reviewed every year, on Level 2 there should be a review every six months, and one every three to six months for people on the Supervision Register. But you need not wait for these formal reviews to let people know if you are unhappy with the services you are getting – ask your key worker (see below) to review your care plan. If this does not work you can make a formal complaint to the trust who is leading your care – they are obliged to investigate your comments and give you a response. A guide to making complaints is given in chapter twelve.

Key workers

Each person on the care programme approach is allocated a key worker who will normally be someone well known to them as provider of care and support – a community psychiatric nurse, a social worker or possibly an occupational therapist. In some parts of the country there are key workers who are not mental health professionals. Whatever their background the key worker's job is to provide a single point of contact and to make sure that the patient is getting (and using) the services listed in the care plan.

Care management

Everyone who has a care plan who also has social care needs will have a care manager. This may be the same person as the key worker, but not necessarily. Social care includes support services which help people to live independently but which are only indirectly linked to their physical and mental health (work experience or retraining, housing or supervised accommodation, or leisure services come into this category). The care manager's job is to co-ordinate services across the different agencies. They may be involved in pulling together the different sources of funding for services.

Mental health care in hospital

Most of the old mental hospitals – the old-style asylums on the outskirts of cities – have closed. Shut away for years, people became institutionalised, and this was often much worse than the original mental health problem. Patients stayed in so long that they forgot how to do things that we take for granted, like choosing which breakfast cereal, handling money or paying bills. Today, if you do need a spell in hospital it is more likely that you will spend a few days to a few weeks in a small unit attached to or part of a district general hospital, although there are still some separate psychiatric units. The NHS also buys some places in private psychiatric hospitals.

Rather than the large wards of twenty or more beds, you are more likely to have your own room or share a small dorm with two or three other people. Although some units offer little planned activity for patients other than a television set, others provide social as well as therapeutic activities. These may range from cookery classes and art therapy to group therapy and Tai Chi. There may be a small gym that you can use and if you are in hospital voluntarily you may be able to leave for short periods and go to the local shops or park if you wish. It's likely that a stay in hospital will be much better than your worst fears. However, the lack of privacy, restrictions and other people's behaviour can be difficult to adjust to.

Forensic mental health care

At the most custodial end of the mental health service spectrum are the forensic services. These are locked environments for the most disturbed patients. There are not many people who need such services so it is not uncommon for patients to have to travel slightly further to these facilities. All patients in need of forensic mental health care will have been detained under a section of the Mental Health Act.

THE LAW AND MENTAL HEALTH: KNOW YOUR RIGHTS

Most people who have mental health problems will have no reason to come into contact with mental health law. But the more severe the illness the more that person's care will be governed by legislation. Legal provisions, such as the 1983 Mental Health Act, aim to balance the rights and safety of the person who is ill with those of the wider community. People with more severe forms of mental illness can be forced to stay in hospital under a section of the Mental Health Act. If this happens they will be referred to as a 'formal' patient. Informal patients, by contrast, have greater choice over when they leave hospital or how much contact they have with community services. A formal patient can only be discharged by a hospital manager or psychiatrist.

The legal side of mental health treatment can be hugely distressing to those affected, particularly if it is their first encounter. Challenging the legal machinery to get your rights recognised and observed can seem like an impossible task, particularly if you are unwell. On the more positive side the mental health legal system is designed to be balanced between patients' and societal rights – there are appeal procedures built in if you are unhappy with decisions about your care. There are also some highly experienced voluntary groups that represent the rights of people with mental health problems which may be able to help. The most widespread of these is MIND, but there may be groups which are specific to your area.

So what can the law enforce on people with the more severe forms of mental illness?

1. It can enforce admission to an inpatient unit for assessment. These provisions tend to be short term and cover only a fixed period.
2. It can enforce certain types of treatment – these are mainly restricted to patients with either a psychopathic disorder, or severe mental impairment. Because these classifications involve a degree of judgement, two doctors have to agree that the patient needs to be 'sectioned' under the Mental Health Act.
3. It can enforce detention in hospital or a transfer to a mental health facility if the person is involved in criminal proceedings.

Chapter eleven deals with your rights in more detail.

If you think you have been detained unreasonably then you have the right of appeal to the Mental Health Review Tribunal. They have the power to investigate your case and make recommendations on future treatment. You can ask for the appropriate forms and contact details of the local tribunal from hospital staff – they are obliged to give you this information.

The Mental Health Act is currently under review but it is likely that provisions for enforcing admissions to hospital and treatment will remain. The main focus of the review is to make sure that the Act covers situations where patients are being cared for in community settings.

CHAPTER 7: PALLIATIVE CARE – A GOOD DEATH

This chapter covers what happens when you or someone you know dies. People who have a degree of warning that they are dying have a choice about where they die. The following pages describe the options available, and what people have a right to expect in the final stage of their life. They also cover what happens if you are left to handle matters when someone dies.

WHAT OPTIONS ARE AVAILABLE?

Until you come across the likelihood of death, either personally or through someone you know, it may not have occurred to you that you could choose where to die. Many people spend their final days in hospital, unless, of course, their death is sudden, but this is not the only option, more and more people are choosing to die in a hospice or at home. But even if hospital is the only practical option there are things that you and your family can do to make sure that quality of life in the final stages is as good as possible.

Dying in a Hospice

Hospices provide special care for people with a terminal illness, not only those with cancer, but also those with degenerative diseases such as motor neurone disease or AIDS-related disorders. There has been a steady growth in the number of hospices over the last few years. Most are supported in part by the NHS although some rely entirely on voluntary donations and bequests. Hospices make no charge for the services that are provided. Most can be accessed by referral from your GP. There is a myth is that you have to be religious to be cared for in a hospice. Many such facilities were originally founded by religious bodies but they do not require their patients to have particular beliefs or faiths.

The pros of hospital care The advantages of a hospice over hospital is that every effort is made to make the environment as like home as possible. There will be far fewer of the hoists, drips, tubes and wires that are characteristic of the more intensive care in hospital. This does not mean that hospices have an aversion to technology, simply that it will be used as discreetly and unobtrusively as possible. Hospices are run by medical and nursing staff who have a special interest and expertise in palliative care. Such care is not about treating people in order to cure them, but about relieving their pain and symptoms in the final phase of an illness. That is why it is seen as 'terminal care', care in the final phase of a life.

The cons of hospice care The disadvantages of a hospice are very much a matter of personal preference. As a general rule there will be less emphasis on keeping the patient alive at all costs, which may be more common in a hospital. For some that is one of the attractions of a hospice – that there will be no heroic but undignified last-ditch attempts to prolong survival. Other people prefer to try everything right to the last, and however low the odds. Also, a hospice can never be exactly like your own home, despite the efforts made to try and achieve this. Some people choose hospices because they cannot bear to put their family through the ordeal of dying at home, but want to go somewhere that is 'home like'.

If you would like further information on the specific palliative care and hospice facilities in your area you should find what you are looking for in *The Directory of Hospice and Palliative Care Services in the*

UK and Ireland, which is published by the St Christopher's Information Service. The service can be contacted by telephone on 0181–778 9252 or by fax on 0181–776 9345.

Dying at home

A deep-seated fear held by many people is that of discovering a dead body. If it is someone you know or if you have never seen a dead person before the stress factor may understandably shoot off the end of the scale. If you die in a hospice or in hospital there will be clinical staff who will take care of the details, but what if there is no one there?

Death is a natural event and although stressful not something of which to be scared. If the person's death was expected the first thing to do is to call their GP. If appropriate, you can also call a priest, rabbi or other minister of religion. The same people should be contacted if the death is very sudden. Depending on the circumstances, you may also need to call the police.

If the person has a terminal illness and has chosen to die at home this need not mean going home to a bed and never leaving the house again. There are now over 200 day hospices across the country for those who prefer to be cared for at home but who need short spells of additional treatment or who have carers who need a rest. Day hospices are normally attached to the larger hospitals and may provide services such as pain relief and symptom control, counselling, physiotherapy and occupational therapy, chiropody and social activities.

If the person who is dying needs intensive nursing care this will often be provided by Macmillan or Marie Curie nurses who provide specialist nursing support to people with cancer and other life-threatening diseases. District nurses may also provide some of the practical care, such as giving chemotherapy or treating the side-effects of being bed bound, which may be anything from pressure sores to constipation. Although most people have heard of Macmillan nurses there is often confusion about what they do. Patients who are offered a Macmillan nurse, or indeed a Marie Curie nurse, can often refuse or get very upset believing them to be less angels of mercy and more angels of death (or at least angels for the dying). The offer of a visit by one of these nurses does not necessarily mean that the patient is expected to die imminently or even has a terminal form of cancer. Their specific expertise is in pain and symptom control, and in counselling, which could be applied to a range of conditions. It is normally your GP or a district nurse who requests this nursing care on your behalf.

Dying in hospital

The quality of palliative care provided in hospitals is slowly improving and many now employ their own palliative care support teams – often staffed by cancer specialists (oncologists) or anaesthetists who have expertise in the pain relief aspects of the disease. Some hospitals now have Macmillan Cancer Care Units – palliative care facilities funded by the NHS and voluntary sector which are attached to the main health care services but which feel less like a high technology hospital environment. These units aim to provide a mix of the good bits of hospices and hospitals. Standards in hospital vary. There is no guarantee that the dying person will be able to have a single room or privacy from the rest of the ward. This is often what relatives find most distressing – the lack of opportunity to spend the final minutes in private without the gawping of other patients or the staff. Nurses similarly may find such situations upsetting. The advantage of dying in hospital is that the relatives will not have to deal with the distressing details of what to do with the body. But again this is a matter of choice. Some find that seeing the dead person and having time to prepare the body or be with their loved one for the last time is a comfort and helps them adjust to the facts. When a person dies in hospital they may be left temporarily on the ward to allow a time for immediate family to pay their last respects. Shortly after, however, the body will be taken to the mortuary.

In certain circumstances doctors may need to report the death to the coroner (a doctor/lawyer responsible for investigating the causes of death). Deaths will normally be reported where there is suspected violence, suicide or other suspicious circumstances, where the patient died whilst having an operation or was in prison. The reason why they have to report such cases is that the coroner is the only person who can sign the cause of death for the certificate. A death is also referred to a coroner when it is more than two weeks since the patient has seen their doctor. If a coroner arranges for a post-mortem they do not need the next-of-kin's permission. If you hear the term inquest it means a more formal investigation which is sometimes held in public and, on occasions, in front of a jury. Relatives are allowed to go to the inquest and ask any witnesses questions but only if they are about the medical cause and circumstances of death.

Depending on the cause of death, hospital staff may ask relatives if they will consider allowing organs to be donated for transplant from the person who has died. This may be a difficult decision to make when relatives are shocked and upset, particularly if the death has been unexpected. Some hospitals have staff specially trained to help relatives decide about transplant. There are, of course, strict time limits within which organs can be removed and some causes of death will determine which, if any, organs can be transplanted. It helps if the person who has died made their wishes clear by carrying an organ donor card, and discussing organ donation with relatives.

DEALING WITH SOMEONE ELSE'S DEATH

If the person dies at home the first thing to do is notify the GP to confirm the death. The GP will normally take you through all the necessary steps that you need to take.

For people who have to face the trauma of a friend or relative dying in hospital, one of the worst things can be returning to the hospital to collect any personal possessions and collect the paper-work. It's not the type of experience that you will have been prepared for until you actually go through it. And the type of questions that pop into your head might be difficult to voice. Each hospital will have different arrangements but a typical set of events might be these.

Where to go When you get to the hospital and if you want to see the body, check first whether the person is still on the ward where they were cared for. The reception desk should be able to help you establish this. If you have been notified by phone of what has happened try to remember to ask where you need to go. If you simply want to do the necessary paperwork and leave, most hospitals have a relatives support or liaison officer whose main job is to meet with the bereaved and help them do this. They will usually have their own office or quiet place where you can go and talk in private.

What will happen? You will be given the patient's personal belongings either in their own bag or in a bin liner, and you might be asked if you want to check it. If you are certain that you do not want to take the clothes and belongings away – and many people do find small personal things like a pair of glasses some of the most distressing things to deal with – you could ask for them to be donated to a charity. Even so, the hospital will still need you to sign a form to say that you have picked them up.

What paperwork will I need to deal with? There are two main bits of paperwork. The first is the death certificate – this records the date, time and cause of death. Do not worry if there are two causes recorded, this is quite normal. For example, the primary cause of death might be written as a heart attack, but this might have been brought about by physical deterioration caused by cancer. If you are lucky you will be shown the death certificate, but some hospitals will give this to you in a sealed envelope. If this is the case, what you will actually be given is an even more impersonal 'Formal Notice to Informant'. This basically tells you that the doctor has signed the death certificate. Anyone can act as the informant but it is normally a relative. The notice tells you what you need to do next, which is register the death with the registrar. The second bit of paperwork is a form which you will need to complete and then sign saying you are happy for the undertakers to collect the body from the hospital. If the person who has died is to be buried you will need an Order for Burial. If they are to be cremated then you will need to get a Certificate for Cremation. The latter has an extra piece of bureaucracy requiring the signature of two doctors who are prepared to say that the person is actually dead. For this simple service you will need to pay the doctors a total of £65 which the two of them will normally share. Strictly speaking, to earn their 'ash cash' as it is known, the doctors have to see the body and do a thorough examination. You will not have to pay for this if the death is referred to the coroner. This double testimony is to prevent any nasty incidents of patients being pronounced dead when they are not and to satisfy the law which states that no one can be cremated until the cause of death is known.

What if they ask for a post-mortem? If the death was brought about by natural causes but was either unexpected or the doctors wish to find out more about the precise cause of death they may ask for permission to carry out a post-mortem. This means that the body will be examined. It will normally mean that the body will need to be cut so that samples can be taken and the internal organs examined. Having a post-mortem should not delay any arrangements you need to make for the funeral.

How do I register the death? The hospital should be able to give you full details of when, where and how to do this. The registrar may operate an appointments or drop-in system. If you can, try to make an appointment as you will probably want to avoid waiting around in a building where more joyful things such as marriages and birth registrations are going on.

What details will I be asked to give? The registrar will ask you for the standard details – the full name and surname of the person who has died (the deceased), their maiden name, if relevant, their address and date and place of birth. You will also be asked for the person's occupation or that of the husband in the case of a woman who does not work. This information may seem strange but is important in collecting national statistics on occupationally related deaths, and the information cannot be identified with the person by name or on the death records. You may also be asked if the deceased had a pension or allowance payable from social security and you may be given another form to fill in so that this can be notified to the authorities and the payments ceased.

Do I need to arrange a funeral? This very much depends on what type of funeral arrangements will be made and how quickly they need to be put in place. It is a little-known fact that there are very few legal controls around the disposal of bodies in this country. It is quite possible to have a 'DIY' funeral, although most choose to put the arrangements in the hands of a funeral director.

What does arranging a funeral entail? This varies from culture to culture and by religion but as a general checklist consider the following:

- Arranging a service or ceremony to be conducted by a priest, vicar, rabbi or other religious leader.

- Selecting an appropriate funeral director to handle the burial or cremation. The funeral company will discuss with you the details of the event and what else you may need to do.

- Notifying family and friends of the death and funeral arrangements (when, where, what will happen afterwards and whether flowers or donations are invited).

- Ordering flowers, if appropriate.

- Putting a notice in a national or local paper.

- Organising any catering before or after the funeral (the wake).

- Thanking family and friends for their support and any donations or flowers.

- Looking at how the deceased's affairs may need to be wound up, such as notifying their solicitor if there is a will, informing life insurance companies, banks, etc.

- Exploring whether you are eligible for financial support for the costs of the funeral from the Benefits Agency. They produce a useful leaflet, 'What to do after a death in England and Wales' (form D49), which covers the main points in a straightforward way.

PLANNING FOR A GOOD DEATH – WHAT YOU HAVE A RIGHT TO EXPECT!

People have very different reactions in the final stages of their lives. Some become stoic and worry about being a burden to health care professionals and to their families. Others are incredibly angry at having their life cut short. And some harbour such entrenched fears that they will become addicted to pain relieving drugs that they put up with far higher levels of discomfort than they need do (in fact psychological dependence on drugs rarely happens where those drugs are used to treat pain). Whatever the reaction, planning for a 'good' death means summoning the strength to think about what you really want and need and making sure you or your representative ask for it. It is tempting to say 'Why bother?'. But if you ask people who have lived through the death of someone close many will tell you how much easier it would have been to cope if they had talked about how they wanted to die to each other and to the clinical staff. Making such plans can also be a helpful way of overcoming the natural fear that people have when confronting their own mortality.

Some things that you can rightly expect are:

For your pain to be acknowledged No one knows your pain better than you. Macmillan nurses are taught the basic principle that 'pain is what the patient says it is and exists when he or she says it does'. The flip side of this is that no one can tell what pain you are going through unless you tell them.

For the professionals to try to understand the type of pain that you are in so that they can treat it There are lots of types of pain and different people will have different levels of tolerance in what they can endure. Try to describe the symptoms that you have in as much detail and let your carers know the things that you find most difficult to bear.

To agree with your carers some simple goals in your treatment which are important to you For example, you may want to aim for as much standing time as possible pain free to enable you to continue with particular activities. For other people it will be hours of uninterrupted sleep that will be important.

To have the potential effects and side-effects of drugs fully explained Knowing what you can expect can help you feel confident that you can recognise when things are not going well. Too many people spend their last few days and hours in fear or panic because they don't know whether what they are feeling is to be expected or not.

To be offered options for the administration of medicines It is now possible to administer medicines in an increasingly wide range of methods. Syringe drivers are automatic battery-operated devices which will deliver a measured amount of a drug into your body over a long period of time, a particularly effective option if you find it difficult to take medicines by mouth, if you feel nauseous or have a horror of regular injections. Suppositories are another option but they tend not to be widely used in this country.

To have your plans for the place and manner in which you want to die acknowledged and followed where possible Your GP or consultant should discuss the options with you and not make assumptions about what is best for you.

To choose who visits you in hospital With family structures becoming increasingly complex through re-marriage, divorce and cohabitation there have been well publicised instances where people have been refused access to visit their relative or partner in the last stages of their life by other members of the family. If you are concerned about potential family feuds make sure that ward or hospice staff are very clear about who you want to be allowed to visit you.

LIVING WILLS

There has been a great deal of publicity in recent years about euthanasia or people receiving assistance to die. Doctors who help their patients in this way still face being struck off the medical register if they are found out. There has, however, been a gradual shift in public opinion on this matter and a growing acceptance of the plight of those whose death is very certain and very imminent and who want to accelerate the process.

The term 'living will' refers to a system which is well established in countries such as the Netherlands. In the UK there is not yet sufficient legal clarity for these wills to be acceptable or widespread. But as people take more and more interest and control over decisions which affect their health, life and death it is perhaps only a matter of time before they become so.

Living wills are useful for people who have a terminal illness, who know that they will die at some point in the not so distant future and want to be able to choose the moment at which treatment is stopped or the manner of their death. The will summarises what they want to happen should different circumstances arise. For example, people with conditions such as muscular dystrophy know that the disease will cause a deterioration in both their physical and mental powers whereby they may not be fit enough to make their views known at the point when they are most needed.

The law does allow something called an 'advance directive' but these are very limited in application. Advance directives are only binding when they relate to refusing treatment – they cannot be used to specify a choice between treatment options. This is because the doctor's professional code of conduct obliges them to exercise clinical judgement about what is in the patient's best interests which overrides any preferences to types of treatment that a patient may express. If you or your relative want to make an active decision to refuse treatment at some specified point in the future then bear in mind the following points which have emerged from case law:

- The patient has to be over 18.

- The patient must be able to understand and remember information relevant to the decision being made. They have to be capable of assessing that information in order to make their choice.

- The consequences of refusing treatment must be fully understood.

- The patient must not have been subject to any undue influence by other people.

No particular format appears to be required so the decision to refuse treatment can be made in writing or given to a doctor verbally. In most hospital settings you are seen by several different professionals so it makes sense to go for belt and braces. Put the request in writing, make copies and let as many people know as you can. If you can, get them to put a copy of your request right at the front of your medical notes. That way you will be able to check that it is there when doctors or nurses refer to the notes in front of you. Finally, keep your fingers crossed that the advance directive works and is followed. The main problem with advanced directives are the conditions listed above – it is very difficult to prove whether, say, a verbal directive was made without influence being brought to bear. For written ones, professionals may doubt the document's authenticity.

An alternative to the advance directive is to allocate the power of proxy to a friend or relative. Unlike the living will or advance directive where you make the choice yourself at a time when you are able to make that decision, giving someone power of proxy means that you give your expressed permission for them to make decisions about your future treatment. The expectation is that the proxy will either make a decision which is similar to the one that you would have made or that you trust them enough to know they would make a decision in your best interest. It may sound like a good idea, but there is not a great deal of research to show whether or not it works. There is always the risk that proxies will not make the decisions expected by those who have invested that power! Pick your proxy carefully seems to be the key message.

PART II

THE BODY IN QUESTION

CHAPTER 8: CLINICAL SPECIALISTS AND WHAT THEY DO

Doctors, like any professional group, are fond of their technical terms. It may be useful shorthand to them but they often forget that the rest of us have little idea about the 'ologies' and 'ologists' they use to describe clinical specialisms and specialists. This chapter gives a 'head-to-toe' guide to who looks after the different parts of your body and its functions. Doctors are not the only professionals with confusing job titles so we have also included some non-medical specialists who are commonly encountered in the health service.

At the top

Neurologists specialise in the diagnosis and treatment of nervous system disorders. These can range from neuralgia (nerve pain) to various diseases of the nervous system.

Neurosurgeons often work closely with neurologists and specialise in surgery of the brain, spinal cord and nerves.

Ophthalmologists diagnose and treat injuries to and diseases of the eye. They can perform eye surgery, such as the removal of cataracts.

Otolaryngologists are often referred to as ENT – ear, nose and throat-surgeons. These parts of the body tend to have inter-related problems, hence the specialism in these three organs.

Plastic surgeons specialise in the reconstructive and cosmetic surgery of the face and other parts of the body. As well as cosmetic surgery such as nose jobs and breast implants, plastic surgeons play an important role in the treatment of burns and cancers of the head and neck.

Psychiatrists are involved in diagnosing, treating and preventing mental illness. They are often confused with psychologists who are not medically qualified and who specialise in human behaviour. Psychiatrists have a range of different treatment methods ranging from psychoanalysis, group therapy, drugs, electro-convulsive therapy (now comparatively rare) to surgery.

Psychotherapist is a generic term for professionals who treat mental illness or personality disorders using psychological techniques. They may or may not be medically qualified. There are different types of psychotherapy which have different theoretical bases. These tend to be named after the people who first described the therapeutic techniques – thus there are Jungians, Freudians and Kleinians. Partly because of these different routes there is no single national registering body for psychotherapists. It is worth doing a little research on therapists' backgrounds before you select one to whom you will bare your soul.

In the middle

Cardiac surgeons are the specialists who perform heart by-passes and transplant operations. In some cases they will be referred to as **thoracic surgeons** – literally surgical experts of the chest cavity, which includes the lungs and trachea (windpipe) as well as the heart and major blood vessels.

Cardiologists deal with the diagnosis and treatment of heart disease. The types of procedures that they perform include stress tests, pacemaker implantation and cardiac catheterisation (inserting a small tube through a vein or artery to examine the circulatory system or widen blood vessels which have become blocked or narrowed).

Gastroenterologists diagnose problems to do with the stomach, intestines and digestive tract.

Nephrologists are specialists in diseases of the kidneys.

At the bottom

Gynaecologists diagnose and treat problems associated with women's reproductive organs. In Britain, gynaecologists also tend to be **obstetricians**, specialising in the medical aspects of pregnancy and birth.

Urologists diagnose and treat diseases of the urinary system and men's sexual organs, including the prostate.

Orthopaedic surgeons cover the treatment and correction of damage or deformities to the skeleton, muscles and ligaments. They may also be specialists in trauma – major injuries caused by accidents or violence.

THE SYSTEMS SPECIALISTS

This group of specialists deal with internal systems or things that affect the whole person.

Anaesthetists are the doctors responsible for the administration of anaesthetics – the drugs that render you unconscious and which relax your muscles before surgery. Increasingly, anaesthetists are extending their work to include the treatment of pain for people who have a terminal illness or persistent pain. This area is known as palliative care.

Dermatologists are specialists in diagnosing and treating skin problems.

Endocrinologists are specialists in the endocrine glands and deal with problems such as obesity, diabetes, growth problems and other conditions which are regulated by hormones and enzymes secreted from glands in the body.

General medicine doctors or **physicians** are experts in the diagnosis and treatment of conditions which do not require surgery. Some specialise in dealing with particular conditions such as asthma or diabetes.

Geriatricians deal with the diseases of older people and the problems associated with ageing. Older people can suffer from complex patterns of illness and disease and geriatricians tend to get involved in the social well-being of their patients as well as their physical condition.

Haematologists diagnose and treat diseases and disorders of the blood and those parts of the body involved in the production of blood – the lymph glands and bone marrow, for example. They are involved in the treatment of conditions such as leukaemia, haemophilia and sickle cell disease.

Immunologists focus on the study and treatment of the immune system, including allergies and diseases such as HIV/AIDS. These latter conditions may also be treated by specialists in **Genito-urinary medicine (GUM).**

Oncologists are cancer specialists – they may also be qualified **haematologists**.

Paediatricians look after sick children and are specialists in children's growth and development.

Pathologists are specialists in diagnosing disease from tissue and fluid samples from the body. Patients do not normally meet the pathologist, although their samples and specimens will. Pathologists tend to act as advisors to other consultant specialists.

Radiologists specialise in the study and treatment of the body using various types of radiation such as X-rays, MRI (magnetic resonance imaging) scans and ultrasound. They are sometimes confused with radiographers, who are not doctors (see below).

Rheumatologists deal with the diagnosis and treatment of problems with joints and connective tissue, particularly arthritis and rheumatism.

Medicine is becoming more and more specialised. It is no longer enough to be a general physician, most will now have a sub-specialisation in a particular technique, age group or disease. Job titles can vary slightly from one place to the next so if you do come across someone with a description you do not understand don't be afraid to ask what it means. Understanding what the person you are dealing with is qualified to do is a first step in understanding your care.

NON-MEDICAL THERAPISTS

It is an unfortunate way to refer to highly skilled professionals on the basis of what they do not do – medicine. But the terms non-medical, or para-medical are widely used in the health service. The NHS has a collective term for its paramedics – Professions Allied to Medicine or PAMs for short. Some of the more widely available therapists that you may encounter are:

Chiropodists Strictly speaking chiropodist means a specialist in the care and treatment of feet and hands. In practice they are best known for the treatment of feet – as a consequence the profession now prefers the term **podiatrist**. Their expertise stretches much wider than cutting off hard skin or treating corns and bunions. Many postural problems and back pain can be due to foot conditions. Podiatrists may also do minor surgery on feet.

Occupational therapists have a job title that does not really describe what they do. They are specialists in assessing people's physical, mental and social capabilities and advising on how to overcome disabilities. They use a whole range of techniques ranging from art and music therapy to teaching domestic skills.

Paramedics are mainly ambulance crew who have received a higher training which enables them to assess and stabilise patients who have been involved in accidents. The care they provide is normally highly regulated by protocols as they are not medically qualified.

Phlebotomists are specially trained to take blood samples and conduct blood tests.

Physiotherapists use movement and exercise to treat muscular and joint problems. As well as these traditional approaches they also use hydrotherapy (movement in water), electrotherapy and massage.

Psychiatric or **approved social workers** are not strictly speaking therapists but are included here as they are specialists who are fairly regularly encountered. They have special training to equip them to work with people with mental health problems. They may also act as an individual's key worker.

Radiographers are non-medical professionals who work closely with radiologists. They are typically the people who take X-rays and other images such as ultrasound. The interpretation of what the images mean and how that person should then be treated is the domain of the radiologist, although in some hospitals the boundaries are being blurred with radiographers extending their skills.

Speech and language therapists assess, treat and advise people who have difficulty in speaking, swallowing or who have eating disorders. These conditions may be inherited or been caused by injury or disease.

WHO'S WHO IN THE MEDICAL HIERARCHY?

Doctors have some peculiar terms to describe their grades and positions. It seems odd that, after being called doctor throughout their careers, when they finally become a consultant – the top grade on the career ladder – they revert to becoming Mr or Ms. It is a piece of inverted snobbery perhaps but very confusing to patients who could be forgiven for thinking the consultant is not a 'proper doctor'.

The terms that doctors use to describe their position in the medical heirarchy seem almost perfectly designed to confound. There is an apocryphal story about an unfortunate man with a particular fear of doctors and hospitals. Having suffered a mild heart attack he was recovering well until the nurse on the ward told him the 'registrar' would be round to see him shortly. As the only registrars he had encountered were those who recorded births, marriages and deaths, the patient feared the worst. Already happily married and with his children grown up, the registrar's attendance could only mean one thing – that he was at death's door. In fact registrar is also the title of a doctor in a training grade.

So as an antidote to heart attacks brought on by misunderstandings, here is a guide to the different titles and grades that doctors use. We'll start from the bottom rung – the new doctor straight out of medical school – and work on up the career ladder.

Pre-registration house officer When medical students have got their initial degree, they spend one year in hospital as part of their training. This leads to their full registration as a medical practitioner with the General Medical Council – the official body which registers (and can strike off) doctors. Once registered they can call themselves doctor.

House officer/senior house officer Having become a registered doctor, junior doctors (strictly speaking they are still called doctors in training) spend two or three years working as generalists in hospitals. It is this experience which helps them decide what they will specialise in. Most of their time is spent working with children, with general medical cases or in Accident and Emergency departments. These are the grades which attract most public attention for working long hours. If you are in hospital during the evening or at weekends you are most likely to be seen by a house officer or senior house officer – the more senior the doctor the more they tend to work 'office hours'.

Specialist registrar These are doctors who are training to work in a specialist field, for example obstetrics or rheumatology. In tandem with their practical work in providing medical care they will be undergoing a supervised programme of training. When they have completed this successfully they get a Certificate of Competence in Specialist Training (CCST). This certificate allows the doctor to apply for consultant jobs.

Consultants The top of the medical career ladder. If you see a doctor privately they will typically hold an NHS consultant job on full- or part-time basis. Most consultants work in 'firms' – normally one or two consultants and a group of junior doctors who share work rotas and organise how they will see their patients.

Some other terms you may come across:

Locums These are effectively 'temps' who fill vacant posts for a short period of time. Locums are also found doing 'out-of-hours' work for GPs, such as visits at night.

Clinical assistants These are doctors who are taken on to work a few sessions a week in a particular specialty. They may be GPs interested in maintaining their skills in hospital medicine or in looking after children.

Staff doctor These posts are not that common but fit in somewhere between a specialist registrar and a consultant. In some cases they will be GPs, in others they will be doctors who keep missing out on getting a consultant appointment.

Principal This is the term used to describe a partner in a group of general practitioners.

Clinical director This is the person in charge of a specialist department of a hospital. For instance the director of oncology is the person responsible for cancer services.

Medical director The most senior doctor in a trust who is either a manager of the doctors or an advisor to the Trust's senior managers on medical matters.

WHO'S WHO IN THE NURSING WORLD?

Most nurses have job titles that have the term 'nurse' in them, and their seniority is reflected in their grade, not in what they are called. The grades range from A to I but it is unlikely that you as a patient will find out what grade a particular nurse is unless you are very pushy in your questioning. Nearly all NHS trusts will have a director of nursing. She (or he) may be an advisor on nursing matters or may have a management responsibility for all nurses in the trust. Below the director will be some other types of managers with names such as team leader, ward manager, sister or charge nurse, and then the staff nurse.

Some nurses do have confusing job titles – something that may become more common as nurses develop specialist skills in particular areas.

Ward manager A senior nurse who has overall responsibility for managing a ward or other section of a hospital. Also known as sister (female) and charge nurse (male). When in doubt about anything in a hospital, ask for the ward manager!

Staff nurse Your named nurse will be a staff nurse, who may also be called an associate nurse.

Macmillan nurse A nurse who specialises in counselling and treatment of patients with cancer or terminal illnesses.

Nurse practitioner A relatively new role, these are nurses with extra training which allows them to do work independently of doctors. They are allowed to do some tests, assessments or treatments which have traditionally solely been done by doctors. Nurse practitioners may also prescribe a limited range of drugs.

Health visitor Qualified nurses who specialise in taking a health rather than illness perspective in their work. They work mainly with children, but occasionally also with older people, and can advise on general health care, development, diet and behavioural problems.

District nurses These nurses work in community settings or from clinics and support people who do not need hospital care or who are convalescing. They can give certain types of drugs by drip and syringe, change dressings and advise on what the patient and carer can do to help the patient to get better. District nurses also provide support to people who are terminally ill.

Community psychiatric nurses These nurses specialise in working with people with mental health problems. They often have overall responsibility for co-ordinating the various services that an individual might need. In this latter capacity they may be referred to as 'key workers'.

A guide to professionals who are part of the primary care team (health visitors, district nurses, etc.) can be found in chapter two.

CHAPTER 9: MEDICAL JARGON MADE EASIER

Long words and abbreviations are part of the medical profession's working life. They were never designed to help explain things to patients but as a shorthand to help doctors and other clinicians communicate with each other. This chapter gives you two different tools to help crack the codes and understand better what doctors are saying to you, to each other and to the other people in the health care team.

The first tool is a translator's guide to the longer words. Once you understand that most complex medical words are made up of smaller bits then understanding what they mean becomes much simpler – all you have to do is divide the word into its constituent parts, work out what each of the bits mean and then join them together. For example, the word *arteriosclerosis* is a bit of tongue twister. Cut it into bits and you get *arterio* and *scler* and *osis*. The first part of the word refers to the part of the body, in this case the arteries (large blood vessels), the second part means hard or hardening and the third part means a disease or abnormal condition. Put them all together and you can see that arteriosclerosis is a disease which involves a hardening of the arteries. Even if you do not fully understand what this means it gives you a better basis from which to ask your doctor questions.

The second tool is a dictionary of the abbreviations that are most commonly found on forms, prescriptions or medical records. Patients are increasingly being allowed to keep their own medical records, and it is already the norm for pregnant women and for young children. But if you cannot understand what they mean there is little advantage in having them. At the back of the book you will also find a glossary of some of the more frequently used bits of management jargon in the health service. It would be good to say that you will never have to encounter these but this is far from the case; managers – like doctors – can easily slip into the habit of thinking that everyone knows what they know. And few seem to have perfected the art of writing and speaking in plain English that the average patient can understand.

TOOL ONE: THE *PATIENTPOWER* GUIDE TO MEDICAL TERMS

Some doctors have accomplished the art of communicating well with their patients. They strike the right balance between explaining what is wrong and what will happen without sounding patronising or using the sort of language that is rarely used by people above the age of eight. Others go too far in the quest to make things easier for patients. This is most typified by a dumbed down form of questioning as in 'And how's your tummy today then?' or in the more euphemistic, 'Any problem's "down there"?' If you do get the full barrage of medical jargon you can normally read this as a compliment – the doctor is convinced that you are a moderately intelligent person who wants to know what is happening in scientific terms and will understand the explanation. Sad to say we could do with more doctors who fill the middle ground between these two positions. *PatientPower* means trying to encourage the clinical professionals looking after you to both take you into their confidence and provide full explanations of anything that is remotely confusing.

Until that time arrives here is the *PatientPower* guide to some of the more common medical terms and phrases you may hear or read. This is how it works:

Table *1a* is a list of prefixes – the short parts at the beginning of words which refer to where, when and how much.

Table *1a*: the prefixes or first syllables	
Prefix	**Meaning**
a, an	not, without
ab	away from
ad	near
ambi/amphi	both, twice as much
ante	before
anti	against
contra	against, counter to
cryo	cold
dia	through, going apart
dys	difficult, painful
e, ex	out from
ecto	outside, external
endo	inside, internal
epi	on, over
exo	outside
hemi	half
hyper	increased, above
hypo	under, below, lacking
in, im, ir	not
infra	below
inter	between
intra	within
macro	large
mal	bad, ill, disordered
meta	after, beyond
micro	small
para	beside, beyond
peri	around
poly	many, multiple
post	after
pre	before, in front of
pseud(o)	false, fake
re	again
retro	backward
sub	under
super, supra	beyond, above, extra
syn, sym	with, together

Table *1b* contains the root parts of words that normally indicate the parts of the body that are affected by a disease or illness.

Table *1b*: word roots	
Root/combining word	**Meaning**
abdomin	stomach or abdomen
adeno	gland
adip	fat
angio	blood vessel
arterio	artery
arthro	joint (usually knee, leg or arm)
aur	ear
bronch, laryng, trachea	windpipe
cardio	heart
cephal	head
cerebral	brain
cervic(x)	neck (also used to refer to the neck or entrance to the womb)
chole	gall bladder
chondr	cartilage
colo	colon
colpo	vagina
cranio	skull, head
cuta	skin
cyst	fluid filled sac
cyto	cell
dent	tooth
enter(o)	intestine, gut
fasci(a)	face
foetal	concerning the foetus
gastro	stomach
haema(o)	blood
hepat(o)	liver
hyster(o)	uterus, womb
ile, ili	intestines
labi	lip
lapar	abdomen
lipo	fatty tissue
lumbar	back or lower torso
maste	breast

Table *1b*: word roots (continued)	
Root/combining word	**Meaning**
men(o)	menstruation
myelo	bone marrow
myo	muscle
nephro, renal	kidney
neuro	nerve
ocul, ophthal	eye
orchi(i)	testicle
orthodont, dent	teeth
osteo	bone
ot(o)	ear
ov	egg, ovaries
phleb, veno	vein
pneuma(o)	lung, air
pod	foot
procto	anus or rectum
pulmo	lung
rhino	nose
splen	spleen
teno	tendon
thorac(ic)(o)	chest
thromb	clot, lump
uro	urinary tract
vas	vessel
vesic	bladder

Table *1c* contains the suffixes – the end parts of the word that tend to describe what is wrong or what is being done.

Table *1c*: suffixes	
These bits of words combine with the prefixes (Table *1a*) and/or roots (Table *1b*) to indicate what is wrong.	
Suffix	**Meaning**
algia	pain
blast	the early stages of a growth
dynia	pain
ectomy	surgical removal
gyna	rotation

Table 1c: suffixes (continued)	
These bits of words combine with the prefixes (Table 1a) and/or roots (Table 1b) to indicate what is wrong.	
Suffix	**Meaning**
hydr	water
iform	resembling
itis	inflammation
lysis	freeing up or of
megaly	enlargement
oma	type of cancer or tumerous swelling
oscopy	viewing of an organ or internal parts
osis	disease or abnormal condition
ostomy	creation of an artificial opening, e.g. in the intestine or windpipe
otomy	incision, cutting into or out
pathy	disease or abnormality
plasty	reconstruction or formation of
proxia	ability to do
rrhagia, rrhage	bleeding, bursting forth
scope	look
tonic	tension
topic	site
trophic	seeking
uria	urine – usually condition or presence of

When you come across a bit of medical jargon that you would like to decipher, such as the word dysmenorrhagia this is what you do. Take the first syllable of the word and look up it up in Table 1a. In this example the first syllable is 'dys', meaning difficult or painful. Next refer to Table 1b and look for the appropriate root of the word. In our example the second syllable is 'men', meaning concerned with menstruation. The final part of the word, which in our example is 'rrhagia', meaning bleeding, can be found in Table 1c. Put all three together and the interpretation of this word is literally 'painful bleeding associated with menstruation' or – for the lay person – period pains.

Table 1d gives a list of words used to indicate numbers – confusingly there are two alternatives as both Latin and Greek roots are used in medical terms. Finally, Table *1e* shows commonly used colours in medical terminology.

Just to confuse us, some medical terms have a Latin root whilst others have a Greek root. This table shows how some of the more commonly used numbers are referred to in medical circles.

Table *1d*: numbers used in medical terms		
Number	**Greek root**	**Latin root**
1	mono	un
2	di	bi
3	tri	ter
4	tetr	quadr
5	pent	quinqu
6	hex	sex
7	hept	sept
8	oct	oct
9	ennea	novem
10	dec	decem
½	hemi	semi
100	hect	cent
1000	kilo	mili
1st	prot	primi
2nd	duttero	second
3rd	trit	tert

Colour is an important part of a doctor's diagnostic kit. With no more sophisticated equipment than their eyesight a doctor can use colour to assess swelling, temperature and certain types of infection.

Table *1e*: words used which describe colours	
Colour	**Use in medical terms**
black	ater
blue	cyanos
gloomy	amblys
golden	aurews
green	choros
pale	palliders

Table *1e*: words used which describe colours (continued)	
Colour	**Use in** **Medical terms**
pink/rosy	eos, rhodon
rainbow	iris/iridus
red	chroma, erythros, ruber
silver	agentum
tawney/reddish	cirros
white	albus
yellow	flavus, galbus, luteus

TOOL TWO: A GUIDE TO MEDICAL ABBREVIATIONS

Most medical abbreviations are in common currency. They are based on scientific terms and frequently Latin or Greek words. But health professionals also use their own shorthand. Some of it may be unique to them but more often than not it will reflect some form of 'in-joke' between doctors – you can almost imagine it being a core part of the medical student's education. The initials FLK, for example, on a child's medical record would generally be recognised as 'funny looking kid' rather than a technical term referring to some deficiency or illness. Without delving too deep into this playschool humour here are some of the more typical and scientific abbreviations you may find on your health records.

A	before
aa	of each
ac	before meals
ad	to, up to
ADL	activities of daily living (a set of common activities, for example washing and dressing, which are used to assess a person's physical and mental independence)
ad lib	as needed or wanted
AMA	against medical advice

Ap	appendicitis
Aq	water
BE	barium enema
bds or bid	twice per day
BM	bowel movement
BP	blood pressure
Bx	biopsy
CA	cardiac arrest
CBC	complete blood cell count
Chol	cholesterol
CNS	central nervous system
cont. rem	continue the medicine
CPA	care programme approach (see chapter six for details on long-term mental health care)
CT	also known as a 'CAT scan', computerised tomography is a high-resolution imaging process that can scan the whole body
CXR	chest X-ray
d	day
dd	give
D&C	dilatation and curettage
DOA	dead on arrival
Disp	dispense
DM	diabetes mellitus
DNA	did not attend (i.e. failed to turn up to a clinic appointment)
Dos	dose
Dx	diagnosis
ECG	electrocardiogram (a machine that measures the pattern of heart beats under different conditions)
emp	as directed
febris	fever
FH	family history
GA	general anaesthetic (i.e. affects the whole body)
GB	gallbladder
h	hour
Hb	haemaglobin (red blood cells)

HPI	history of present illness
hs	before bed
Hx	history
ICU	intensive care unit
IM	intra-muscular
LA	local anaesthetic (i.e. just one part of the body is numbed before an operation)
LMP	last menstrual period – date on which it started
neg	negative
NPO	nothing to be given by mouth
N&V	nausea and vomiting
OD	once per day (not overdose!)
P	pain
p	after
pc	after meals
PE	physical examination
PI	primary infection/present illness
post op	after an operation
PTA	prior to admission
qds or qid	four times a day
qn	every night
qv	as much as needed or wanted
rbc or RBC	red blood cell count (an indicator of anaemia)
RT	radiation therapy (or radiotherapy)
Rx	prescription or treatment
SC	subcutaneous – under the skin
SID	sudden infant death (commonly referred to as cot death)
Stat	immediately
Sx	symptoms
tds or tid	three times a day
TPR	temperature, pulse and respiration (breathing)
TOD	took own discharge
Tx	treatment
UTI	urinary tract infection
VD	venereal disease
VS	vital signs

CHAPTER 10:
TESTS, TESTS, TESTS

The chances are that someone performed a test on you before you were even born. Someone else may perform a test on you after you die. There's no escaping medical tests! But what is the point of them all?

WHY WE GET TESTED

We get tested for three main reasons. First, we get tested when there is nothing apparently wrong with us. These tests are called screening tests, and they are carried out as early warning systems to reassure us that nothing is wrong; or to tell us that something is beginning to go wrong; or something might go wrong in the future. Some screening tests are carried out to find more out about a health issue in the general population. One of the first mass screening tests were chest X-rays to pick up TB. TB is less common these days, so routine X-ray testing is neither needed nor carried out, particularly as we now understand the harmful effects of radiation from X-rays. Modern screening tests are used to detect cervical cancer and breast cancer, and may be introduced in the next few years for other cancers, such as ovarian or bowel cancer, or for genetic disorders. Screening tests are discussed in more detail in chapter thirteen.

The second type of test is diagnostic, and is carried out as part of an investigation to help identify an illness or health problem. These tests are designed to pick up things in the body that are different from normal – abnormalities – and which will be caused by a particular disease. An example is a blood test to count the number of white blood cells in the body: if it is abnormally high, it would indicate that the body is fighting an infection.

A third reason for tests is to see whether a patient is responding to treatment. Tests to measure the air capacity of the lungs after a course of treatment for asthma would measure whether this was helping the patient's lungs to function properly.

What's it for?

Like everything else in your health care, it is worth asking a few questions before you are led off for a test. Before someone puts you in front of a machine, sticks a needle into you, or cuts a bit out of you it seems reasonable to ask: 'Why do I need this test? What is it for? What might it tell you about my health that you don't know already?' Here are some more specific questions to consider.

Could you find out this information without doing this particular test? What is it going to tell you and why is it important that you know this?

Far too many tests are performed on patients. Partly this is because the doctors who are trying to form a diagnosis of what is wrong use tests as their insurance policy to cover themselves. They decide to order a full battery of tests, just in case they miss something which later turns out to be important. They imagine being bawled at by a senior doctor for not trying hard enough, or worse that you will sue them for misdiagnosis and wrong treatment.

Please tell me exactly what is going to happen and how I am likely to feel during and after it.

Some tests are also painful or uncomfortable. It is really important that the doctor explains exactly what the test will involve. You will also want to know what the effects of the test will feel like, and how long the effects will last.

Is there any risk or possible side-effect with this test? How likely is the risk of something going wrong by performing this test?

Some tests have risks. Sometimes this is nothing more than a bit of bruising or a sore limb for a day or two. But there are other tests which have more serious risks – X-rays are a form of radiation which increases, very slightly, the risk of cancer. Amniocentesis, a test used in pregnancy to check for any genetic abnormalities in the baby, carries a small risk of harming the baby and in a very few cases it may cause a miscarriage.

If this test shows that something's wrong, what can you do about it?

It is also important to know that if your test reveals that something is wrong then there is a form of treatment that can improve the situation. You have as much right to refuse to take a test because the result is not going to change anything, as you have to request that a particular test is carried out. This is true at certain times of genetic testing. Knowing that your gene type shows that you will get a wasting disease about which nothing can be done may not be something you would wish to know. In the case of screening for prostate cancer the test is good at detecting the problem, but medical experts are divided as to whether treatment is effective or whether it is better to leave it alone.

Can you explain what the test result means for my health?

Make sure you know what the test result actually means. If you are told that your test was positive, that may be good news (a confirmation that you are pregnant, for instance), bad news (you have an infection) or neutral news (your blood group is rhesus positive).

How reliable is this test – how many false results (positives or negatives) are likely? Is there a way of double-checking its accuracy by getting a second test done?

It is sensible to ask about the accuracy and reliability of the tests. We often hear about 'false positives', when a test shows something to be abnormal, when in fact it is normal, but there are also such things as 'false negatives' when a test shows that things are normal, when in fact they are abnormal. For example, there have been several high-profile cases of inaccurate cervical screening where women have been told that their test is clear when in fact the labs have missed some early cell abnormalities. In order to be worthwhile, tests have to be sensitive, which means that they will detect a high proportion of the true cases; and they have to be specific, which means that they will have few false positives. It is impossible to get tests which are 100 per cent accurate, so they are measured by sensitivity (the number of false positives likely in every batch) and specificity (the number of false negatives likely in every batch). This is a measure of the test itself, and is nothing to do with human error.

Testing yourself

The most common test, and one of the oldest, is to take your temperature. As well as the good old thermometer that you stick under your tongue or armpit there are new clever bits of equipment – temperature sensitive tape to hold on your forehead and a sort of torch that you shine in the person's ear. Like many other tests, taking your temperature may tell you that there is something wrong or abnormal, but it won't tell you why. To do this you have to move from the symptoms (the effect) to diagnosis (the cause).

Pharmacists now sell a range of over-the-counter tests and will be able to advise you on how to do the test and how to understand the results. But be aware that these home-test kits vary greatly in their value and ease of use. The common home-test kits for pregnancy are now very accurate and very easy to use. Machines which promise to test your heart rate or blood pressure may, by contrast, be pretty useless. This is because, even if the kit is working, you may not be in your 'normal' state when you take the test, particularly if you are in a rush, under stress or have just eaten. So two DIY blood pressure readings taken an hour apart may well show that you are (a) super-fit and (b) you are about to suffer a fatal heart attack when, more often than not, you are about average.

In GP surgeries, the GP or the practice nurse may do the test and get the result almost immediately (for example when testing blood pressure, or testing for diabetes). Alternatively, the GP or practice nurse may take a sample (blood, urine, etc) and send it off to the hospital pathology labs for analysis.

Hospital tests

If the test is carried out in hospital, or is sent in for analysis, the general procedure is roughly the same. One group of staff will do the testing, either by taking an image or using chemical changes in the pathology labs. The tests will then be screened to point out anything which is abnormal, and the abnormalities will then be interpreted by specialist doctors who will advise on how to proceed. So, a GP may ask for an X-ray which will be carried out by a radiographer, the technician who operates the X-ray machine. The image is then read by a radiologist, a doctor who specialises in interpreting what the X-rays tells us. The radiologist then reports the results of the X-ray to the GP or to another consultant. For example, a radiologist will review a mammogram to see if there is evidence of breast cancer. The surgeon will then use that information to guide the way that they do an operation to remove a breast lump.

Dissatisfied? Confused?

Remember that no test is 100 per cent certain. Sometimes a test will suggest that something is right when it is wrong; sometimes it says it is right when it is wrong. There are tens of thousands of tests performed each day in hospitals. With that volume, the false positives and negatives, and human error, things will go wrong. The important point is to have ways of trying to spot when things are not right. So if you are not satisfied that the test was carried out properly, or the result doesn't make sense, ask if it can be repeated, or if a back-up test of another type can be done.

And remember, everyone who is involved, from the technicians who operate the machines, to the doctor who ordered the test, should treat you courteously, should explain exactly what is going on, what to expect, and how the results of the test will be interpreted. If they don't tell you, or if they do, and you are still unclear what is going to happen to you, then say you would like to talk again to the doctor who has referred you for the test. Don't allow anything to happen until you are comfortable about it happening to you.

WHY ARE THERE TESTING SCANDALS?

Over the past few years there have been a number of occasions when hospitals responsible for 'reading' the screening tests have had to re-check thousands of tests, recalling and retesting women for cervical screening or breast screening. What is going on? In the flurry of news headlines generated by such scandals, and the telephone hotlines that are set up, it is often impossible to tell what has happened. After all, it is hard to imagine that every single test over a period of time could have been wrong.

One thing to remember is that the tests themselves cannot be 100 per cent accurate. A test which is too sensitive will give false positives; a test which is too specific will give false negatives, so all test methods strike a balance. Second, it is not necessarily the case that any one person has been incompetent in carrying out or reading the test. Tens of thousands of test results are read every week by technicians, who will pass on the abnormal ones to be looked at by a cancer specialist. The technicians are looking for changes from normal. But how much change? If they recalled everyone who had very small changes, thousands of people would be brought back to hospital, most of whom are simply showing normal variations, and have nothing 'wrong' with them. So the health service works with the idea of 'acceptable variations' and with that 'acceptable risks', that is, they set a level of difference from normal in tests, and they recall everyone who is beyond that difference for further investigations. And sometimes they get the level of change wrong. This can mean that hundreds, maybe thousands of people fail to be recalled for more tests, sometimes with fatal results. It is not quite as simple as that, for the 'risk' in health care is not very well understood. It means one thing if you are a patient (I would prefer no risks to be taken with my health). And it means another if you are approaching the problems from a scientific or accountant's perspective (the level of risk to these patients is so small that it would not be cost-effective to do more tests).

Conclusion

Although you should approach medical tests with your eyes open, you should also welcome them when they are well directed at your health needs. Medical tests are like map coordinates: well used they should allow you to pin-point your situation with amazing accuracy. But you only need a limited number of tests to get an accurate fix, just as you only need a couple of coordinates to pin-point where you are on a map. After that both patient and professional should be able to use other information – looking and listening to find out what is going on.

A TABLE OF TESTS

Below is a table of the most common medical tests that are in use today. It describes each test under the following headings:

- **Part of the body tested** – starting with the whole body and then going from the head to the foot.

- **The name of the test** – they are usually called after the sort of process they involve, and are often shortened to acronyms, for example MRI is magnetic resonance imaging, but as it is always known as MRI, there is no reason to learn the full name.

- **How it is done** – a quick guide to what will happen if this test is done on you.

- **What it shows** – what the doctor, nurse or technician sees.

- **Discomfort** – how it feels for the patient.

- **Why it is done** – what the professionals can conclude from what it shows.

What to expect from your medical tests

Part of body tested	Test	How it is done	What it shows	Discomfort/pain/ side-effects/time	Why it is done
brain, body in general	CT scanning, (computerised tomography) also known as CAT scanning (computed axial tomography)	lying down, low-dose X-rays pass through the body at different angles giving cross-sectional images (slices) of the area, converted to pictures by computer	computer pictures of the soft tissue in the brain or the body, showing up abnormalities, such as tumours, bleeding, injuries	no discomfort and safe; images produced instantly	very effective in finding problems, particularly in tumours, and in directing needle biopsy (removing a tissue sample)
body in general	MRI (magnetic resonance imaging)	lying down, surrounded by a large electromagnet which fires short bursts of powerful magnetic fields and radio waves	high quality images of cross-sections or 3D images of organs in the body	no discomfort, very safe	better images than CT scans, shows tumours in brain or spinal cord, internal structure of ear and eye, heart, blood vessels, joints and soft tissues
body	biopsy	cutting out a small amount of tissue or cells for examination under a microscope	looked at under a microscope, the tissue or cells show normal or abnormal growth	biopsies can be cut from skin or muscle, or taken from needles (with CT scans) under local anaesthetic. From organs such as lungs, bladder, stomach, colon, biopsies are taken using endo-scopes (viewing tubes) under sedation. Biopsies are also taken during surgery to examine tissue that has been removed	examinations will show difference between malignant and benign tumours, and other changes in normal growth of tissues or cells
brain	EEG (electroencephalography)	small electrodes are attached to the scalp – no shaving necessary	shows wave patterns of the brain – some medical problems have special wave patterns	painless, no side-effects, about 45 minutes	helps with diagnosing epilepsy, dementia, brain tumour, etc.

Part of body tested	Test	How it is done	What it shows	Discomfort/pain/ side-effects/time	Why it is done
brain	PET scanning (positron emission tomography)	radioactive substance is injected into the blood and sensors around the body show how it is taken up in the brain	shows how quickly the substance is taken up into the brain, so how active the brain is.	painless, no side-effects; an hour or two	helps with diagnosis of a variety of brain problems
spinal column	lumber puncture	hollow needle is inserted into the fluid of the spinal canal between two vertebrae	fluid is taken to be analysed for infection or bleeding	very little discomfort, though may be headache afterwards; about 20 minutes	infections such as meningitis, haemorrhage or bleeding around the brain
spinal cord and nervous system	myelography – X-ray of the spinal cord and nerves	lumber puncture needle injects heavy liquid that X-rays can't get through, causing shadow	shadows around the spinal cord shows where the fluid has 'leaked' through damage	little discomfort, about 20 minutes, though bed-rest after for several hours	damage to spinal column, damaged nerves, tumours
nerves, muscles	EMG (electromyogram)	small disc electrodes are attached to skin over the muscle	wave pattern of messages passing through the muscle	no discomfort, 30–60 minutes	changes in electrical wave can detect disorders in muscles, such as muscular dystrophy and nerve disorder
blood	blood tests	up to 20ml of blood is taken from a vein, usually in the arm, and sent to the laboratory, where one or more of hundreds of tests are carried out. The results can be almost instantaneous, or can take several days for the most complex tests	gives information on the blood cells and any of the chemicals, gases, antibodies and bacteria or viruses that have invaded the main transport system of the body	small amount of discomfort from the needle	tests can be used to check the health of the blood itself, the health of major organs, as well as the breathing, hormones, immune system and how well the body processes food
blood	blood count	number of red cells, white cells and platelets in one cubic centimetre of blood is counted	anaemia with low or misshapen red cells or abnormally high or low white cells	small amount of discomfort from the needle	tests for infections and some cancers

Part of body tested	Test	How it is done	What it shows	Discomfort/pain/ side-effects/time	Why it is done
blood	platelet count	number of platelets in one cubic centimetre of blood is counted	platelets are used to clot blood – shows how well it will clot	small amount of discomfort from the needle	clots in blood vessels lead to strokes – particularly in pregnancy
blood	blood group	tests for the different proteins on red blood cells known as antigens	ABO and rhesus blood groups	small amount of discomfort from the needle	essential to know a person's blood group for safe blood transfusion by matching the grouping of the blood to be transfused
blood	biochemical tests		measures the chemicals in the blood, such as proteins, carbohydrates	small amount of discomfort from the needle	may point to long-term illnesses
blood	blood sugar level	measures the amount of glucose (type of sugar) in the blood	the amount of sugar in the blood is controlled by insulin produced by the pancreas	small amount of discomfort from the needle	high sugar levels in blood show diabetes, failure of the pancreas. Untreated diabetes kills
blood	blood pressure	a sphygmomanometer is a cuff with an air bladder which is attached around the upper arm and pumped until it stops the blood flowing through the main artery. As air is released from the cuff the blood begins to flow again. The pressure at the start and end of this process is recorded	the pressure on the flow of blood as it is pumped by the heart through the main arteries	nil	blood pressure is measured as systolic (heart contracted) and diastolic (heart between beats). Very high pressure (hyper-tension) or low pressure (hypotension) need treating

Part of body tested	Test	How it is done	What it shows	Discomfort/pain/side-effects/time	Why it is done
blood vessels	angiography	a liquid which shows up under X-ray is injected into a blood vessel where a problem is suspected through a catheter (fine plastic tube) that is threaded to the site from an entry point such as the groin or elbow. A rapid sequence of X-rays is taken	the dense liquid shows how the blood is flowing through the blood vessel and will show ballooning (aneurysm), narrowing or blockage (thrombosis or embolism) or a tumour. It is especially used in looking at the heart and brain blood supply	carried out under local or general anaesthetic, a few minutes to two or three hours. The main risk is damage to blood vessels and the catheter is being inserted.	now combined with computers to enhance the X-ray images, it can give a large amount of information about problems, allowing treatment to take place, sometimes without the need for surgery
veins	venography	similar to angiography to look at veins. Sometimes the liquid is injected directly into the veins to be studied	X-rays are taken of the veins once the liquid has been injected	as for angiography	particularly useful for studying varicose veins
heart	ECG (electrocardiogram)	electrodes are attached to the chest, wrists and ankles and connected to a recording machine	the electrical impulses that immediately precede the contraction of the heart muscle (the beat of the heart)	no discomfort; can be carried out at home, the GP surgery or hospital. Can monitor the heart over 24 hours	abnormal electrical activity shows that the heart is beating irregularly and the upper chambers are not beating in sequence with the lower chambers (fibrillation)
heart	echocardiography	an image of the heart is produced from high frequency soundwaves (ultrasound)	shows the structure of the heart and picks up abnormalities in the heart wall, values and the blood vessels	the ultrasound transducer is put on the chest. No discomfort at all	valuable for problems with heart valves and inherited heart disease, as well as inflammation of the membrane around the heart, and blood clots
heart	catheterisation	a fine tube is inserted into the heart through a blood vessel	a way of investigating inside the heart – the catheter can be used to measure pressure, take a blood sample or a biopsy of heart lining	local anaesthetic, little discomfort, but it may cause a disturbance of the heart rhythm and is thus only done if necessary	another way of testing for a range of heart problems

Part of body tested	Test	How it is done	What it shows	Discomfort/pain/side-effects/time	Why it is done
lungs	bronchoscopy	a hollow tube or a fibreoptic fine tube is inserted into the trachea through the mouth or nose	examines the bronchi, the main airways of the lung, to look for problems and may take samples	either local or general anaesthetic	helps in detecting and diagnosing some lung disorders
lungs	spirometry	patient breathes out through a tube into the spirometer	records the rate at which a person breathes out and how much lung capacity there is	no discomfort	detects lung disorders which obstruct air flow such as asthma and bronchitis
breast	mammography – X-ray of the breast	machine compresses the breast to X-ray as much of the tissue as possible from several angles	breast lumps and other disorders. Women between 55–65 are now regularly screened for breast cancer	simple and safe, but may cause discomfort or some pain	detects tumours that are too small to be detected by self-examination. A biopsy is taken of any abnormal area of the breast
liver	liver function tests	series of chemical tests on blood samples	show how well the liver is breaking down and making new chemicals for the blood	minor discomfort	helps to show acute liver problems such as hepatitis, with long-term problems such as cirrhosis and liver cancer
gall bladder	cholecystography	X-ray of gall bladder and bile duct after they have been filled with a liquid that shows up on X-ray	for looking for gall stones, usually after an ultrasound scan has not provided enough detail	patient swallows tablets which in within 12 hours are excreted as an opaque liquid from the liver to the bile	gall stones show up as holes and can be clearly seen on the X-ray
pancreas and bile duct	ERCP (endoscopic retrograde cholangiopancreato-graphy)	endoscope (flexible tube with light) is passed down the mouth, stomach and duodenum (small intestine) and a fine catheter is then passed through the endoscope into the bile duct and then releases a dense liquid opaque to X-ray	mainly used when ultrasound or CT scanning have not shown very much	sedative and local anaesthetic; 20–40 minutes	abnormalities in the ducts will show up on X-rays, or the catheter could take a biopsy for analysis, or scrape cells for examination

Part of body tested	Test	How it is done	What it shows	Discomfort/pain/side-effects/time	Why it is done
liver, pancreas, gall bladder, ducts	ultrasound scanning	a monitor is placed on the skin over the site of the liver and high frequency sound waves are sent into the body and reflected off the liver and build up a picture of the organ	these organs are very clearly viewed by ultrasound and disorders such as cirrhosis, cysts, abscesses, tumours, stones and obstructions can be seen	no discomfort	ultrasound is a very useful technique for soft tissue organs (such as the liver) and fluid-filled organs (such as the gall bladder). Also used in obstetrics
stomach, intestines, colon and rectum	barium X-ray	barium sulphate powder mixed with water is swallowed or introduced by tube into the area to be investigated	barium is a metal and X-rays can't go through it, so will show changes in the digestive tract	sedation is sometimes used for discomfort; 20–40 minutes	shows a variety of changes including narrowing, hernia, ulcers and tumours, polyps, etc.
body cavities	endoscopes	there are two types: rigid narrow viewing tubes with a light source attached; or fibreoptic bundles with light and lens at the tip and power source, viewing lens and steering system at the head	virtually any hollow structure can be looked at directly and photographed, or a biopsy performed by attaching cutters to the tip of the endoscope	usually under sedation or local anaesthetic	allows operations to be carried out without major surgery, and very useful for emergency examinations and treatment, such as taking a foreign object out of a lung
oesophagus, stomach	gastroscope	flexible tube, inserted through the mouth	investigates severe pain or bleeding, may use a video camera	sedative can be given, as some discomfort and pain in throat afterwards; 5–20 minutes	attachments allow biopsy for examination
bladder, urethra	cystoscope	rigid with lens, inserted into the bladder or rectum	looking for bladder stones, tumours, bleeding or infection	local anaesthetic. No risk of damage but discomfort passing urine for several days afterwards	
colon	colonoscope	flexible tube, inserted through the rectum	investigates bleeding from the bowel and diseases of the colon	laxatives for two days before to empty colon, local anaesthetic; ten minutes to two hours	attachments to colonoscope to perform biopsy

Part of body tested	Test	How it is done	What it shows	Discomfort/pain/ side-effects/time	Why it is done
abdomen	laproscope	hollow needle is inserted into the abdomen below the navel and carbon dioxide is pumped in to expand the abdominal cavity. The laproscope is then inserted through another excision to view the internal organs	used to assess someone with acute abdominal pain, from e.g. appendicitis or pancreatitis; and used to diagnose pelvic pain in women	performed under anaesthetic, gas in abdomen may cause discomfort for a day or so afterwards	surgery in the abdomen is now carried out with a laproscope, including removing appendix and gall bladder, infertility treatment and sterilisation of women
kidney	kidney imaging	ultrasound scanning, angiography, CT scanning, MRI (see above for these techniques)			
kidney	urography	an iodine-based liquid is injected into the bloodstream via a vein in the arm and travels to the kidneys and urinary tract. X-rays are taken at intervals over next 30 minutes	X-rays show the size, shape and position of kidneys, the urethras and the bladder and whether there are any obvious obstructions	safe and without discomfort	performed to investigate repeated urinary tract infections, blood in urine, and suspected stones. Also to investigate cause of hypertension in young people
urine	urinalysis	a battery of tests under the microscope and chemical tests on urine	can be used to check that kidneys are operating properly and to diagnose urinary tract problems	safe and simple	microscope may show red blood cells, indicating kidney damage; bacteria, parasitic eggs, or crystals suggesting a disorder. Chemical tests include acidity and concentration (kidney function), sugar (diabetes), human chorionic gonadotrophin (pregnancy), or illegal drugs

Part of body tested	Test	How it is done	What it shows	Discomfort/pain/side-effects/time	Why it is done
reproduction	pregnancy tests	tests on urine or blood, most commonly using an indicator which changes colour	looking for the presence of human chorionic gonadotrophin produced by the placenta	urine tests most often performed, and can be done a few days after a missed period, with home-testing kits. Results are 97% accurate for positive test and 89% accurate for negative test	blood tests are only normally used when very early diagnosis of pregnancy is needed
foetus	amniocentesis	a needle is inserted through the abdomen into the amniotic sac avoiding the foetus and placenta and a small amount of fluid is taken from the amniotic sac which surrounds the foetus in the uterus	the fluid contains cells and chemicals from the foetus which can be tested to detect genetic abnormalities such as Down's syndrome, haemophilia, cystic fibrosis, or developmental disorders such as spina bifida	local anaesthetic, and 24-hour rest after is advised. The incidence of miscarriage or early rupture of membranes is slightly greater, so only advised if an abnormality is suspected because of family history. Another side-effect is that this also reveals the sex of the foetus	detecting abnormalities in a foetus allows the mother to decide whether to proceed with the pregnancy. However the results of the genetic tests may not be known for up to four weeks, pushing the option of a termination back to 20 weeks.
foetus	chorionic villus sampling	a needle is inserted through the abdomen and takes sample cells from the edge of the placenta	cells from the placenta have the same genetic make-up as the foetus. This test can be performed earlier than amniocentesis and the results can be ready earlier	can be done under sedation; about 30 minutes. Small in-crease in miscarriage rate of around 1%, and occasionally causes complications, such as puncturing of the amniotic sac, bleeding and infection	main advantage over amniocentesis is that it can be performed earlier and allows the choice of a termination in the first three months of pregnancy.
cervix	cervical smear test	with the vagina held open by a speculum, cells are scraped from the cervix by a spatula which are analysed under the microscope	changes in the cells of the cervix may indicate cancer of the cervix, one of the most common cancers affecting women worldwide	risk free, and with minimal discomfort, the smear takes only a few seconds	abnormalities will be followed up with colposcopy examination and a biopsy may be taken
knee joint	arthroscope	rigid steel tube with optical fibres, lens and light source is inserted into the joint through small skin incision	inspect the inside of the knee joint when X-rays will not show surfaces of bones, ligaments, cartilage and the membrane that lines the joint	general anaesthetic or nerve block	arthroscopic surgery is now used to repair damaged joints, reducing hospital stays and time off sport

PART III

GREAT EXPECTATIONS

CHAPTER 11: RIGHTS AND RESPONSIBILITIES

This chapter provides an overview of the rights that patients have concerning their health care. With rights, however, come responsibilities. PatientPower is not about making unreasonable demands of the health service – it is about being a responsible user of services that are provided to everyone else as well as to you.

PATIENTS' RIGHTS

The rights of patients are rather different from human rights. Governments, including that of the UK, are signed up to several charters of human rights, including the UN Charter and the European Convention on Human Rights, and these try to set down the moral basis for the laws of individual countries. There is no Bill of Rights in the UK, so there is nowhere that you can go to find out whether your rights as a citizen have been violated. Your rights as a patient are legal rights: if you believe that you have not received the care and treatment that you should have received, you have to go to court to get the courts to interpret the laws which govern the NHS.

When particular cases have come to court, the courts have interpreted the responsibilities of the government to be the general provision of health care, not the health of a particular individual. This is a very important distinction, but not very well understood. It means that as long as the government, in the form of the Secretary of State for Health, can show that there is reasonable provision of health services – medical, nursing, ambulance, hospital beds, etc. – in a particular area, then the government has carried out its duty. So the government is not required to provide an individual with any specific health services. So if you have to wait 18 months for a particular treatment, or if you are not offered a treatment which is generally available, the law has not been broken and so your rights have not been violated. However, if the NHS were to deny a large number of citizens health care treatments which were known to be beneficial, it would be failing to provide comprehensive care and so would be acting illegally.

Some guidelines on rights

While there is no written definition of rights, the following is a useful set of guidelines to how your interests are protected within the NHS.

1. The treatment you are offered must give you a benefit which is greater than any risk that could be associated with it, including side-effects, and it should be free from significant risk to your future health or lifestyle.
   Example: If a GP offered you a drug to reduce your weight which could significantly increase your risk of heart attack this would be against your interests – the risk would outweigh the benefit and so the advice would be considered illegal. If a GP offers you a heart operation to reduce your chance of long-term heart disease, even though the operation has an associated risk, it is in your interests and is thus legal.

2. Health services must present themselves honestly and without misrepresentation. They should not 'oversell' themselves by leading you to expect more from services or from the benefits arising from these services. You must be given the facts about services and treatments to allow you to make informed choices.

Example: A doctor cannot claim to be 'the best' specialist in cancer treatments, nor to have a treatment which will cure cancer, as these claims would give you false expectations about the benefits of care. Where there are alternative treatments, say for treating cancer, you should know enough about the alternatives to decide for yourself on the evidence which you would prefer.

3. Your access to care should depend solely on your need for care. This is written into the 1946 NHS Act and is seen as fundamental to the health service, although the more explicit rationing of services has weakened this principle in the last few years. The NHS still works on the basis of priority need, so that if you have a life-threatening emergency, you will be treated immediately; and if you have a life-threatening condition, such as a tumour, you will be seen as a priority.

   Legally you also should not have to wait for treatment if there is likely to be a significant deterioration in your condition while you wait. In reality, with limited resources in the health service, not everyone gets treated as quickly as they should (people with heart disease die of heart problems while waiting for treatment). What care you get depends on what the NHS can afford. The courts have recognised that in what they have judged is reasonable for health authorities to offer.

4. You have a right to be consulted about changes to the health service in your area. This means that the health services must publish their plans if they are proposing to close, change, relocate or develop health services and must actively seek your views on their proposals. All health authorities and NHS trusts are now required to hold their meetings in public so you can see how decisions about your local services are made. However, the system of consultation and local representation in the NHS does not work well. In the last few years decisions about the future plans for health services up and down the country have frequently been taken in secret, often against the wishes of local people, who have had to resort to petitions and demonstrations because they have no say in these decisions. This is slowly changing, but NHS managers

– who are only accountable to the national government not to local people – too often fail to engage in proper consultation. See chapter thirteen for more on getting involved in health service decisions.

Access to information

Access to information on health services is controlled by a government 'Code of Practice on Openness in the NHS' which states that the health service should make information available to people unless there is a good reason not to release that information, for example it is confidential to a patient. The Code of Practice gives each part of the health service the duty to have a named officer responsible for arrangements to release information. If you want a particular piece of information or want to ask about what information on the NHS is available, you should contact your local hospital or health authority.

Personal information and confidentiality
Information on a named individual which has been given by the person or from someone else should remain confidential and is exempt from the Code of Openness. This information can only be disclosed if permission is given by the individual. This means that even family and close friends may be denied information unless the person concerned has given approval. However staff are allowed to release information if it is thought to be in the public interest, for example in response to police enquiries.

Medical records
It is only in the past 15 years that patients have had any rights to see their medical records. As doctors wrote and kept these notes, they often assumed that they owned them and that patients would never get to see them. As discussed earlier in chapter nine, doctors often use shorthand in their notes that has no scientific basis – along with the example of FLK (funny looking kid). Dr Phil Hammond, the media GP, has collected some of the more popular examples, such as PAFO

(pissed and fell over); TATT (tired all the time); OAP (over-anxious parent); SIG (stroppy ignorant git).

NHS records legally belong to the Secretary of State for Health – not to you and not to the doctor who wrote them. Health authorities and NHS trusts are delegated the legal powers to decide who has access to those records. Patients' legal right of access to their medical records was strengthened in 1991. This means that you have a right to see any health record about you which was written after 1 November 1991. Furthermore, you don't have to explain why you want to see your records. If you want you can authorise someone else to see the records on your behalf, for example a lawyer, or you can see your child's record. These rights of access allow you to inspect the records directly, have a copy made and require the trust to arrange for any terms which are unintelligible to be explained. You can also ask for any inaccurate statements to be corrected. So there should be fewer acronyms like FAS (fat and stupid) in medical records these days. While you have a right to access, you may be charged a fee of no more than £10, plus the cost of making photocopies.

Doctor's reports

Doctors are asked to provide reports on your medical history and current state of health for life insurance; for welfare benefits and private medical schemes; for evidence in court; and by your employers. Doctors are paid to write these reports, but they must ask your consent to pass on confidential information. If information is to be released to an insurance company for example, you will have to sign that you agree to the disclosure. Doctors' reports which are used in court have legal validity and must always be a disclosure of all the medical facts about you. As doctors' reports are by their very nature information about a patient then, according to the law of access, the patient should give permission before a health professional writes a report, even to another health professional. In fact there are hundreds of examples every day when that does not happen, when doctors are reporting their findings to other doctors as part of a referral. However it also happens when relatives are informed about a serious or terminal illness in advance of the patient being informed, often because staff are worried about upsetting the patient.

CONSENTING TO TREATMENT

The idea of consent is one of the foundations of the relationship between a patient and a health professional. If there is evidence to show that a particular treatment was carried out without a patient's consent, even if that treatment could be shown to have given a benefit, the patient will be able to seek compensation. A surgeon who does not have the permission of a patient to carry out a particular operation would be guilty of assault. This applies if the surgeon carried out a different operation without the patient's express permission, even if that operation was beneficial. For example, a woman who had given consent to a sterilisation could not have a hysterectomy performed at the same time, even if the surgeon had very good medical grounds for doing this.

Consent does not need to be written: it can be verbal or even (in the event that someone is unconscious at the time of needing treatment) implicit. Attending an appointment with your GP is an implicit consent to allow them to examine you and treat you, but doctors are required to explain treatments and cannot act if you decline the examination or treatment, even if it would count as beneficial. So a doctor treating a Jehovah's Witness, whose beliefs prevent them from having a blood transfusion, would be guilty of assault if that person had refused a life-saving transfusion and this wish was ignored to save their life.

Despite the very well-established basis of the law of consent – the notion of trespass against person or property is centuries old – a minority of doctors seem to believe that they have complete authority over their patients, carrying out procedures that they have not discussed with their patients and certainly have not had consent to perform. The argument that this is beneficial to the patient is not one which should sway a court of law, although judges are not infallible on this point.

When is consent not needed?

Treatment can be given legally to someone without their consent if the person is acting out of necessity in the best interests of another. This common law power is most obviously used in emergencies, when someone is unconscious or otherwise unable to give their consent, but it has also been applied to a wide range of other cases. For example, until recently this was used to justify decisions by professionals to sterilise women with severe learning difficulties, to preserve their day-to-day well-being. The courts are increasingly siding with patients, and doctors are much more careful about what they have been given consent to do. Recently a woman was detained under the Mental Health Act because she had refused to have a caesarian delivery, even though her life and that of the baby were at risk. She was then obliged to have a caesarian delivery. The woman later successfully sued the NHS for assault.

Legal powers to treat without consent

The 1983 Mental Health Act allows treatment to be given without the consent of patients who have been detained under the Act. Drugs can be given for three months without the patient's consent before the treatment is confirmed by a second doctor appointed by the Mental Health Act Commission. In emergencies some treatments can be given to patients detained under the Act without their consent. For details of the working of the Mental Health Act see chapter six.

If someone has a notifiable disease, or could spread a notifiable disease, then, with an order from a Justice of the Peace, they can be examined and detained in a hospital, even without giving consent, without this being an assault.

Informed consent

Giving or not giving your consent for medical care is one thing, but giving consent to a course of treatment knowing all the facts about the likely result or side-effects of treatments is entirely different. We all look back on decisions that we have taken in our lives – about a purchase, a relationship or a job – and have thought that if only we had known more about the options at the time, we might have chosen differently. With health care, we should know as much as practical, about the relative benefits and risks of the different treatment options that are available. Sometimes it is obvious that a particular treatment will vastly improve your life at very little risk of side-effects or long-term problems, but much of health care is not that clear. Medical procedures have mixed experiences. Sometimes the benefits are not obvious; the risks of a particular procedure may be high; success cannot be guaranteed: for some cases there may be complications or long-term problems. Understanding the pros and cons of each treatment and weighing up the options in order to pick the one that is suitable, is making an informed choice and thus giving informed consent.

Many doctors are still reluctant to give all the possibilities of treatment, worrying that patients would be so put off that they would opt to do nothing. The law is not much help on the matter of informed consent, and when cases have come to court, the judgment has often gone in favour of the doctor, even when it has been shown that information has been withheld, on the grounds that it might be too confusing for the patient to know all the options.

Consent forms

Before planned treatment such as surgery, you will be asked to sign a consent form. As this is the basis of the agreement which might allow the doctor to carry out major surgery, it is important that you check that the form is accurate. In particular check that the consent form has your correct personal details, that the procedure that is going to be undertaken is written in full and that you have had it properly explained to you, including any complications that could arise. Sometimes a consent form will include the words 'and proceed'. This is written when the doctor is going to undertake exploratory surgery because he or she believes that surgery is necessary, but is unsure what is wrong. This wording means that you are giving consent to the doctor to carry out whatever treatment is needed to sort out your problem. It does not allow the surgeon to carry out unrelated surgery. For instance, a surgeon cannot cut something out if you have only consented to an exploratory operation, even if the surgeon believes that it is in your best interest. Surgeons who have, in good faith, carried out other procedures without gaining consent for these have found themselves subject to very serious disciplinary and legal charges.

If there is anything on a consent form that you are unsure about, get the doctor to explain it to you. If there is something on the consent form that you object to do not be afraid to cross it out and initial the change that you have made.

Consent for young people

Young people of 16 and 17 have a right to give consent to examinations and treatments. Patients of 16 and 17 years old can also give consent, and if there is a clash between parents and children, the doctor will take the wishes of the child as paramount. Under the age of 16, the parents have the right of consent, but if consent is not given and the doctor believes that the health or life of the child may be jeopardised, he or she can apply to the courts for a ruling on whether or not to treat the child and, in an emergency, can act without going to the courts.

Many young people are confused about their rights to get prescribed contraceptives. This is partly due to the 'Gillick case' in the mid-1980s. This case established a precedent whereby if a person under the age of 16 has the maturity to understand the proposed treatment and make a decision themselves, then it is not necessary to get parental consent. In prescribing contraceptives to a person under 16, a doctor will need to show that this action is to protect the young person against the harmful effects of sexual intercourse, such as an unplanned pregnancy or sexually transmitted disease.

HUMAN GUINEA PIGS – YOUR RIGHTS IN MEDICAL RESEARCH

Each week seems to bring a new treatment that gives hope to people suffering from incurable disease. What is never made clear is that these treatments are experiments, carried out under strict research conditions and that the people who have agreed to take part in these experiments are human guinea pigs. While people want the chance to get a new treatment which might help, they are rightly nervous about being experimented on, so the way in which medical research in carried out in human trials is very carefully controlled.

Every hospital or health care institution where medical research goes on has to have an ethics committee which looks at all research proposals. No medical research can go ahead unless the ethical committee has approved the research and the methods that will be used. The rights of patients in research trials depend on whether they may benefit from taking part in the trial. If a benefit is expected, it is not necessary to give the patient all the information. If there are doubts about the outcome, then asking people to volunteer for a clinical trial without giving them all the information could be interpreted as getting consent with deception.

One of the most common research techniques used is the randomised controlled trial or RCT. In these trials some patients are given the new treatment and some are given a placebo – a treatment which looks like the new one but which is either a harmless substance or the old treatment against which the new one is being tested. No one entering the trial knows whether they get the real thing or the placebo: if the trial is a double-blind one, the patient's doctor will not know either – only the researchers will know who got which drug or treatment. If you are enrolled in an RCT you should be told what the trial might mean for you.

Parents can find it very difficult to give their consent for research on their child. It is natural that parents will only consent to treatments which will cause benefit to a child, and will not give approval to treatments which have no expected benefit or which carry a degree of risk.

For peace of mind check and double-check that you are aware of what any research trial involves.

Health service decisions – your right to be asked for your opinion

Health service decisions are usually made about what sort of services people will get locally and where they will be sited. So there may be plans to close or relocate hospitals or health centres; or to cut the number of beds (or, more rarely, increase bed numbers); or to change specialist medical care. Health authorities are usually responsible for these plans and they have to involve local people in the discussions, listen to their ideas on the proposals, and take notice of local people in arriving at the final plans. When there is a significant change in services, then the local health 'chiefs' are required to consult formally with a large range of bodies, including community health councils (CHCs) and all health trusts, local authorities, MPs, major voluntary organisations, user groups and people directly affected. Chapter thirteen has more on this right.

Going home

Doctors and nurses often talk about 'allowing' you to go home after a stay in hospital, but this is perhaps misleading. In hospital you are free to leave at any time, just as you are free to refuse to consent to any examination or treatment. You can discharge yourself at any time, although you can expect to be told that you are 'to do no such thing!' by the ward sister. If you insist, as you have a right to do, you will be asked to sign a discharge form which says that you are leaving the hospital at your own request and against professional advice.

Planned discharge of a patient from a hospital should be made at the right time and in the right manner. The right time is when the patient no longer needs the intensive support of the clinical team of an acute hospital and can be moved home to recover or to some form of long-term nursing care, if appropriate. All discharges should have a care plan, which means that hospital staff have planned the sort of care that you will need, from relatives, neighbours, the primary care team and social services and that the health care professionals in the community are ready to take over your care. Sounds straight-forward? It should be, but sadly it does not happen very well in many cases. GPs, in particular, often complain about not being told when their patient has left hospital. Other reasons which tend to be given for poor co-ordination include lack of money and the difficulties of getting the different organisations who provide health care to work together. You may hear the term 'bed-blocking' used to refer to patients who, through no fault of their own, cannot leave the much-pressured acute hospital bed, because no plans are in place for their discharge. This is one of the big problems facing the health service today.

The only patients who don't have the right to discharge themselves are those detained under the 1983 Mental Health Act; patients detained because they have an infectious disease; and patients whose health or incapacity means that they are no longer capable of taking care of themselves.

Right to die

Just as you are free to decide whether you want to accept treatment or not, you are free to refuse treatment even if it leads to death. A doctor cannot help you to die, and still faces criminal charges if evidence emerges that this has happened, but doctors do have the duty of care to their patients to bring about 'a good death', and many will hasten the death of a patient by prescribing pain-relieving drugs, such as morphine. This is known as the 'law of double effect' and is legal. If it is clear that the death of a patient was hastened as an consequence of the primary motive of the doctor, which was to relieve suffering, then no crime has been committed. See chapter seven for more on this topic.

THE PATIENT'S CHARTER

As we have seen earlier in this chapter, you do not have very many rights as an NHS patient. Rights, such as they are, tend to be those that you can claim as a citizen, or because of a general provision of health services from the NHS. It may be very satisfying to say, 'I have a right to be seen by Dr X!', but actually you have no such thing.

Under the previous government the NHS published a 'Patient's Charter', which tried to set out the standards of service that everyone in the country had a 'right' to receive. The 'Patient's Charter' brought the issue of long waiting lists and waiting times to everybody's attention, by first stating that no one should wait more than two years for admission to hospital for treatment. But it also introduced many other 'consumer' ideas, such as information on health services, ways of dealing with complaints, patients' privacy and the need for the NHS to respect cultural and religious differences.

Although there were many good things about the 'Patient's Charter', it was very confused about people's rights to health care. So if the NHS didn't measure up to a particular standard of care, there wasn't very much you could do about it. Nonetheless the old 'Patient's Charter' did provide a spur to the NHS to take seriously the very reasonable calls to provide more flexible and patient-focused services. The Labour government is now reviewing what sort of values and standards should form the basis of a new NHS Charter.

Patient responsibilities

'With rights come responsibilities' is the old adage. Another of the problems with the old 'Patient's Charter' was that it was all one way. It was all about what the health service should provide for the patient, with no mention about how people should use health services responsibly. Recently, the government has begun to look at the other side of the relationship between patient and professional: what health professionals should expect from patients. It is in nobody's long-term interest for patients to abuse the care that the health service provides, but unfortunately it happens every day. When we refer to patient responsibilities, we are thinking of rules of behaviour that everyone could have an interest in supporting, because in that way everyone gets the best from their health care.

So here is the *PatientPower* list of patient responsibilities:

1. The NHS can only be sustained if we are willing, as a society, to continue to contribute to it, irrespective of the demands that individually we may make on it.

2. The NHS will only remain viable if we are willing, as individuals, to take from it only what we need, when we need it.

3. Staff in the NHS provide a public service and do their best, as professionals and as individuals, to provide for your health care. They deserve to be treated with courtesy and dignity at all times.

4. Violence and abuse of any kind against anyone involved in health care is unacceptable, and should not be tolerated, whatever the cause.

5. Health care is a partnership between you and the health professionals to get the best possible outcome to your care.

6. Consenting to treatment should be a responsibility which is more than a passive acceptance of things being done to you, but indicates that you have taken an active role in deciding your health care choices.

7. You have a responsibility to attend appointments and carry out whatever you have agreed as part of your health care. If you can't do something you have agreed to do, you should let someone know as soon as possible, so that they can make other arrangements, both for you and for others who will benefit.

8. People should have a basic understanding about the health service, so that they can make informed judgements about what to use. Going to A&E with a minor illness is not proper use of the

health service. Neither is phoning your GP at 3 a.m. because you can't get to sleep.

9. The NHS will only improve its services if it listens to its users. You should be encouraged to give feedback and should feel that you have a responsibility to make things work better, when you have ideas to contribute.

10. You should act in such a way as to minimise risks to your health. Smoking or drinking yourself into chronic and debilitating illness, for example, is not a responsible approach to your health care or your well-being.

CHAPTER 12: WHEN AND HOW TO COMPLAIN

The vast majority of people who use the NHS are satisfied and grateful customers. There are, however, many people who get a poor deal from the health service but who never voice their concerns or put their views in writing. This might be due to a lack of information about how to do this or uncertainty about where to start. People may also worry that their treatment will be affected in the future if they make a complaint – perhaps that the doctor they moaned about will take it out on them later.

The current NHS system for investigating complaints from staff or patients has been in place since 1996 and is a vast improvement on previous arrangements. But although the process is now much clearer, it can still take several months for your complaint to be dealt with. Few people appreciate that there are several different ways of making a complaint about their health care. This chapter will help you consider what outcome you are looking for and to choose which of these routes is best for you.

IT'S NOT REALLY A COMPLAINT BUT ...

Before we look at the various options for making complaints it is worth pausing to define what constitutes a complaint. The health service sees 'any expression of dissatisfaction which requires a response' as a complaint. Health service managers should take it seriously whether you just make a comment to a member of staff or are looking for a more thorough investigation.

One thing you can do to help yourself is to dismiss the idea that your comments will be seen as a bother or that nothing will be done. Even if you think your issue is not very important – just a niggling irritation or feeling that your care was worse than it could have been – the health service is obliged to reply to you, explaining what went wrong. They should also tell you what action they have taken to stop such incidents from happening again. In most places patients' views are taken seriously and are seen as having a positive role in improving services. In a few others complaints may not be dealt with as effectively as they should be. If this happens to you there are several further levels at which your concerns can be heard and investigated which are discussed later in this chapter.

Why do you want to complain?

From the outset it is worth being clear in your own mind what you want to happen as a result of your complaint. What would make you feel satisfied that the issue had been taken seriously? Is it:

- an apology?
- a recognition of what you have experienced?
- financial compensation?
- an assurance that the same thing could not happen to someone else?
- retribution?

The way you answer this question should help you decide how far to take the complaint. For example, if what you are looking for is a quick apology then this will suggest one course of action; if you require financial compensation a different path would need to be followed.

Preparing your complaint

Many complaints are made verbally – at the time and place when you receive your health care and realise that it has not lived up to your expectations. But if you want to make your complaint in writing, or are looking for a thorough investigation, you will need to do some homework. As soon as possible after the event put together all the information that you have about your case. As far as possible this should be written material. For instance, if you have had your operation cancelled for the second time, try to gather together the appointments cards, any correspondence telling you about the cancellations and why they happened, and any letters that you may have sent. Try to write down your own account of what happened, starting with the events leading up to the incident or experience and what was done in response. The longer you leave this the more likely you are to forget the details of what happened. You may need to put this account forward during an investigation into your complaint.

Getting help in making a complaint

Making a complaint or voicing concerns whether it is in a bank, restaurant or health centre can be daunting, particularly if you are still suffering the physical or mental aftermath of the thing you want to complain about. But there are independent public bodies called community health councils (CHCs) whose specific role is to represent patients' interests in the health service. They do not provide health care themselves, but act as an independent 'watchdog' working with health care providers and the health authority to ensure that they take account of people's wants and needs.

A large part of the work of any CHC is to offer information and advice to patients and to act as their representative. They can also help you put your complaint together and guide you through the right procedure. CHCs are staffed by a small number of paid workers, although the council members themselves are lay people who tend to be active in the local community and voluntary bodies. They will be in a strong position to tell you whether what you have experienced is typical or extraordinary.

Choosing the right route for your complaint

There are several routes through which complaints can be heard and investigated in the health service. The right one for you will depend on who was responsible for the problem, the outcome you are looking for and whether you are satisfied with the way your complaint is then handled. Having these different routes makes sense as complaints range from relatively minor difficulties (such as a rude receptionist) that might be resolved on the day (often by an apology from the organisation or member of staff), through to more complex cases involving litigation and claims for damages. But if you are approaching this territory for the first time the choice of routes can be bewildering, particularly if you are feeling a bit bruised after a less than pleasant experience from your health care. To help you decide which approach is best for you we start with an overview of the routes, then describe each one in more detail. The diagram provides a further illustration of the options.

One word of warning, complaints processes do vary slightly from place to place and what is outlined here is a description of the more typical elements. It is therefore worth checking out the specific local procedures before you take your complaint forward.

Complaints about your health care

These are dealt with by health authorities and NHS trusts. Health authorities can deal with complaints about GPs, local chemists, dentists doing NHS work, opticians, the overall health service in the area and whether certain treatments are not available or are rationed. Complaints about a GP can also be made to the practice itself. NHS trusts which run hospital and community health services deal with issues directly concerned with the care they provide and with complaints about their staff.

Complaints about health care professionals

If you want to complain about a clinician you can either take the matter to the organisation that employed them (an NHS trust) or make a complaint to the appropriate professional regulatory body. The professional conduct of doctors, nurses, midwives, health visitors and most of the clinical professionals is governed by regulatory bodies. In the case of doctors it is the General Medical Council. In the cases of nurses, midwives and health visitors it is the UK Central Council. These bodies have specific procedures for investigating the behaviour of health care professionals and in severe cases can take action to stop them working in the NHS again. You will find the addresses and contact numbers for these organisations at the back of the book.

Complaints about social services

Complaints about social workers, home helps, day care, assessments for community care or other services such as housing should be made directly to the director of social services, to the department concerned or to the chief executive of the district, county or borough council (which one it is depends on where you live). If you feel that you have not been given an adequate response you can take up the matter with your local councillor as an elected member of the local authority. Failing that the Local Government Ombudsman will investigate complaints which have a) already been brought to the attention of the authority concerned who have been given a reasonable time to reply and b) are about some personal injustice which is caused by an administrative fault, such as a delay in responding, bias in decision making or actual neglect.

Complaints about complaints that have not been successfully resolved

If you are not happy with the way your complaint has been dealt with locally you have two choices. You can ask for an independent panel to review the complaint or you can go direct to the Health Service Commissioner (formerly known as the Ombudsman). The Commissioner will look at all the records on your complaint and how it was investigated and can make the performance of the health service or trust very public – something that no chief executive would relish.

Complaints about treatment for mental illness

These can be made to a body called the Mental Health Act Commission. They have power to investigate complaints made by patients who have been formally detained as inpatients. The Commission can also step in in situations where the organisation providing the patient with hospital treatment has been unable to provide a satisfactory answer to the patient's complaint.

Claims for negligence

You can sue your health authority or trust if you believe that they have failed in their duty of care. Legal action is a costly option that is normally only considered if financial compensation is sought – in situations where there has been medical negligence resulting in disability, for example.

Below we take you through the ways you can make a complaint.

COMPLAINING ABOUT YOUR GP

Considering the number of people who consult their GP every day, very few make a complaint against them. Even fewer GPs end up being sued by their patients, although it does happen. This is partly because patients tend to see themselves as having long-term links with their GP and worry (sometimes unnecessarily) that their GP will give them worse treatment, victimise them or remove them from their list if they complain. The two main routes for complaints are *a)* directly to the GP practice or *b)* to the health authority which covers the area in which the practice is located.

Complaints to the practice

Each practice should have its own complaints procedure which describes who you can talk to about your concerns. It might be the practice manager, nurse, receptionist or a doctor. Ask for the leaflet which explains that procedure if you need to know more. This is likely to be the quickest way of getting your complaint heard and recognised, but you may feel that you need to talk to someone who is not directly involved with your care, which is where the health authority comes in. As discussed earlier in chapter two developments in primary care are in a state of flux and new primary care groups are being set up which will include all GPs. The role of primary care groups in investigating complaints is not yet clear, so you are best taking your complaint to the health authority.

Complaints to the health authority

Most complaints against GPs are dealt with by the local health authority with whom they have a contract of employment. You need to put your complaint in writing and send it to the complaints manager or to the chief executive. The health authority's investigation will centre on the terms and conditions of service under which GPs are employed. These are national rules which are strictly defined in what is known as 'The Red Book'. The process is not a judicial one in that lawyers are not involved. But be warned, the proceedings can feel legalistic. You will be allowed to bring someone who can speak on your behalf. The community health council will be able to do this or help you put your case together.

Figure 1 shows the key stages in the process from writing to the chief executive or complaints officer explaining your concerns to the action taken at the end. Your letter will be acknowledged and a copy will be sent to the GP concerned for his/her comments. The GP's response will in turn be sent to you. If you are not happy with it and you want to take the complaint further the health authority may offer you a meeting with a conciliator. Conciliators are lay people who are appointed by the health authority to mediate between patients and GPs. They try to help resolve the complaint or find some middle ground between the two opposing viewpoints. If conciliation is unsuccessful or if you do not want to go through that process, your case can be passed to the chairman of the Health Authority's Medical

Services Committee (MSC). This body has both lay people and representatives of GPs, dentists and pharmacists. The chairman will decide if there is enough evidence to warrant a hearing in front of the whole MSC and will then make a recommendation about this to the health authority. It will vary from place to place but some health authorities meet only every other month so it could take some time for the chairman's recommendation to be confirmed.

If your case is referred to the full MSC you and the GP will each be given the opportunity to present your side of the story. You will both be able to call witnesses and put your questions to the other party's witnesses. You will then be asked to sum up your case and the committee will go away to discuss the facts and think about the recommendations they wish to make. These then have to be approved by the health authority at its next meeting. If the committee finds that the GP was in breach of the terms and conditions of their contract then normally what will happen is that he/she will be reprimanded.

The long drawn out process and its quasi judicial nature is stressful for patient and GP alike. There are two common mistakes that people who want to complain about GPs make. The first is that they don't understand that the MSC who will hear the complaint have to concentrate on the GP's terms and conditions. These are not comprehensive and are open to interpretation – in theory a doctor could be considered grossly negligent and still conform to the conditions specified in their contract. The second mistake is that they go into the proceedings expecting that the GP will be 'struck off' or that something can be done to stop him/her repeating the mistake. The MSC does not have that sort of power, only the doctor's professional regulatory body – the General Medical Council – can do this.

COMPLAINTS ABOUT HOSPITAL AND COMMUNITY HEALTH SERVICES

The majority of complaints made by patients are about the quality of care they receive. Many are about staff being rude, the condition of

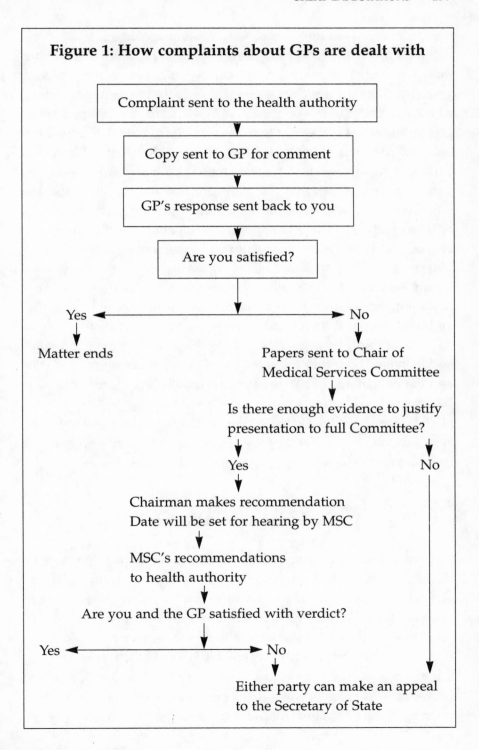

Figure 1: How complaints about GPs are dealt with

Complaint sent to the health authority

Copy sent to GP for comment

GP's response sent back to you

Are you satisfied?

Yes — Matter ends

No — Papers sent to Chair of Medical Services Committee

Is there enough evidence to justify presentation to full Committee?

Yes

No

Chairman makes recommendation
Date will be set for hearing by MSC

MSC's recommendations
to health authority

Are you and the GP satisfied with verdict?

Yes

No

Either party can make an appeal
to the Secretary of State

the facilities or waiting times to see a specialist. All NHS trusts have to have a procedure for investigating complaints and must make sure that it is well publicised. In 1994 a new system was introduced whereby there are clearly specified standards for responding to a complaint and for investigating it. This means that there is now greater similarity in the way that different bits of the NHS respond to patients' concerns. Having said that, there will be subtle differences between trusts in the importance that they attach to complaints and in their approach to handling them. In practice you may find it takes what seems like an unreasonable amount of time to get an answer.

Trusts will accept complaints either from patients or their representatives, but if the latter they will need evidence to indicate that a patient has given someone else permission to complain on their behalf. Any complaint should be made within six months of the event that triggered it. Beyond that deadline a trust is not obliged to conduct an investigation, although they can choose to do so if there are good reasons for the delay and if it is still possible to establish the facts after such a long time. If the case is reliant on the distant memories of staff and the patient it is likely that a trust would refuse to look into your complaint.

There are two stages to the NHS complaints procedure. First there is local resolution. If that fails to give you a satisfactory response you can ask for the second stage, an independent review.

Local resolution

Most complaints are made verbally at the time and place they happen – when you point out that the doctor has been patronising or that the receptionist has been unhelpful, for example. The majority of these complaints can be resolved in an informal way by the member of staff concerned or their manager – usually by an apology or quick explanation. But if, for example, the complaint raises fundamental questions about administrative systems in the organisation or the professional competence of a member of staff, the issue will then be referred to the complaints manager for advice.

If the matter is a very serious one or you get nowhere with your verbal complaint then you should write down your concerns in a letter to the complaints manager or the chief executive. You could also write to the chairman of the trust but what will normally happen is that he or she will just pass it on to the chief executive or complaints manager. It is tempting to believe that you will attract the personal interest of the chairman who will make sure that your issue is properly dealt with, but although they are the most senior figures in the NHS, chairmen of trusts are only part time, and few will have the time or detailed knowledge to be able to deal with your problem.

If you make a complaint in writing this is what you can expect to happen:

- Your letter should be acknowledged by the chief executive within a couple of days. The response should tell you what is being done to investigate your complaint and how long this will take. The better organisations will give you the name of the person conducting the investigation (the investigation manager).

- The investigation should be completed within three weeks of your complaint being received. If it is going to take longer you should get a letter describing what progress has been made and explaining why the investigation has been delayed.

- The investigation manager should make sure that any person who is the subject of a complaint is told about it and given the opportunity to put their side of the story

- You (or your representative) should be offered a meeting with the investigation manager. This can be a useful opportunity to clarify the details of what happened or simply to talk the matter through with someone.

- When your complaint has been investigated a report will be produced with recommendations. If appropriate, an action plan will be drawn up to ensure that similar mistakes are not repeated, although the trust is not obliged to show it to you. Trusts should keep a record of all complaints and monitor any trends to see what can be learnt from them. The chief executive should write to let you know the conclusions and apologise if this is justified. You may be offered an opportunity to discuss the findings with the manager who investigated the complaint.

- Once the investigation is complete the health authority will be sent a summary of the complaint but personal details such as your name and address will be kept confidential. This is so that they can look at any trends over time.

Independent review – taking your complaint a step further

If, when you have had the response back from the trust, you still feel that your complaint has not been properly addressed you can ask for it to be reviewed by people who are independent of the trust. You can ask for an independent review verbally or in writing but you need to do this within one month of receiving the final letter telling you about the investigation of your complaint, any longer and your request for a review may be refused. Your request will be considered by the trust's convenor, normally one of the non-executive directors (members of the trust board who are appointed for their business skills or local community interests to help the trust manage its work).

The convenor will discuss the case with a panel chairman nominated by the NHS executive. The chairman will be totally independent of the trust. Together the panel chairman and the convenor decide whether or not to set up a full independent review panel. They will use two criteria in making their decision:

a) Could the trust do anything more to look into your complaint without an independent review panel being involved?
b) If the trust has done everything they can, would a review panel be able to do anything further?

If the answer to both questions is no, then your request for an independent review will be turned down. If this happens you should be told within one month.

If you get the go ahead your complaint will be heard by an independent panel made up of the following members.

- An independent lay chairman who will be approved by the Secretary of State (in practice it is the regional office of the NHS executive who does this on the Secretary of State's behalf)
- A convenor (a non-executive director of a trust)
- A representative from the local health authority
- Two clinical assessors (if your complaint involves a health care professional)

It can take some time to establish an independent review panel due to the other work commitments of the members. Independent review panels normally work in a relatively informal and conciliatory way. They will look at any documentary evidence (such as case notes or your own written account of what happened). They may also interview the various people involved. You will be able to take along a friend or representative if you meet with the panel. The panel are expected to publish a completed report within 12 weeks of being formed. What normally happens is that a draft report will be produced for each party to check. The final report will be sent to you and a number of other people, including all of those involved in the inquiry, the chairman of the trust and the local health authority. Directors of the regional office of the NHS executive, the body which holds health authorities and trusts to account for the quality of services they provide, will also be informed. This is so that they can make sure that any wider lessons are learned and acted upon.

Once you have received the final report from the panel, the chief executive of the trust should write to you within one month to let you know what action has been taken in response to their recommendations. That letter should also remind you that you can take the matter further with the Health Service Commissioner (Ombudsman) if you wish (see below).

Going to independent review is no quick fix and you will need a good deal of determination and energy to persist down this road – all in all it can take as long as six months from making the request to receiving the final letter from the chief executive. Adding this to the time it takes for your complaint to be investigated it may be as much as one year after the event which caused you to complain. You should think about how comfortable you feel with the details of your complaint being shared with a wider group of people (although typically the report will refer to you only by initials rather than your full name). One small crumb of comfort is that you should be able to claim travel expenses from the trust for any meetings that you need to attend with the review panel.

COMPLAINTS TO PROFESSIONAL BODIES

All professional groups in the health service have some form of professional body which both represents and regulates the standard of work – this is called 'self-regulation'. Indeed most professions, from lawyers and architects to accountants, have professional regulatory bodies along similar lines. It may sound like a cosy affair and indeed some professional groups have been accused of protectionism in the past. But no profession wants its reputation to be tarnished by those whose work is poor or even dangerous, so there is every incentive for them to ensure that standards are maintained. Many people who complain are not motivated by revenge for their own situation, just a desire to see that similar events do not happen again.

If you want to complain about the work of an individual doctor, nurse or therapist on the grounds of incompetence, and if you want that complaint to be heard at the highest level, then you can make your complaint directly to the relevant regulatory body. The process again is complex and lengthy and the standard of proof you will need to provide is high. To give you an idea, there was a recent case of a GP who had served a prison sentence for assault on a patient yet the GMC concluded he was still fit to practise as a doctor.

How are the professions regulated?

Both doctors and nurses have a professional regulatory body which oversees their activities and maintains the register of those who are eligible and safe to practise. The General Medical Council (GMC) for doctors and the UK Central Council for Nursing, Midwifery and Health Visiting (UKCC) are both keepers of the ethics of their profession. They are essentially run by doctors and nurses, although both councils also have lay representatives, some of whom are appointed by the Secretary of State for Health. Any member of the public or a member of that profession can make a complaint to the professional body. Complaints can also be referred by community health councils, health authorities and NHS trusts.

Complaints about doctors

In investigating complaints against doctors the GMC's powers cover four situations:

- Where the doctor has shown *professional misconduct*, that is behaviour which makes the GM question that doctor's ability to practise medicine without restriction.

- Cases where the doctor has been convicted of a *criminal offence* in court.

- Where the doctor's performance is *seriously deficient*, meaning that he or she has shown consistently poor practice below expected standards as opposed to one major error (misconduct).

- Where the doctor *is ill* to an extent that it affects their work.

The GMC provides a standard form which you can use to submit your complaint. Alternatively, you can describe the complaint in a letter. The form will mean that you include all the pieces of evidence that are needed by the committee who will consider your complaint. At a minimum you need to make sure that you provide the following information:

- the full name(s) of the doctor(s) involved

- a summary of your complaint and when it happened

- any other letters that you have sent or have received about the matter – for example if your complaint has already been investigated under a trust's local investigation process then include the final letter that you got from the chief executive

- any other relevant evidence such as copies of medical records

- your name, address and a daytime phone number

Unlike NHS trusts the GMC does not have a formal time limit within which complaints have to be made, although they do encourage complaints to be made as soon as possible after the event. You can make a complaint to the GMC at the same time as lodging one with the trust that employed the doctor (or the health authority in the case of a GP). However, the GMC may well wait until those local investigations have been completed before they start their own.

The GMC's complaints process has several stages.

Stage one: screening
When a complaint is sent to the GMC it will be assessed by a doctor who has the job of 'screener'. Screeners look at how serious your complaint is and at the strength of the evidence that you have sent in. They also check to see if there is any other information that the Council holds on the same doctor. Normally they will discuss the complaint with you informally. They may also give you advice if they think the matter should be dealt with elsewhere. For example, they may suggest that you first go through the complaints procedure with the trust which employs the doctor.

The purpose of screening is to decide whether any further action should be taken. For a complaint to be rejected at this first hurdle the decision has to be agreed by two GMC members, one of which has to be a lay member whose job is to look at the matter from the patient's viewpoint. This does provide some insurance against professional protectionism. Some of the most common reasons for not investigating complaints are:

- where the complaint is not serious enough to warrant a review of the doctor's registration

- where the doctor cannot be identified

- where the complaint did not actually involve the doctor

- where the complaint was not related to the doctor's medical work

- if the patient does not agree to the complaint being discussed with the doctor concerned or wishes to remain anonymous

Stage two: investigation
The second function of screening is to decide which procedure will be used to investigate the complaint. The GMC has three distinct procedures.

Conduct procedures These are for professional misconduct and criminal offences and require a standard of proof similar to a criminal investigation. There are different stages involved, the final one being a public hearing which is similar to a trial.

Performance procedures These are for generally deficient clinical practice. Both the performance and health procedures focus on day-to-day performance and health rather than a specific event. The aim is to get the doctor to co-operate with either re-training, supervision or medical treatment. If the doctor refuses then there will be a formal hearing. There are various stages which involve observation of the doctor at work and assessments by peers. Both the performance and health procedures take place in private and you will not have to appear as a witness.

Health procedures These cases occur where a doctor is ill, and normally involve mental health problems, drug or alcohol abuse. If your case is to be investigated under the conduct procedures it will go first to the Preliminary Proceedings Committee, who will review all the papers on the case, including any response from the doctor concerned. They then decide what action will be taken. The options are these:

- They can send the doctor a written warning or a letter of advice.

- They can decide that the matter warrants a public hearing by the Professional Conduct Committee.

- They can refer the case to the Health Committee if the doctor's health is the underlying problem to the complaint.

- They can decide to take no further action.

They will write and tell you which of these options they have chosen.

If your case is to go to a public hearing you will be asked to appear as a witness before the Professional Conduct Committee. The seriousness of these investigations is indicated by the fact that doctors are allowed legal representation at the hearings. You will have to make a sworn written statement, and other people involved in the complaint or who had personal knowledge of what happened may also be asked to make statements. To make a sworn statement you will need legal advice from a solicitor; you may also be able to get help from your local community health council. If you cannot afford to pay for a solicitor you can ask the GMC to pay this for you – they have some discretion on this matter.

The GMC should make all the arrangements for the public hearing and will pay your expenses. You will be able to take a friend or relative with you for support. Unfortunately, if you want the support of a solicitor you will not be able to claim legal aid. The GMC do make available the services of their own solicitors to complainants free of charge. In exceptional circumstances the GMC may agree to pay for the services of your own solicitor. It is worth checking whether this applies in your case.

The public hearings of the Professional Conduct Committee are normally well attended by the press and radio and TV journalists because very few cases ever get to this final stage. This is worth bearing in mind if you have a horror of the details of your case reaching the attention of the public. The 1998 case of the Bristol childrens' surgeons found by the GMC to be guilty of poor practice, for example, was a very high-profile affair.

If after all the investigations and observations on the doctor's performance your complaint is upheld there are various options open to the GMC. It is not automatic that the doctor will be struck off the register for good – this happens only in the worst of cases. It is more likely that he/she will be given a public warning which will stay on their record in case a similar event happens again or that some limitations will be placed on their medical work (one of the Bristol surgeons, for example, was forbidden to operate on babies but was allowed to continue surgical work on adults). A doctor can also be suspended from practising for one year. The GMC publishes an annual report summarising the cases they have dealt with and the results. This may give you some clue as to the likely outcome for your own case.

This is not quite the end of the process – a doctor can appeal against the GMC's decision to the law lords who form the Judicial Committee of the Privy Council. This will be a private hearing and you will not be asked to appear before them.

Complaints about nurses, midwives or health visitors

Anyone has the right to complain about the actions or errors of a registered nurse, midwife or health visitor either to their employer (usually an NHS trust) or directly to their professional regulatory body, the UK Central Council for Nursing, Midwifery and Health Visiting (UKCC). So how do you decide whether or not to take your complaint to this level? If your complaint is about whether the nurse should continue to work in her/his present post then you should take your complaint to the NHS Trust or GP practice that employed them. If you believe your experience raises questions about the person's ability to work with any patients or clients in the future then your complaint should be addressed to the UKCC. Put another way, ask yourself whether the outcome you are seeking is for the nurse/midwife to be suspended or removed from the professional register. If the answer is yes, then it is the UKCC you should approach with your complaint.

The way in which the UKCC conducts its business is defined in statute. Like the GMC the UKCC is required by law to have two levels of committee to investigate nursing practise. The first is the Preliminary Proceedings Committee, which considers allegations of misconduct and fitness to practise and decides whether the individual should be referred to a hearing. The second is the Professional Conduct Committee, which decides whether the practitioner should be suspended or have her/his name removed from the register. This effectively stops the person from working as a nurse in the NHS.

If you choose to make a complaint to the UKCC be prepared for it to take several months before your complaint is investigated and heard. Again the standard of evidence required to demonstrate misconduct is akin to a criminal burden of proof, i.e. the committees have to hear evidence that proves beyond reasonable doubt what has happened. They also have to be assured that the facts offer conclusive proof of misconduct. This can lead to anomalies. For example, a trust may dismiss a nurse for hitting a patient, an act which would be considered to be gross misconduct, but the UKCC may find insufficient evidence to justify that nurse being prevented from practising again. As with doctors, what is being looked for is not the highest standard that a nurse, midwife or health visitor might attain but what could be expected of the average practitioner.

If the allegation concerns fitness to practise, the committees look at the person's health. The illnesses which normally lead to removal from the register are alcohol or drug dependence or mental illness.

Making a complaint

As with all other complaints procedures the UKCC recommend reporting your complaint as soon as possible after the event. Complaints have to be made in writing to the UKCC addressed to the

Assistant Registrar, Professional Conduct (you will find the address at the back of this book). Your letter should include as much information as possible on the incident. It is also worth looking at the UKCC's published code of professional conduct for nurses, midwives and health visitors or their guidelines for professional practice as these give a guide to the standards which are expected (you can get this from the same address).

The UKCC does make an effort to pursue complaints where the patient cannot remember the nurse's name. If this applies to you try to include as much detail as possible to help them identify the practitioner on the register (what they looked like, the time of the day they were working, the name of the ward and the date of the incident, for example). In putting your case bear in mind the sort of evidence that you put forward. Hearsay (or indirect) evidence will not provide an acceptable level of proof. An example of hearsay would be if you were making a complaint on behalf of a patient who had been given the wrong dose of a drug. If you saw the nurse in question give the dose to the patient that would be considered as fact. If you assumed that it was the particular nurse because she was giving the drugs to other patients, this would be considered hearsay.

The UKCC publish some helpful guidance on typical successful and unsuccessful cases. Situations which the UKCC are very unlikely to uphold include the following:

- employment issues, for example false overtime claims

- mistakes made when the practitioner was under pressure of work

- cases where the failure was effectively a failure to do the impossible given the circumstances

- where the complaint was assessing the actions of the practitioner against outdated practice or norms

Cases which are more likely to be successful in getting a nurse, midwife or health visitor removed from the professional register include the following:

- wilfully unskilful practice

- concealing untoward incidents

- failing to keep essential records or falsifying them

- physical or verbal abuse of patients

- failing to act when a colleague is improperly treating or abusing patients

- theft from patients or employers

- breach of confidentiality

- administering drugs that were not prescribed (if that nurse has not got the authority to prescribe the medicines herself) or an excessive amount of prescribed drugs

HEALTH SERVICE OMBUDSMAN OR HEALTH SERVICE COMMISSIONER

This is the only stage in the complaints system which is totally independent of the organisation against which you have a complaint. The Commissioner is independent of both the NHS and the government. No charge is made for this service. You can refer your complaint to the Commissioner if:

- You were refused an independent review – For example if you did not manage to make your request for a review panel within a month of local resolution or if the convenor decided that a panel would not be able to help

- Your complaint has been investigated locally and by an independent review panel and you were still not satisfied with the decision.

Since 1996 the Commissioner has had the power to investigate complaints about primary care services and actions concerned with clinical judgement, so the remit is much wider than in the past. The

Commissioner is not allowed to investigate matters where the complainant has taken the matter to court. In fact the Commissioner has no legal obligation to take on any particular case; it is for them to decide whether your case is worth investigating. The process tends to be lengthy and thorough, not least because it can take some time for the organisation involved to supply all the relevant documents. When the investigation is finished a report will be written and you will be sent a copy, as will the health authority or trust concerned.

The Commissioner's main weapon is publicity. A case described in the annual report to the Secretary of State and in turn submitted to the House of Commons and the House of Lords is something that no chief executive would relish. In theory the Commissioner has no power to tell a health authority trust or practitioner to do anything – he/she can only make recommendations or ask the organisation to reconsider the issue. The Commissioner can also bring matters to the attention of the Parliamentary Public Accounts Committee, which in turn can summon the managers and professionals in a trust to give evidence before it. In practice no organisation has ignored the Commissioner's recommendations for fear of a similar event occurring in the future.

LITIGATION: THE FINAL FRONTIER

An increasing number of patients are choosing to take legal action against the health service. Claims against the NHS went up by 15 per cent between 1997 and 1998 and similar increases were seen in damages paid. The cost of negligence claims to the NHS is now over £200 million per year. In 1997 the Medical Protection Society paid out a further £15.5 million on behalf of the GPs that they represent and UK consultants who work in the private sector.

The odds on success

Litigation is the route to choose if you are seeking financial compensation. If you decide to take legal action one of the first things to consider is whether you can afford it. Legal aid is available to some people and charities and trade unions are also known to sponsor cases that are likely to raise the profile of an issue or test the boundaries of the law. But for the majority of people litigation can be an expensive option even if they win their case. So you need to be aware of the odds on winning or losing.

The media attention given to rare cases of negligence which win the victims hundreds of thousands of pounds can be misleading. The medical negligence system is often referred to as a lottery: the success rate for claims is actually around one in four. Only about 17 per cent of cases ever reach a court hearing, most are settled out of court with appropriate payments of damages which will be far more modest than those reported. Legal costs in even simple cases are not insignificant. Even if you win you will probably have to meet some of your legal fees and this can easily take up the lion's share of your compensation if you are lucky enough to be awarded damages.

If you think the odds on a case being successful seem promising you may change your mind when you compare the success rate for negligence in non-medical cases (around 85 per cent). Part of the reason for the difference is that all doctors are represented by one of three specialist medical defence bodies: the Medical Defence Union, the Medical Protection Society and the Medical and Dental Defence Union of Scotland. These organisations have a wealth of experience and case law to draw on which is far beyond that of the average lawyer who will act on your behalf.

Recent developments in managing negligence claims

Taking or defending legal action is a lengthy and expensive business for NHS organisations as well as patients. This is why the health service insures itself against clinical negligence claims through the Clinical Negligence Scheme for Trusts. This is administered by a body called the NHS Litigation Authority. A body called the Medical Protection Society is responsible for the day-to-day management of the claims. This may not be of much interest to you in taking out your claim for negligence but it may help to know which body you and your solicitor will be dealing with behind the legal letterheads.

The civil justice system is undergoing some radical changes following a review conducted by Lord Justice Woolf. His recommendations were designed to make it easier for people to make negligence claims, although many consumer groups have opposed the changes. The new arrangements have streamlined the process and introduced new arrangements to encourage resolution of disputes before matters come to trial. These include the following:

Pre-action medical negligence protocols These procedures are designed to encourage both parties to put their cards on the table at the outset. This can help narrow the issues at dispute and improve the process of incident investigation. In theory this should also help keep legal costs down. The protocols also encourage earlier explanation from the health service and earlier disclosure of a patient's records. The aim is make the patient more aware of the full picture so that they can fully understand the options available to them.

Greater use of conciliation and mediation This process, although similar to that used by trusts and health authorities when complaints are made, is confusingly called the alternative disputes resolution when potential litigation is involved.

Standard forms for patients to use when requesting their medical records. Timescales have also been specified within which trusts must respond (40 working days).

A fast tracking system for dealing with medical negligence claims through the courts.

Curtailing costs awarded in negligence cases This provision has yet to be fully tested.

Approval of lawyers who operate conditional fee systems This is perhaps the most contentious of the changes. Conditional fees mean that you only pay legal fees if you are successful in winning the case. A solicitor who works on this basis who is willing to take on your case is effectively giving you a vote of confidence that your case is a strong one. Contingency arrangements should come with two public warnings. First the lawyers may charge a success fee of up to double their normal fee, which will be deducted from any damages that you are awarded. The second is that 'no win no fee' arrangements do not mean 'no cost'. If you lose your case then you will have to pay the other side's costs and probably some of your own expenses. Alternatively, you may be able to qualify for legal aid to take forward your claim in a civil court (see below).

Getting legal aid

Legal aid is for people who need the services of a solicitor or barrister but who are unable to meet the full costs themselves. The financial support covers both initial advice and assistance in taking your case to either a civil or criminal court. Not all solicitors do legal aid work – your local Citizens Advice Bureau or a law centre should be able to give you a list of those that do and details on whether or not you are eligible for this support.

What counts as medical negligence?

Having looked at the procedures involved in making a negligence claim and how to pay for it, let us take a step back to consider what the term negligence actually means. Most people would assume that failed sterilizations, complications in childbirth which resulted in injury to the baby, surgical errors or errors of diagnosis were all likely to have been the result of negligence. But these examples may be a little misleading – it is not the severity of the condition which is important but whether fault can be proved. Negligence then is another way of describing fault and it is tightly defined in law. The definition states that a person or organisation is not necessarily liable to compensate another who has suffered an injury as a result of that person's act or omission. There has to be some fault or negligence on the first person's part. In simple terms you can only recover damages from another party if you are able to prove three things:

- that they owed you a duty of care

- that they failed to show reasonable care

- that you have suffered injury as a result of that failure of care.

A lawyer will be able to explain the ramifications of the three criteria and how they relate to your particular case. However, there are some simple guidelines which should be relevant to most cases.

Duty of care

According to their own professional body, the GMC, doctors providing diagnosis and treatment owe their patients a duty of care. But most doctors are unclear how far that duty stretches and there are indeed some grey areas. For example, if a doctor warns you not to do something which would cause you harm but you go ahead and do it, has their duty of care been fulfilled or should they take further steps to prevent you from taking that action? Another area where the duty of care may be unclear is where treatment is refused. For example, a patient walks into a psychiatric unit and asks to be admitted but the doctor on duty turns them away without giving any treatment. If that patient then commits suicide a few hours later, the doctor would have failed in their duty of care by not properly assessing the risks of refusing treatment. The duty of care issue is also relevant where a doctor or nurse acts as a Good Samaritan by providing first aid to someone who has collapsed in the street. A doctor or nurse who failed to help the stranger in the street could be in breach of their professional code of conduct rules. At the end of the day the legal duty of care is something that is difficult to define in absolute terms and will often be for a judge to determine.

Aside from individual behaviour there is one other circumstance where patients can take legal action concerning the duty of care. This is when local facilities or treatments are not available, for example there are insufficient paediatric intensive care beds or dialysis machines. Although no individual is at fault a claim could be launched against either the health authority or the Secretary of State on the grounds that they have failed to fulfill their statutory duty to provide health care facilities. Such claims are rarely successful for the reasons outlined in chapter eleven. The most likely interpretation of such claims by the court is that it is for the Secretary of State to decide what is an acceptable distribution of available resources – there is no requirement to provide any individual with a particular service. The Secretary of State's judgment would need to be proved completely unreasonable if such a claim were to succeed.

Strictly speaking someone who commits an act of negligence is personally liable for their actions. But if they are acting in the course of their employment then their employer is also liable – this is called vicarious liability. Generally employer organisations have more resources than their employees so lawyers will try to sue the organisation rather than the individuals.

A reasonable standard of care

The key issue here is who judges what is reasonable? Medicine is not a black and white science. So the courts now follow some well-established guidelines to inform their decisions about the standards expected of doctors. These include the following:

- A doctor is not guilty of negligence if he/she has followed practice which would be accepted as proper by a responsible group of peers working in the same specialism, even if different opinions also exist within the profession. This is called the 'Bolam' principle and comes from the case of the same name. With more medical practice being subject to guidelines and protocols it remains to be seen whether the Bolam test will, in time, prove unnecessary.

- The doctor does not have to demonstrate the highest standard of care and competence, simply what is reasonable for that profession. So you could not claim that a doctor was negligent simply because you found another doctor who had a greater skill or success rate in a particular treatment.

- Errors of judgement are accepted in the eyes of the law. To prove negligence you have to show that the errors have been made by an ordinary doctor acting without an ordinary degree of care. This can be quite difficult.

Lawyers generally use expert witnesses to help them determine what is a reasonable standard of care. However, it is not uncommon to find two sets of experts holding contrary views which support either the plaintiff or defendant's case.

Injuries resulting from failure of care

A large proportion of the disputes in medical negligence cases focus on whether the injury was caused by a failure of care. For this clause you have prove that the defendant's actions contributed to your damage. This can be the most difficult of the three clauses. For example, if the person was suffering from a pre-existing condition which is made worse as a result of medical treatment the relative or extra damage will be difficult to prove. Most treatments carry a degree of risk even if carried out properly. A further point to bear in mind is that the law expects you to show that you have taken reasonable steps yourself to limit or control your loss or injury. For instance, if you suffered a complication from a failed operation on your knee and then refused to have a second operation which you were told could improve your situation, your claim against the original act would be unlikely to be upheld.

Medical negligence claims: what you can claim for

If you have been injured as a result of medical negligence, you will need to put together a claim for the sum of money for which you are seeking recompense. There is some evidence that public expectations of the damages that should be awarded are much higher than those which judges award in practice. This may be partly fuelled by high-profile cases in which the damages total hundreds of thousands of pounds.

The things that you can claim for include:

1. damages for pain, suffering and loss of function
2. financial loss and expenses incurred by the time that the case is heard
3. damages for future financial loss and expense
4. interest – available on (1) and (2) at a fixed rate.

Under (2) you are entitled to claim for any private medical and nursing expenses or other costs of care such as engaging a home help which have been incurred as a direct result of the injury. It is also worth bearing in mind that you can also claim damages for the value of nursing services which were provided free of charge, for example by a friend or relative. The carer does not have to have given up employment for these damages to be recoverable but you would need to be able to prove that the level of care was over and above what you would normally get in the course of family life. Another point that is not always appreciated is that you are entitled to claim for any medical or nursing care which has been provided by the private sector, even if that care is available on the NHS. Once you decide on the litigation route make sure you keep detailed records of any expenditure associated with your health care in case you are asked for proof when putting your claim together.

Damages for bereavement under (2) are very low – there is a ceiling of £7,500 which is defined in statute. If you cannot prove dependency then this may be all you are entitled to.

Under (3) you can claim for damages if you are unable to return to work. If you work at home or in the home you will also be able to recover costs if you have to engage paid or unpaid help from someone who has to give up work to provide it. So if the victim is a child and the main breadwinner in the house has to give up work to look after them you could claim for the loss of their income. The travel and living costs of relatives visiting the injured patient in hospital can also be claimed, but relatives cannot claim for any income they lose taking time off work.

Increasing use is being made of structured settlements. These allow for the costs to be paid over a lifetime or agreed period rather than a lump sum. These settlements have benefits for both the health service and for patients. For the former it means that damages are paid in relation to need and the financial effects can be handled over a longer period of time – it can often be difficult for a hospital to find a large lump sum, even if it is covered by the Clinical Negligence Scheme. One version of the structured settlement is where the NHS buys an insurance policy which will pay out a regular sum to the injured party whilst they are still alive. For the patient the main advantage is that settlements can be structured so that the payments are made tax free. If a structured settlement is to be awarded by the courts both parties have to be in agreement that this is acceptable.

The new changes to the civil justice system make it easier than ever for patients to take legal action against the health service. Within the NHS the growing use of protocols and defined care pathways should result in tighter definitions of what is or is not acceptable clinical practice. It remains to be seen whether the upward trend in litigation will continue and how these new factors will work to the benefit of patients, the NHS or both.

PART IV

SELF-HELP HEALTH

CHAPTER 13: YOUR HEALTH AND HEALTH CARE – TAKING CONTROL

The earlier sections of this book give an introduction to the health care system and explain both what you can expect from the health service and, in turn, what your responsibilities are to it. This chapter shows you how to implement your new understanding by taking an active part in your own health care – short of getting training as a health service manager or health care professional.

WHY DO PEOPLE GET ILL?

We all know that cigarettes and too much alcohol are bad for you. But then we all also know someone who smoked 60 a day who lived to be 99. We all know that keeping fit and eating a low fat diet are good for you, yet we have all heard of someone who dropped dead at 45 after playing a game of squash. The food brigade tell us that the only really healthy produce are pure organic vegetables grown a thousand miles from any pollution or additives. Sociologists tell us that how long you live depends on your social class and wealth, and scientists say that illness is all locked up in your genetic make-up. The only thing everyone can agree on is that you're going to die one day. So the sensible advice might be to enjoy yourself and ignore the experts – particularly the doom merchants.

As yet, we only get one body and one life. The really smart thing to do is to get the most out of it. Your body as a machine is a million times more sophisticated and efficient than the most fantastic car, plane or computer, but all these share some common features with your body. All need feeding the right fuel, they all need to be handled with attention and be maintained regularly. But unlike mass-produced cars each human being is different – despite what we would like to think, we are not all equal. It is the differences between us which make general statements about what will happen if you do this or don't do that so difficult to apply to individual people. So why do some people stay healthy and fit and others seem to get routinely ill?

We are not all equal: nature

Human beings are not clones of each other. We all have our own unique code, written in the genetic make-up on our 52 chromosomes. The material which makes up the genes is called DNA (short for deoxyribonucleic acid). The race to crack this genetic code is now the subject of a massive worldwide research programme called the 'genome project' . The aim of this research is to get a complete map of all the genes in the human body and what they mean. For example, we know that there is a gene for eye colour and one for cystic fibrosis. But we don't yet know whether genes regulate things such as intelligence, aggression, skin cancer or the ability to determine right from left.

We are not all equal: nurture

'Give me a child until he is seven, and I will give you the man' was the famous slogan of the Jesuits, the strict Roman Catholic teachers, who set out to show that children, whatever their birth and origins, could be moulded into a particular type of adult if they were taken out of their environments at birth. As well as our genetic make-up the circumstances in which we live and the environment into which we are born have an important influence on our health and well-being.

What our parents do, the way they bring us up, the education we have, our friends, work and play opportunities are hugely significant. The statistics indicate that if you are born to professional parents you will, on average, live longer and healthier lives than if your parents have manual or unskilled jobs. Not fair is it?

We are not all equal: behaviour

So we know that nature (our genes) and nurture (our upbringing) affect the sort of lives we are likely to have. But we are not just creatures who are programmed to live our lives without being able to do anything about it. We make choices in how we live our lives and all of us gamble with fate. Every time we cross a road, take a holiday, make love or have a meal we take a risk, but we balance living life to the full, with the chances that accident or illness will carry us off. Some of these choices have a positive bearing on our health and some of them don't. So whilst we cannot yet select the genes that we have, and until we are adults we cannot change the environment in which we live, here are some steps that everyone can take to improve their health and increase their longevity.

TAKE CONTROL OF YOUR HEALTH

PatientPower is about taking control of your health before you need health care. It's about minimising the time we have to spend as a patient. Some of the things we can do are mentioned earlier in the book but they have been brought together here for reference.

Early warning systems – screening

Screening tests are the early warning systems to things that might go wrong with your body, or which may have already begun to go wrong. The idea behind all screening is that the sooner something is found, the sooner action can be taken to tackle it. This sounds like a model of good health care. But some screening tests can detect things for which there are no cures. Why should people who have no symptoms at all be worried about an illness that is not troubling them and for which nothing can be done? Screening without action can diminish quality of life for little or no long-term gain.

There are several types of screening:

- genetic
- antenatal
- infant and child
- adult
- older people

Genetic screening

This is the newest form of screening, because it is only in the last few years that we have known something about the link between particular genes and the illnesses that they cause. Sometimes a problem is caused by a single gene defect, but usually the relationship is more complicated. As more becomes known about the genetic basis of health, families who have a history of a particular disease can be thoroughly screened to see the possible inheritance of a problem in the next generation. Genetic screening is done by taking cells from the body and looking at the chromosomes for abnormal genes, usually by testing the way they react to chemicals and dyes. This is the earliest of early warning systems, because it shows whether you have a chance of passing on a disease to your children. This raises the possibility that every child has the chance to be born without inherited illness and the spectre that we will be aborting children who do not have the ideal genetic characteristics. Genetic diseases that can already be detected include Down's syndrome, cystic fibrosis and some cancers.

Antenatal screening

Antenatal screening ranges from routine checks on weight, urine and blood to more complex tests such as ultrasound scans and amniocentesis. Most pregnant women are routinely tested for syphilis although they will normally be unaware that this is done, unless, of course, the test results prove positive. There is also increasing pressure for routine HIV tests to be done.

Amniocentesis is done by sampling the fluid around the baby to check for certain genetic disorders such as spina bifida and Down's syndrome in the unborn baby. The test can also detect the sex of the baby, which can be useful if there is a family history of certain sex-linked conditions. The chemical make-up of the fluid can also indicate whether the baby is getting enough oxygen. Amniocentesis does carry a small risk that it will cause a miscarriage. It is worth remembering that although some babies are born with inherited disorders, most of these conditions come out of the blue with no family history. Ultrasound can be a very powerful tool for detecting physical defects.

Infant and child screening

Newborn children are examined by specialist doctors and health visitors, who check for a variety of disorders of the blood, heart, brain and nervous system. There are some routine tests done when a baby is first born – its reflexes, heart rate and skin colour are all noted, for example. All children under five also have regular check-ups with health visitors to monitor their developmental progress.

Adult screening

Routine screening is currently only available on the NHS for certain types of cancers. At present the only population wide screening is that available to women within certain age bands for breast and cervical cancer. The former is available every three years to women between 50 and 64 and the latter every five years to women between 20 and 64 although there are local variations. Other cancers which are common in adults, such as cancer of the colon, ovary and prostate, are not yet routinely screened for various reasons – partly for those based on the balance of cost and effectiveness and partly relating to the availability of a successful treatment.

Next to cancers, heart problems are the biggest cause of premature death in this country, and a regular blood pressure check will detect possible problems ahead.

Older People Screening

Some diseases, such as Alzheimer's, osteoporosis (in women) and prostate trouble (in men) are many times more common in older people than younger. To keep older people living healthy lives (known as adding 'life to years'), GPs are now paid to carry out yearly health checks on everyone on their list aged 75 and over. The attitude that older people should lead staid, sedentary lives has rightly passed. With good diet, regular exercise and periodic health checks, older people will increasingly lead very full and active lives into their 80s and 90s.

Early warning systems – health checks

These are a sort of human MOT – testing you every year or couple of years to see what shape you are in. These health checks are only available on the NHS when you register with a GP and when you reach 75 years. Private and company health insurance schemes often offer an annual health check. Opinion is divided in the medical profession about the value of such routine testing. Chapter fifteen gives you some hints about whether buying a private health check is worth while.

Ten tips for do-it-yourself health

When all is said and done, the person who has most control over your health is you. It's your body, your health, your life, and you can mess it up if you want, or you can get the most out of it. Here are some basic things that you probably know already.

1. *Smoking* This is a legalised way of killing millions of people worldwide every year. Until tobacco is made an illegal substance you should do all you can to stop smoking or cut down on the number of cigarettes you smoke. Tobacco companies need to recruit ten of thousands of new smokers each year to fill the ranks

of those their product kills each year. Smokers are victims, because the active drug in tobacco – nicotine – is highly addictive. If you smoke and enjoy it enough not to mind the diseases that accompany it, then fine, carry on (but remember you're harming your children, your friends and those around you). If you do want to stop, check the self-help section in the Appendix.

2. *Alcohol* This is another drug which has been used by humans for thousands of years. Small daily amounts of alcohol (a couple of glasses of wine or the equivalent) probably improve your general health, but drinking excessively (over six glasses a day) increases your chances of accidents and heart and liver problems, simply because you are overloading your body and cutting down your mental functioning.

3. *Food* Food scares and fads have become so common in recent years that a lot of people have grown tired of hearing what is good or bad for them. The best advice it to try to get a good balance in the range of things that you eat. Excess of anything clogs up the biological systems and stops things working properly, so again a little of what you fancy is better than overdosing on one substance. And try to eat at least five portions of fruit or vegetables each day – this sounds like a lot but you can include potatoes or frozen vegetables in your five. Processing food cuts out some nutrients and breaks down others, so it is sensible to eat fresh food as well as processed.

4. *Weight and fitness* Too many people in the UK are above their ideal weight to the extent that it interferes with their health and fitness, and obesity is on the increase. The simple answer to people who say that they are too busy to get in shape is that they had better get busier, because their chances of living longer are not good. The latest thinking suggests that you need to exercise for about 45 minutes a day to get yourself into a state where your whole body (and mind) will perform better. You don't have to run a marathon for the exercise to work: brisk walking, cycling or swimming can be just as effective. If you can't manage 45 minutes

don't give up and reach for the biscuit tin, start with just ten minutes of something you enjoy and build up to more.

5. *Stress* Work, travel, children, parents, money, mortgage, colleagues, friends: the pressures of life are stressful for all of us. Many of these things are also challenges and are exciting – a new project, change of job or house, the children growing up. But if we don't feel in control of the situation, we can get stressed out by it. The health service is not very good at dealing with patients suffering from stress – the usual response is a prescription for drugs that knock out the areas of the brain which register the effects of stress. This addresses the symptoms associated with stress but not the causes. It is far better to think about what you need to do to control or manage your stress: not easy but not impossible. Recognising when you are stressed and talking through the reasons for it with someone who you trust is one way of dealing with it. Exercise, too, can be an effective way of relieving stress, with the additional benefit that you will be getting fit.

6. *Sex* Healthy sex is a great pleasure and is good for mental and physical relaxation. But sexual activity is also a way of transmitting disease between individuals and, in the case of HIV, it is the way of passing on the potentially fatal AIDS disease. Unwanted pregnancy, with the mental and physical stress of a termination, is also another consequence of not taking control of your health. Whatever sexual activity you chose, with different sex or same sex partners, make sure that you plan your sex life so that it works for you, not against you.

7. *Relationships* Human beings are instinctively social creatures and naturally form into social groupings. This is not the same as forming into the small family units that are the pattern of life in much of western society today. Small families can bring tensions, particularly across generations in a society which is changing rapidly, and the breakdown of close family relationships is one of the biggest causes of mental and physical ill health. As a result, we now have more people living alone, cut off from close relation-

ships, physically separated from family and friends, and isolation brings its own health problems. Your health is not just about you, but about the quality of relationships you have. And these need to be worked at, protected, improved.

8. *Risk taking* We are not very good at understanding risks and chances. If we were, we would never play the national lottery, with its chance of winning less than that of being hit by a meteorite. Life is a gamble, and most of us should probably count ourselves lucky to have got through it so far. But as the chances for each of us of dying one day are 100 per cent our luck will run out. Before then, we can think a bit about how we behave so we can act with our eyes open. Smokers are many times more likely to die earlier than non-smokers. Motorbike drivers are many times more likely to be killed or seriously injured than car drivers. The group most likely to die before their time are young men, because the social behaviour of this group is all about risk taking. If you are male and 18–25 you are at greater risk from accident, violence, suicide, sexual and mental health problems than any other group. On the positive side young men today will on average live to be 80 or more.

9. *Environment* Some parts of your surroundings you can't do much about, except through political action. It is unlikely that you will be able to tackle air pollution on your own other than pressuring local and national politicians to do something about the causes. But in your own behaviour you can make a contribution by using public transport or lead-free petrol if you have to drive, for example. You can also help yourself by avoiding some of the known environmental causes of ill health, such as long periods of exposure to sunlight, as well as checking your home and workplace to remove potential accident hazards, fitting smoke alarms and being doubly careful of the surroundings that children grow up in.

10. *Check yourself* There are some forms of cancer which you may be able to detect yourself through self-examination – women can do

their own screening by making regular checks on their breasts, and men can check for changes (lumps) on their balls. Being aware of your own body and how it changes can be one of the most effective pieces of diagnosis. It may take a professional to name the problem or to confirm or disperse your fears, but no one knows or feels your body like you do, so learn to trust yourself.

TAKE CONTROL OF YOUR HEALTH CARE

There are numerous tips and suggestions throughout this book on how to take a more active part in decisions about your health care – starting with asking questions about anything you don't understand. Here are ten things you can start doing to feel and be more in control of what happens to you.

1. *Be prepared* This is about knowing what you want from your health care and finding out how you can get it. One of the reasons why, as a nation, we are not powerful patients is that we choose not to be. We have also been conditioned into this in the way our health professionals treat us. Put aside a little time before any health consultation with a doctor or other professional to think about:

   - how you will explain what is wrong with you

   - what you know already and what you want to find out more about

   - how you will present yourself (remember doctors respond better to questions or descriptions of symptoms rather than the patient's attempt at self-diagnosis)

   - what you want to come away with at the end of the consultation.

2. *Do complain if you are not satisfied* The majority of people who are unhappy about the health care that they or their relatives received never tell anyone other than their friends. If health

services are not told about what they are doing wrong the chances are they will never put any effort into putting it right. Remember, all complaints have to be acknowledged and investigated.

3. *Get informed* If you have a particular condition that has been diagnosed read as much as you can about it. The internet is proving an increasingly valuable tool for helping people find out about the latest treatments and prognosis for their condition. Libraries in medical schools and charitable bodies are good sources of material and most will have trained library and information specialists who will be able to help you find what you are looking for. Phone ahead to book some time with them to be sure of getting the help you need. Even the health and reference sections in local libraries stock an increasingly wide range of health related material and some even have terminals where you can access the internet.

4. *Use your right to choose* Using the health service does not feel like shopping for clothes or food when you can choose between one brand and another, and select a different colour or flavour. Most of the time you are offered Hobson's choice. Before you accept what you are given think about whether there are other options that you would like to explore – a referral to a different consultant that you have heard has a good reputation, a different hospital which is more convenient for your family to visit, a second opinion. It is up to you to find opportunities to choose as you will rarely be offered them.

5. *Help yourself by getting networked* There are thousands of self-help groups in the UK for almost every health condition. They are led by people with similar problems to your own and so they will have a bank of expertise based on real experiences. For conditions which are relatively rare, such as Lupus syndrome, self-help groups may well be better informed than the average GP who may see only one or two cases a year. If going to meetings is not your style some self-help groups publish leaflets and pamphlets which might be helpful or have telephone advice lines. With so much

choice the problem can be finding what is available in your area for your region of interest. For further information see the Appendix.

6. *Follow the instructions* If your GP or doctor prescribes a course of medicines or tablets play your part and finish the pack as instructed. Many people stop taking medicines when they begin to feel better because they believe that the rest of the course is unnecessary, but this can put you at a high risk of getting another infection or worse still allowing the bugs to build up an immunity to the medicine.

7. *Treat yourself* The flip side of staying healthy is knowing what to do when you or your family are sick. A few home remedies and medicines allow you to cope with many minor health problems. The NHS has published a Home Healthcare Guide which you can get through your GP. An understanding of first aid (St John Ambulance run courses around the country) is a valuable asset for everyone to have. You can pick up a basic knowledge in a relatively short time. By the year 2000 a 24-hour health telephone helpline, NHS Direct, will offer over the phone advice to the whole of the country. Pilot projects started in Milton Keynes, Preston and Northumbria and others will be added so that in April 1999 about 40 per cent of England's population are covered. The idea of NHS Direct is that everyone will be able to get telephone advice on how to treat yourself and advice on getting the best care that you need. If you want to know if you are covered by NHS Direct, phone directory enquiries or the Health Information Service – 0800 665544.

8. *Seek screening tests* Women, in particular, need to make use of the screening tests that are available for breast and cervical cancer. If there is a history of bowel cancer in your family it is worth arranging an annual check to detect any problems as early as possible – or at best to keep your mind at rest. None of us find screening tests an enjoyable experience, they can be uncomfortable, embarrassing and in some cases nerve racking, but this is nothing compared to the problems you could experience if you

ignore those screening appointments and find yourself with advanced cancer with no chance of cure.

9. *Understand the risks* One of the hardest things for clinicians to explain to their patients is the concept of risk. People's attitudes to risk vary significantly and a great many of us are not very good at understanding what a 1 in 500 risk actually means. If you are told that this was the risk of your baby being born without a handicap the burning question is likely to be what chance has my baby got of being that 1 in 500. Trying to understand risk is an important step in making decisions about your health and making an informed judgement about what you want to happen. So don't be afraid to ask the nurse or doctor to explain the issues again. Ask them to explain it differently or ask them to give you some examples which could illustrate the problem – simply repeating what they have told you will not necessarily help you to understand it better. The answer to the 1 in 500 question, by the way, is that everyone in a group of 500 people has the same chance of being the one who has the handicap although only one will actually have it.

10. *Get involved* One way of influencing your health care is from the inside. This need not mean retraining as a doctor or nurse, there are many different options to choose, which are described in the following pages.

Get involved

There are lots of ways to play your part as an informed consumer within the NHS. But if the idea of getting involved conjures images of kindly old people selling tea and buns in the League of Friends snack bar or wheeling trolleys of books around the ward, think again, you don't have to put on a pinny and you may find that the traditional stereotype of the volunteer is some way away from reality.

Become a volunteer
It has been estimated that around 70,000 volunteers put in over 13

million hours of service for the NHS, and that's not including the
work of organisations such as the Women's Royal Voluntary Service
(WRVS). Volunteers can be involved in many aspects of hospital and
community health services. They may be drivers, helping people get
from their homes to hospital or day care appointments. They may be
fund raisers, organising all sorts of events to help buy new equipment
or contribute to improving a hospital site. They may be running a help
desk to assist patients find their way around a hospital or involved in
the hospital radio station. Or they may be working as visitors and
friends to people with learning difficulties or long-term mental health
problems.

Volunteers are not meant to be substitutes for paid professionals
and mostly they are used appropriately – the fact that the main health
care unions are broadly supportive of the use of volunteers supports
this. Not all volunteers provide their support for entirely altruistic
reasons. An increasing number of young people, for example, are
getting involved as volunteers as a way of obtaining some work-
related experience or as something to strengthen their application to
university. Others find volunteering gives them access to new friends
and acquaintances. If you want to find out more about what you can
do the easiest thing is to contact the voluntary services manager in
your local NHS trust whose job it is to find volunteers and co-ordinate
the work that they do. Alternatively there are national organisations
such as Community Service Volunteers which might be able to help
match your skills and interests with existing projects. For those that
are not averse to fundraising and visiting patients there are the better
known routes such as the League of Friends and the WRVS. Another
possibility is to get involved with a self-help group, most of which are
run almost entirely on the contributions of volunteers.

If you are retired and are interested in voluntary work, you can try
REACH at Bear Wharf, 27 Bankside, London SE1 9ET, telephone 0171
928 0452, fax 0171 928 0798, who find part-time, expenses-only jobs for
retired professionals in voluntary organisations with charitable aims.

Make a suggestion

An increasing number of health centres and hospitals make use of suggestion boxes to get feedback from patients about their care and ideas about ways of improving it. Popping a note in the box is an easy way of putting your views across without the embarrassment of telling someone face to face or the worry about whether it's a harebrained idea. It's a way of making a complaint without having to be formally identified.

Get consulted

Health authorities are legally obliged to undertake a formal consultation with the public on any major plans to change the type or location of health care in the area they serve. For example, if a new health centre is to be established, or there are plans either to move a service half a mile away from its current location or to shut all or part of a hospital the public needs to be told exactly what is planned and why and given three months to make their views known. After that time the health authority will make up its mind in the light of the comments they receive.

Public consultation in the health service has had a bad press. Many people are cynical about whether they will be listened to or whether their views will make a difference. This is partly because, in the past, the health service treated consultation as a formality – something to get over and done with – with the result that the public were given very little real choice about what happened. There is now greater recognition that consultation should be a two-way process, with the health authority putting forward options and the public giving feedback on which one is best. A consultation involving only one option is an advertising campaign, not real discussion.

So how do you find out about what's going on locally? How can you make your viewpoints known about changes to your health care? Sadly there are no easy answers to these questions. There are no standard ways in which health authorities consult with local people. What normally happens is that a paper is written which describes the proposals for change and the reasons for them. There will then be one or more public meetings which may be advertised in the local media or through leaflets pushed through your letterbox. In other cases, the process might be more sophisticated if the health authority wants to get the views of particular sections of the community such as parents with young children or people who use mental health services, in which case you might be invited to a small group discussion (sometimes referred to as a focus group) or be sent a questionnaire to fill in.

If you hear rumours about changes to local health services on which you would like to comment, the first step would be to scour the local press to see if any proposals or meetings have been reported. Alternatively, try your local community health council (CHC), who should be the first to know of any proposals.

Finally, a new development to watch is that the government have made a commitment to public surveys about the NHS. The details are still being drawn up but one thing is certain, your views are going to be in more demand.

Use your MP
A few people are habitual visitors to their MP's 'surgery' but most of us never even consider what our MPs can do. MPs are effective at asking embarrassing questions of hospitals and community health services. They can write letters to the organisations concerned or even more powerfully table questions in the House of Commons. Most trusts will take these enquiries seriously. Use your MP if you are unhappy about the availability or standards of health care in your area or if you feel that local people have not been sufficiently consulted about changes.

Join up
Most health authorities and trusts have set up groups of patients or service users which look at the planning of health services. They may be actively looking for members of the public to sit on those groups. Some of the best established are maternity services liaison committees which combine managers, doctors, nurses and midwives and past or present users of maternity services. Mental health and learning difficulties services also tend to have well-established user groups. If you have a special area of interest to which you want to contribute, contact the relevant manager for the service and ask what form of user involvement they need. Your CHC will be able to give you contact names and numbers.

If getting involved in the health service itself is not your idea of a good or worthwhile time, why not think about joining a voluntary organisation, self-help or pressure group. You will be able to select how much and what type of involvement you want – from a paid-up member, an occasional attender of meetings or a more active role such as treasurer to the organisation. To get a list of the groups which are active in your area you could contact the Citizens Advisory Bureau or local branch of the Council for Voluntary Services.

Join a community health council
If you are happier providing views and criticism from outside the health care system then the health care watchdog – the local CHC – might be the organisation for you. There is roughly one community health council for each health authority. In Scotland they are called local health councils and in Northern Ireland district committees. CHCs have around 24 members, some of whom are political appointments whilst others are nominated by local voluntary sector groups. CHCs largely run on the goodwill and interest of their members and most will have just a few paid employees to keep things on track. Typically, there will be a chief officer and one or two other professional staff plus some administrative support – not much to cover a health authority and the full range of health care provided by two or three trusts. Currently CHCs have no remit to look at the work of GPs and primary care, which with more health care and purchasing decisions planned to be concentrated within primary care means either the power of the CHC could be on the wane or their responsibilities will need to be changed. On a more positive front, the current government is committed to public involvement in health care decisions, although it remains to be seen whether they channel this effort through the formal watchdogs or through informal and less tangible means. CHC members, unlike the non-executive directors of NHS trusts, are not paid for their services. Again, if you want to see what it is like being a CHC member go along to one of their meetings – like those of health authorities and trusts these are open to the public and the dates and times should be advertised locally.

CHAPTER 14: CONVENTIONAL OR COMPLEMENTARY – YOUR CHOICE

The NHS and most of the private health care in this country practise conventional medicine. But conventional medicine hasn't been 'conventional' for that long and there are many other forms of medicine and therapy that have been practised for thousands of years which have a valid place in modern health care. This chapter provides an introduction to the complementary therapies which are becoming increasingly popular.

CONVENTIONAL MEDICINE

Just 150 years ago very little of what is now called conventional medicine existed. It was only as 19th-century physicians and biologists made progress on understanding the cause of illnesses, through advances such as the germ theory of infections and the genetic basis of inherited characteristics, that conventional (also known as allopathic) medicine began to take shape. There were further big medical advances in the first half of the 20th century, particularly in surgery during the First World War, and the development of antibiotics during the Second World War.

Eighty years ago, the first attempt to 'fix' modern medical practice was made with the publication of the Flexner Report which described what should be taught in modern medical schools. The gold standard for this was the scientific method, which appeared to have been so successful in revealing the causes of illnesses. For example, modern medicine teaches that the symptoms of pneumonia are 'caused' by a bacterium which has invaded the body, that antibiotics will 'kill' the bacterium, and the result will be that the 'effects', or symptoms, will vanish. After the Second World War, the success of new drugs, new therapies and treatments cemented the allopathic tradition which is firmly in place in medical schools, in teaching hospitals and training general practices, and in the medical technologies (the drugs and equipment made by powerful national and international companies) which support medical practice. In this way, conventional medicine has become the dominant therapy of western practice.

Why bother with alternatives?

If conventional medicine is so fantastic and successful, why bother with anything else? The reason, of course, is that conventional medicine has not lived up to its promise to solve all the health problems of humanity. There are a number of reasons for this.

First, despite the claims of the scientific method of cause and effect, much of medicine is practised without proof of the causes of illness and therapies. Often we know that something works, but not how or why it works. How does aspirin, which was first produced commercially over a hundred years ago, cure headache? We don't know, nor are we very sure how it protects against heart disease. Aspirin is an old and an important part of conventional therapy, but its workings are still largely unknown.

Second, despite its claim to be able to treat everything, there are some very common things that conventional medicine is not very good at dealing with. Perhaps we will finally defeat cancer with conventional practice, but what about chronic backache, migraine, anxiety or depression? It seems that for many longer-term, debilitating health problems, conventional medicine has relatively few answers.

Third, some conventional medicine seems to do as much harm as good. Chemotherapy is a treatment for cancer. In some cases the doses given effectively poison the person being treated so badly that they die of the treatment rather than the cancer. Many treatments which are less dramatic than chemotherapy still cause unpleasant side-effects and reduce the body's ability to fight disease naturally. Furthermore, we have used so many antibiotics in the past 50 years that many bacteria are now immune to most of them, and new strains of serious illnesses occur all the time. So the treatments in conventional medicine seem very often to be self-defeating.

A fourth reason is the observation that the focus on the scientific and biomedical workings of the body in conventional medicine means that the emotional and spiritual dimensions of health and illness are often ignored. Conventional medicine has very few ways of dealing with these aspects of our health and well-being.

Traditional approaches to healing

If conventional, allopathic medicine has only been around for just over a century, traditional therapies have been present in almost every culture that has existed in the past 3,000 years, and elements of these traditional therapies can be found all over the world. Chinese medicine is perhaps the one tradition that everyone in western therapy knows, but there are many others including native American, Yogic and Hebrew traditions. The traditional therapies often share a belief which is very different from conventional medicine. This is the principle that everyone has the ability to heal themselves, and that illness or disease is often the result of an imbalance in the individual. If you can restore the balance then the individual will be able, with help, to channel their energies to become healthy again.

It is this philosophy which leads traditional therapy to place such an emphasis on diet, exercise, relaxation, balance, self-regulation and self-care in its approach. This is often know as a holistic approach to health care, looking at the individual life as a whole, rather than focusing solely on the immediate symptom or problem.

ALTERNATIVE, COMPLEMENTARY AND INTEGRATED HEALTH CARE

A few years ago it was common for people to talk about alternative therapies. So you would hear acupuncture called an alternative treatment to, say, giving drugs for migraines. This was because people were looking for 'alternatives' to conventional treatment and because the large majority of conventional doctors would not accept that treatments such as acupuncture had any validity at all. They dismissed the whole thing as quackery. But the barriers are being dismantled, partly because many doctors themselves are now using or referring to traditional therapies, and partly through effective lobbying. It is now more common for people to supplement their traditional medicine with a complementary therapy, and for some conditions NHS doctors may well refer patients to complementary therapists rather than sending them to traditional consultants.

An initiative led by Charles, the Prince of Wales, a long-standing advocate of complementary medicine, is bringing together conventional and complementary practitioners to talk about a more integrated form of health care. This work seeks to break down the barriers to using complementary care in the NHS and at the same time improve training and introduce standards and registration to regulate the complementary medicine practitioners.

Choosing a complementary therapist
Most people find a complementary therapist though a friend's recommendation, through a referral from a GP or even the Yellow Pages. One of the main problems is that there is still very little way of knowing who are the reputable and competent practitioners. One

way to find out is to ask the practitioner whether there is an accredited association of therapists and whether the practitioner is a member. Another problem is finding out whether any particular therapy is right for you. It is often a case of try it and see.

Paying for complementary therapies
Some therapies are now available to a limited degree on the NHS, which means that the NHS may meet some or all the cost of a referral to a complementary practitioner. For this to happen, you must be referred by a GP or specialist who has an agreement with an alternative practitioner to provide services. Sometimes these will be provided at a subsidised rate, with a flat rate charged to the patient and the remainder of the real cost of an hour's consultation (perhaps around £35) being met by the health authority or from the primary care group's budget. Remember, though, that all health budgets are stretched, and that if the NHS agrees to fund more osteopathy or homoeopathy it will probably have to stop funding something else. If you cannot get a referral through the NHS you will need to pay for the treatment yourself. Prices vary for consultation time and for any products that you need to take. Ask for an estimate of the hourly rate and the typical time your treatment may take.

A quick guide to complementary therapies

Here is a quick guide to some of the main complementary therapies:

Alexander Technique is a practical technique based on body movement and balance. It is applied to the basic things such as posture, moving, standing, sitting, breathing, lifting, reading and writing.

Acupuncture is a method of treatment created by the Chinese which involves the insertion of special needles into specific parts of the body which lie along 'meridians' or pathways which are the conduits of the two life energies, yin and yang. Health depends on the balance of yin and yang. The acupuncture points, some 800 along the main meridians, can affect the energy flow and bring the body back into balance. Acupuncture is used for a wide number of symptoms, as well as a pain reliever or mild anaesthetic.

Aromatherapy uses aromatic extracts and essential oils from herbs and plants to treat mental and physical symptoms and induce a feeling of well-being. Aromatherapy is widely used as a relaxation technique, but it is increasingly being applied in the NHS, for the treatment of burns, relaxation, and even orientation therapy for Alzheimer's patients.

Chiropractic is often confused with osteopathy. The main difference between the two therapies is that chiropractors focus on manipulation of the spine rather than the rest of the body. The treatment is based on the theory that the root of illness is blockage or impairment of the nerves. They have different manipulation techniques to osteopaths.

Herbalists use their knowledge of the medicinal qualities of herbs and plants to treat physical and mental symptoms. Chinese herbalists have become increasingly popular over the last few years, particularly for the treatment of chronic illnesses such as eczema. Although most natural products tend to be relatively safe, there have been reports of Chinese herbalists prescribing standard packages which have proved toxic. Remember, just because you are using natural herbs and plants doesn't mean that they are free of side-effects, so it is important to check.

Homoeopathy is the method of treating disorders and diseases with minute doses of medicines which, if used in larger quantities, would produce the same symptoms in a healthy person that they are designed to cure. A wide range of homoeopathic medicines and preparations are now available in some chemists. They usually come in the form of small powder tablets or in droplets. Being water based they are particularly suitable for treating children. Even vets are starting to use these products to treat animals. Like all medicines, the preparations work best when prescribed by qualified specialists. A homoeopath will begin your treatment by taking an in-depth history of your condition, feelings and general physical condition.

Hypnotherapy involves hypnotising the patient and suggesting particular modes of behaviour whilst the person is in a hypnotic state. Hypnotherapy has been used to help patients stop smoking or change eating habits as well as in psychotherapy. A number of medically qualified practitioners are also practising hypno-therapists.

Osteopathy uses manipulative therapy or pressure on the muscles, bones and joints. In some cases these therapies are applied with other interventions such as acupuncture or homoeopathy. Osteopaths hold that if the body is properly aligned then it is able to fight disease effectively and heal itself.

Reflexology is an ancient therapy which acts on the basic premise that our internal organs have corresponding reflex points on the surface of the body. The most accessible and sensitive areas are the feet, hands and ears, with the feet being the most commonly used areas. Massage and manipulation of the feet simulate energy zones within the body, clearing tension and removing impurities and so encouraging healing to take place.

Complementary *PatientPower*

If you choose to use complementary therapy rather than conventional medicine, you must still have the inquiring, active, interested attitude that you have towards conventional health care. Just as you prepare for a visit to the GP or to a hospital specialist, you should go armed with questions about the complementary therapy:

1. Can you explain the principles of the treatment?
2. What is the likelihood that the treatment will work?
3. Why is it the right treatment for my problem?

4. Why is this a better treatment than alternatives?
5. Are there any side-effects?
6. How do I know that you are not missing some problem that someone medically-trained would spot?
7. What can I do to make sure that the same problem doesn't occur again?
8. How can I get the best out of traditional and complementary therapy?
9. Will you inform my GP or medical specialist about this treatment?
10. If I need a course of treatment are there any long-term disadvantages or problems?

It is also worth re-reading chapters two and three for the discussion about how to take an active part in your care.

CHAPTER 15: PRIVATE OR NHS – YOUR CHOICE

The reasons for selecting private rather than NHS care vary. Not all are founded on fact – some are based on misconceptions. This chapter is designed to help you think ahead about the choices available before you are forced into making a quick decision and aims to debunk some myths about the advantages of going private. However, whether you opt for private or NHS care, the same principles apply – know what you want and plan ahead. To help you make the right choice for you, there follows a checklist of questions and a guide to the increasingly varied insurance products on the market.

HOW POPULAR IS PRIVATE HEALTH CARE?

If the National Health Service is the envy of many other countries then some obvious questions are: how large is the private health care sector; and why does it exist at all?

The introduction of the NHS over 50 years ago initially reduced the role of private health care, but that trend did not continue. Ever since, health care in the UK has consisted of both public and private provision and public and private funding. Around six million people are covered by private medical insurance in the UK, and there are also those who pay for private health care directly. In total, the sector is worth around £2.2 billion a year.

Private health care has, and continues to perform, two main roles. It provides elective (non-urgent) diagnosis (tests) and treatment of acute illnesses, and in the vast majority of cases this is paid for by private medical insurance. This element increased considerably during the 1980s and early 1990s. Media coverage emphasising cost cutting and lengthy waiting lists in the NHS contributed to this growth. The public perception of the NHS was that you had to wait an incredibly long time to be treated. And once you did get through the doors of the hospital and into the operating theatre you could not expect a personalised service or a high quality environment in which to recover. Both the previous and present governments have been committed to driving down NHS waiting times. This has produced real results and the net effect has been a slowing down of the private health care market. Perhaps in response the private health care and medical insurance market has produced a complex array of new products and services, making it more difficult for consumers to choose what is right for them. More of this later.

The second area of private purchase is long-term care for older people in residential and nursing homes. This care is paid for by a mix of arrangements – by individuals out of their savings, by social security benefits and, more recently, by specific long-term care insurance policies and bonds. Here, too, there is an increasingly wide range of types of homes and payment mechanisms to choose from.

Private medical and nursing home care accounts for as much as 20 per cent of all medical and nursing home care in the UK. About 17 per cent of the population are covered by private medical insurance and over 70 per cent of private health care is funded by medical insurance. So it is probably true to say that without the insurance system private health care would not exist in its current form. Some people who take up private treatment pay directly out of their own pocket, without the back-up of medical insurance cover. But the vast majority pay for private care through an insurance policy, around half of whom have their policies paid for by their employers.

Why people use private health care

The NHS provides health care to the whole population. But as discussed earlier, its performance looks much better when viewed in terms of benefits to a whole community – the care that individual patients receive may feel less good. The typical person who is covered by private health insurance is male aged between 35 and 54 and is looking for speedy treatment to minimise the time they need to take off work – a hernia repair, for example, which the NHS cannot fix for six months.

So why do people choose to go private when they could be treated under the NHS? The usual reasons are these:

A better standard of care Some people are motivated by the expectation that they will get a better standard of medical care if they use a private facility – both in terms of the environment and ambiance of the hospital, and the quality of the clinicians who will look after them.

Services which are not available on the NHS Health authorities are increasingly making choices about what they will and will not provide. In some cases these choices are based on evidence and research, and determine, for example, whether or not a new drug would be available. In other cases the choice is based on a judgement about the best way of using resources to the benefit of the whole population. Some health authorities, for instance, will not fund cosmetic surgery such as breast enlargement, in-vitro fertilisation or tattoo removal. In other cases age cut-offs might be introduced to guide who gets certain services – in most parts of the country, for example, adults under 65 will find it difficult to get chiropody treatments paid for by the NHS. People who still want to get these services will have to pay for them privately.

A choice of doctors and hospitals For some people being able to choose where they are treated and by whom are important factors in their decision to fund private health care.

Short waiting times Paying for private health care can offer people more immediate access to diagnostic tests or that instant hernia operation. Paying can mean less time in pain or greater peace of mind.

More frequent tests The NHS covers people for certain screening tests, such as mammograms to check for breast cancer and smear tests to check for cervical cancer. Mammograms are offered every three years to women between fifty and sixty-four, and smears every five years to women between twenty and sixty-four, although there are regional variations. Some people feel that more frequent testing will give them greater peace of mind.

Do you really need to go private?

At the end of the day the decision is yours. Not everyone can afford to make the choice and they will, by default, stick with the good old health service. But if private medical care might be an option for you, consider the reasons listed above and think about whether these are real or based on myth.

Does going private give you a better standard of care?

It may do, but then standards vary so much from one health service establishment to the next that you could equally say that you might get a better standard of care up the road. It is worth bearing in mind that by and large it is the same consultants who treat you in the NHS who work in private practice. The consultant's contract introduced in 1979 removed all constraints to working in the private sector. This contract means that most full-time consultants employed by the NHS are contracted to spend only 11/13ths of their time in the public sector, the rest can be dedicated to private practice. The extent of private work does vary according to specialty. There is very little private paediatric work, for instance, whereas urologists who deal with the prostate and urinary problems of older men have a very lucrative market.

What the private sector tends to be better at than the health service is the small personal touches which make a stay in hospital more like visiting a hotel – the quality of food, a room of your own, perhaps a higher standard of decor and a more peaceful and less frenetic environment. But just to blur the picture even more, some NHS hospitals provide pay beds or have private patients' wings. They then use the income from these services to reinvest in NHS care. If your health insurance offers you a choice of an NHS pay bed then you need to check whether it is in a dedicated part of the hospital or just a bed that is designated private when a patient is admitted who can pay for it. If it's the latter you could find yourself in the same hospital, the same ward and with the same group of fellow patients as you would if you'd stuck with the NHS.

However, the real determinant of quality of care is the outcome it produces – whether private treatment offers you a greater chance of recovery or a more accurate diagnosis than in the NHS. As there are no comparable figures on health outcomes in both the public and private sectors this is difficult to determine. It is worth knowing, however, that staying in a private hospital after an operation, particularly a complex one, can be a risky business. Private hospitals will not necessarily pay for surgeons to stay on site after the operation has finished on the off chance that the patient may experience complications. So there may well be no surgeon on the premises out of core hours – they will have done the operation and returned home or to their NHS commitments. A private hospital will also not necessarily have the full back-up of other specialties to rely on if, for example, the patient develops kidney failure. This is one of the advantages that NHS pay beds have over some of their private sector rivals.

Will you be able to get services which are not available on the NHS?

Again there is not a simple answer. There are some things that only the NHS can provide. The private sector can only deal with treatments which are relatively planned – it cannot cope with things such as a major accident. Nor are organ transplants widely available in the private sector. But there are situations where the NHS does not provide comprehensive services for all people and all eventualities. Health authorities are allowed to decide which treatments they will not provide if they believe them to be ineffective or too costly – it's their job to balance the demands of the whole population that they serve in relation to the money that is available. If you are told by your GP that something is not available, try a little persistence before you jump on the private bandwagon: ask about the basis for the decision made by the health authority and ask your GP whether there are sound medical grounds in your particular case which could challenge the decision.

Nevertheless there are things that you should find it easier to get if you decide to pay for private health care – a shorter wait (much shorter in some cases), more frequent tests (see below) and techniques such as IVF which may not be available or may be limited in number in your area.

Will you get a choice of hospitals or doctors?

It depends on the conditions in your medical insurance. Some products offer only a limited range of choice from a list of approved hospitals. In some parts of the country there are not many private facilities, so you find yourself effectively having a choice of one place or specialist. If you are paying for the service out of your own pocket your choice will potentially be much wider, particularly if you are prepared to travel.

Shorter waiting times

No NHS patient should wait more than 13 weeks for a first outpatient appointment or 15–18 months for inpatient treatment. In reality a few people will wait longer but most will be seen much earlier than this standard. If you find a lump which could indicate suspected breast cancer, for example, new standards mean that you should be given an immediate appointment – no more than two weeks. Your GP does have a degree of choice over who and where to refer you to. If you don't mind travelling for treatment another option to private health care might be to get your GP to call the NHS Information Service (for contact details see the Appendix) who may be able to advise which hospitals have shorter waiting times. A short stay in a local hotel for a friend or spouse could be cheaper than the annual insurance premiums or paying for private treatment out of your own pocket. However, most people will have heard stories of consultants telling patients that they will have to wait a year for an operation on the NHS with him or her, but that the same operation can be done next week if they go privately.

More frequent tests

Going private does give you a degree of choice about what tests you can get and how often. But the first question to ask is whether you really need them. Of course, if you have had a positive smear test in the past or readings that were wrong you may want to put your mind at rest and get tested every year. The frequency of the screening tests available on the NHS is worked out on the benefits to the population as a whole – balancing the costs versus the number of lives saved. These scientific explanations become more complicated when applied to individuals. Many people are happy to pay for the peace of mind of more regular tests, particularly if someone in their family has died of cancer.

Types of private health cover

The insurance industry is a competitive market and products do tend to come and go or change over time. The whole area can be very bewildering to the newcomer. And although things have improved over the last few years, not all insurance companies produce their promotional material in 'plain English'. It does not help that some terms, such as health insurance or medical insurance, are widely misused or confused in general use. This section aims to give you a feel for the main types of insurance cover that are available and provide some of the questions to ask yourself to see if this is the right product for you.

Some of the products that you can expect to find are:

Life insurance This pays a lump sum or income to your family or dependants when you die. Some mortgage companies insist on adequate life cover which may need to be equivalent to the amount you are borrowing. Life insurance is not a way of paying for health care.

Health insurance Here it is your health rather than your death that you are insuring. This product pays out a regular income if an illness or injury prevents you from working. Payments are normally made only if you have a long-term illness.

Private medical insurance For these products you pay a monthly premium which covers the cost of private medical treatment should you require it. In some cases you will need to pay for the treatment yourself and then reclaim the money from the insurance company. In others the insurer will deal directly with the health care provider. The products vary as to what is or is not included. Most have exclusions for psychiatric illness, childbirth, chronic conditions, cosmetic treatment, fertility treatment, AIDS/HIV and kidney dialysis. Some exclude pre-existing conditions from their cover and not all policies include home nursing cover. Most private medical insurers offer policies with different levels of cover and therefore different prices.

Critical illness insurance This insurance pays you a lump sum if you are diagnosed as having one of a list of specified serious medical conditions or as having a total or permanent disability. The conditions which are normally included are multiple sclerosis, cancer, heart disease, stroke, kidney failure or a major organ transplant. The payment is made whilst you are alive. Like life cover, some people buy these policies as a safeguard to a mortgage endowment. Policies that are linked to repayment mortgages should be cheaper than those that are not as they are designed just to cover the sum borrowed – premiums should go down over time as you pay off the sum borrowed plus interest.

Combined life and critical illness insurance These policies are designed to benefit both you and your family. The payments are made when you are diagnosed as having a critical illness or when you die, if this happens first. The advantage of such policies are that you can benefit from the money whilst you are alive. But it could leave you with no life cover which would leave nothing for your dependants. If you need both then it would make sense to buy separate policies rather than a combined one.

Long-term care policies and bonds A long-term care policy is something which people tend to take out in their later years as it is an insurance which covers you for the costs of residential care should this be needed. More recently, some life companies have introduced a long-term care bond which refunds most of the premium if health care turns out not to be required. The main problem is that these schemes need a big cash lump sum. For instance, a 70-year-old woman looking for the level of cover that would pay for a place in a residential home would pay about £100 per month on a conventional long-term care policy. If she opted for the bond she would need to shell out around £30,000. Bonds may be suitable if you have a life policy that matures or have spare capital to invest.

The pros and cons of insurance versus out of pocket payments

This is a difficult equation to weigh up and will be influenced by your income and outgoings, your health and that of your dependants, and the degree to which you like taking risks. The first thing to find out is the likely cost of a premium. The cost of private medical insurance is calculated on the basis of age and sex, not lifestyle or state of health. Your annual premium could cost from £150 upwards to over £1000, depending on the package you select. The cost of providing the same amount of health care from one year to the next, whether private or NHS, tends to rise more sharply than the national rate of inflation. One of the certainties in private medical insurance is that premiums progressively get more costly – rises of as much as 10 per cent per year are typical. You need to weigh up the annual premium against the average cost of an operation. A hernia repair, for example, costs about £1,200 and a hysterectomy over £3,000. Taking the mid point for an insurance premium this means that you would have paid for the cost of your hernia repair with just two and a half years of premiums. You could be in the position of spending thousands of pounds without ever making a claim. You might be better putting the sum you would have put into private medical insurance premiums into a building society account or other savings scheme, that way you would have flexibility on how you used the money if you did not have to use private health care and you would be earning interest on your investment. However, many people find that private medical insurance gives them peace of mind, and the more comprehensive the package that you buy the greater assurance you will have that your needs will be covered.

How do I choose?

Choosing the product that is best for you will be a combination of what the product includes and excludes. Price may also be significant:

just as the products vary so, too, do the prices. It is difficult to compare like with like as insurance companies try to differentiate what they are offering – they may extend the range of illnesses covered, add cover for travel abroad or make the products cheaper by putting limits on the amount that can be claimed.

Perhaps the easiest thing to do is to collect some general information on the products that are available. Once you have seen what is on offer, write down a list of the features that you must have (such as coverage for maternity care or dental treatment) and a second list of 'nice to have'. Then look at as many companies as you can to see which offers you the features you need. After this it will be simply a matter of price – how much more you are prepared to pay for those things on your 'nice to have' list and which product works out cheapest. As a guide, the costs of insurance will be higher if you have a history of a particular illness or there is someone in your family who has or has had a serious illness. The costs also tend to be higher the older you are when you start the policy. And there is often a sharpish increase in cost once you reach particular age thresholds such as 40 or 50. There are products which cost as little as £12 per week, but these will have quite a few exclusions.

Warning: the small print

As with any form of insurance, insurers do reject claims made for health, illness or medical cover. Don't assume that because you are sick they will feel sorry for you and pay out. To prevent unfortunate situations occurring for which you are unprepared, force yourself to read through the small print before you sign any policy, looking for anything the policy doesn't cover. Is there a limit on the fees that your insurance company will pay for? Do these elements present risks that you are prepared to accept; if not you may need to find another policy which is more suitable. If there are things that you do not understand do not be afraid to ask – better to make a nuisance of yourself to the sales people than find yourself out of pocket when you are sick. If you do have a complaint against your insurer and you are not satisfied with the response you get, you can write explaining your case to the Insurance Ombudsman Bureau, 135 Park Street, London SE1 9EA. If you think you need help in choosing a policy, there are a few independent firms who specialise in advising people on medical insurance policies or you can go through a traditional insurance broker.

Questions to help you get through the insurance minefield

- How would you cope if you needed to wait up to a year for treatment?

- Is there any history in your family which might put you at risk from a serious or critical illness?

- Are you likely to need time off work for non-critical illnesses such as back pain or stress?

- Are you looking for cover for yourself only or do you want your family to be included? Does the policy offer any discount for additional family members?

- How important is it to you to have comforts such as your own room compared with sharing a small ward area with three to five other people? Would having company be better than being alone?

- Are there tests or treatment that you need done for which the NHS will not pay, for example artificial insemination (this varies geographically), certain screening tests, cosmetic surgery, chiropody if you are under 60, etc.? Although the NHS is meant to be a comprehensive service, try telling that to the podiatrist in your local health centre when you ask to get your corns removed.

- How often do you think you will need to use private health care? Do you really need a policy that offers unlimited claims?

- What services would you want included in your insurance cover?

  - inpatient treatment

  - dental expenses

  - chiropody

  - home nursing

  - 24-hour advice line

  - outpatient consultations

  - maternity care

  - alternative therapies

  - hospice care

- Is a low cost plan important to you. What would be the best way of keeping the costs down?

  - a cash sum for nights spent in an NHS or private hospital

  - cash benefits if you are diagnosed as having a critical illness

  - a no claims bonus or discount

  - a bonus if you opt for care in the NHS

  - exclusions on outpatient treatment

- Can you afford to settle the bill yourself and reclaim the insurance or do you want the bill settled directly by the insurer?

- Do you want to be able to select a pay bed at your local hospital if it's available? Some policies require clients to use only selected hospitals from a pre-paid network.

- Would you be better off putting aside regular savings into an interest-earning account and using this as your fund should you ever need private treatment? You then have a choice whether or not to use it for this purpose at a later date.

CHAPTER 16: WRITING IT RIGHT

This book has covered your rights to see your patient notes and the best way of complaining, but where do you begin? This chapter gives some standard letters that can be used if you need to write formally to the HA/Trust.

HOW TO KEEP A DIARY/LOG OF HEALTH CARE

There are many good reasons for keeping a record of your health care, particularly if you are having a long or continuous period of treatment. You may be a compulsive diarist anyway, and this is just another episode in your life and times. You may want to keep a special record of health care to observe your reactions, record your thoughts for a relation or friend or for publication somewhere. If you are a friend or carer of a patient, you may keep a diary as a way of helping you to adjust to someone you love who is ill or incapacitated. You may keep a diary to record the last period of your life, or the last period of the life of a loved one. All these and many more reasons for keeping a diary are important, and the way you do that will be individual and particular to you.

Recording who comes to see you

One thing that many patients remark on is how many different health care professionals they have to see when they are ill. The table below can help you keep track of who is looking after you and what they did. It's effectively like putting together your own medical notes – from a patient's perspective.

Date & time	name/job/title	What was said/done	comments	satisfaction or feeling

How to write a letter that gets you what you want!

In a perfectly fair world, what you have to say would be more important than how you say it. Unfortunately the impression of a letter can carry as much weight as its contents. If you are writing to someone in a position of authority in the health service, a manager, doctor, nurse and so on, it is worth spending time getting the letter right to show that you mean business. Here are some tips which should help you to get the result you want.

- Get the right title and right address with the post code. This should guarantee it gets to the right place! If you don't know some of this, telephone to ask how to address your letter.

- On the line below the salutation ('Dear x') print a single line which gives the subject of the letter, for example, 'Visit to Westwood Surgery' or 'Proposed changes to Mountview Hospital'. Sometimes this appears as 'Re: visit to Westwood Surgery', 're' is Latin for 'about' or 'concerning'.

- If you are replying to a previous letter, look to see if that letter had a reference number and quote it in your own correspondence; alternatively, quote the date on which you got the letter and remember to date your letter.

- Write in short sentences, being as clear and precise as you can. Don't use shorthand or jargon and don't use technical or clinical terms unless you are absolutely sure you understand them. You don't need to pretend to be a professional in order to be treated seriously.

- Sign your letter, but print your name at the bottom so it is clear who has written it.

- If you think someone else should read it, copy it to them by writing the copy line below your name, for example, e.g. 'cc Dr Charles'. Putting a copy line serves the important purpose of making the receiver know that you are bringing the subject to the attention of other people. You can copy it to as many people as you think need to see it, and can use titles if you don't know the person's name, for example 'cc CHC chairman' or 'cc. Chief Executive, Health Authority'.

- Never be rude or abusive in letters, however angry or upset you feel. It weakens whatever case you have and can allow the receiver to dismiss it. If you need to let off steam in a rude letter, do it, then burn it.

- Keep a copy of everything you send. If you have a long correspondence about something, then file it, with replies, by date.

- If you don't get a reply to your letter within a week or so, don't be afraid to phone up the office of the person you wrote to, ask them if they have received your letter, ask how they will be dealing with it, and when you can expect a reply. If they claim not to have received it, tell them a copy will be in the post that day, then phone up again and make sure they have received it. You will certainly get a quick reply!

- Remember that people increasingly use fax and email to send letters. That doesn't mean you have to, but if you own or have access to fax or email, then make use of them.

Bearing in mind the points raised above, here are examples of two sorts of letter you might need to write.

Letter of complaint

In a letter of complaint you need to state what happened; what the impact was of what happened; why you feel this is wrong; what you would like done about it.

Ms S Hallam
Chief Executive
Somewhere Hospital NHS Trust
Somewhere
SW35 1AB

12 March 1999

Dear Ms Hallam

re: Visit of Mr J Holland (dob 4.2.17) on 11 March 1999

I accompanied my father Mr John Holland to Dr Geoffrey's outpatient clinic on 11 March where my father had a 9.30 a.m. appointment. After waiting for 90 minutes my father was informed that Dr Geoffrey had been unavoidably delayed and would not be able to see him that morning. The receptionist suggested we came back next week at the same time. My father is 82 years old, and he and I spent an hour travelling by bus to get to this appointment on time. When we asked if we could wait to see Dr Geoffrey we were told very rudely that he would be too busy when he arrived as he had more urgent cases to see.

In treating my father in this manner your staff were not only rude but they broke the standards which you as an NHS hospital are required to meet. They also failed to explain why my father could not be seen. My father left in a very distressed state and must now go through the whole thing next week.

I am making a formal complaint about his treatment. I hope that you will give this complaint your urgent attention and I anticipate a prompt reply to this letter.

Yours sincerely

Peter Holland
cc B Miles, CHC, Dr Geoffrey

Requesting access to medical records

Medical Records Officer
Somewhere Hospital NHS Trust
Somewhere
SW35 1AB

12 March 1999

Dear Medical Records Officer

re: Peter Holland, dob 2. 8.42, hospital number 4369372

I would like to obtain copies of my medical records kept at your hospital and would be grateful if you could explain how I can go about this. I understand that I have the right to see all my medical records, including letters, hospital tests and hospital notes since 1991. However I was also a patient of Dr Sweetham in the hospital in 1985 and I would like to have copies of these records as well.

What I would like to do is to arrange to see my records and then ask for the ones that I am interested in to be photocopied. Could you let me know how I might go about doing this, and also whether there is any problem in seeing my 1985 records? If I am not permitted to get copies of any of my records, could you tell me if I can appeal to someone to challenge this decision? Please let me know if there will be a charge for photocopying.

I look forward to hearing from you. Please write to me at 11 Broadway, Townscape, SW35 1TG. Alternatively you can email me at pholland@aol.com.

Yours faithfully

Peter Holland

Feedback

Not every letter you write has to be a complicated and high powered letter. It is really helpful for NHS staff to get feedback on the health services they provide, often in very difficult circumstances. If you are even minded to drop the staff a note to say thank you for their work, then that gives staff a huge lift. Combining a thank you with a couple of observations about how the service and care could have been improved is a good psychological ploy. It gives you more of a chance of seeing your suggestions acted on. Although the NHS is getting better at customer research, there is still no substitute for a personal note of personal observations to get to the desk of the most senior person in the hospital or health centre.

Medical referral letter

As discussed in earlier chapters, the referral letter is still the gate that opens or blocks your way as you negotiate the strange paths of the

NHS. Referral letters are 'insiders' letters' because they are written from professionals to professionals and they are not thought of as public documents, although you have every right to see them, if you ask. There is a style to referral letters which mixes the formal and the informal style of people who know they have particular standing in modern British society. So here is a typical referral letter:

Mountview Health Centre
Mountview
Middletown
MG36 7GE

Dr J Graham
Consultant Gastroenterologist
Middletown Hospital NHS Trust
Long Road
Middletown
MG1 6FR

15 January 1999

Dear James

re: Paul Holland, 32, dob 12.4.59

Thank you for seeing this man who came to me last Thursday complaining of a painful abdomen. He has a history of moderate to heavy consumption of beer over many years, and has attended my surgery on four occasions over the past year complaining of stomach pains, for which he has been treated with anti-acids. On examination I found his stomach to be rigid and distended. A stool sample taken that day shows traces of blood but no culture. Liver function tests carried out on his last visit six weeks ago were within normal limits.

I have advised him about his drinking, which seems to be very heavy weekend binge consumption of up to 20 pints of beer and moderate to heavy drinking during the week (60–70 units/week), but he is very resistant to any suggestion that his behaviour is related to his present health problems, which he prefers to relate to an attack of food poisoning (not reported) about 12 months ago. He does however seem anxious to see you.

Mr Holland is married with two young daughters. He is a pleasant man but has low self-esteem, and is particularly worried that his continuing health problems will jeopardise his work as a factory packer.

I would be most grateful for your opinion.

Yours sincerely

Dr H Jamal, MB BS BChir MA (Cantab) FRCGP

APPENDIX: CONTACTS AND SELF-HELP GROUPS

KEY CONTACTS

National Blood Donor Service
Helpline 0345 711711

Association of Community Health Councils for England and Wales
(ACHCEW)
30 Drayton Park
London
N5 1PB
Tel 0171 609 8405
Fax 0171 700 1152

Citizens Advice Bureau – look in phone book under Citizens Advice
Bureaux

National Association of Citizens Advice Bureaux
Myddelton House
115–23 Pentonville Road
London
N1 9LZ
Tel 0171 833 2181
Fax 0171 833 4371

Community health council – look in phone book

General Medical Council (GMC)
178 Great Portland Street
London
W1N 6JE

Laws centres – look in phone book under 'Law'

Local health authority – look in phone book under the name of the health authority

Local NHS trusts (which run hospitals and community services) – look in phone book under the name of the hospital

NHS Confederation
Birmingham Research Park
Vincent Drive
Edgbaston
Birmingham
B15 2SQ
Tel 0121 471 4444
Fax 0121 414 1120
The umbrella organisation for health authorities and NHS trusts.

NHS Direct – a 24-hour nurse-led NHS telephone advice line which is available in some parts of the country and will be extended across the nation by 2000. You can get help on what you can do to treat yourself and which part of the NHS you need to use. Tel 0845 1888. If you want to know if you are covered by NHS Direct, phone Directory Enquiries or the Health Information Service on 0800 665544.

Chief Executive NHS Executive
Quarry House
Quarry Hill
Leeds
LS2 7UE

**NHS Health Information
Service**
Tel 0800 665544

**Health Service Commissioner
for England**
Millbank Tower
Millbank
London
SW1P 4QP
Helpline 0171 217 4051
Fax 0171 276 2099

**British Organ Donor
Society**
Tel 01223 893636

Patients Association
8 Guildford Street
London
WC1N 1DT
Helpline 0171 242 3460
Fax 0171 242 3461

Secretary of State for Health
Department of Health
Richmond House
79 Whitehall
London
SW1A 2NS

**United Kingdom Central Council for
Nursing, Midwifery and Health Visiting
(UKCC)**
23 Portland Place
London
W1N 3AF

SELF-HELP GROUPS

Alcohol and drugs

Alcoholics Anonymous
PO Box 1
Stonebow House
Stonebow
York
YO1 2NJ
Helplines 0171 352 3001; 01904 644026
Fax 01904 629091

Drinkline
(National Alcohol Helpline)
7th Floor
Weddel House
13–14 West Smithfield
London
EC1A 9DL
Helplines 0171 332 0202; 0345 320202
Fax 0171 332 0127

Drugline
9a Brockley Cross
London
SE4 2AB
Helpline 0181 692 4975
Fax 0181 692 9968

National Drugs Helpline
PO Box 5000
Glasgow
G12 9BL
Helpline 0800 776600

QUIT
Victory House
170 Tottenham Court Road
London
W1P 0HA
Helpline 0800 002200
Fax 0171 388 5995

Bereavement

Cot Death Society
1 Browning Close
Thatcham
Newbury
Berks
RG18 3EF
Helpline 01635 861771
Fax 01635 861771

Cruse Bereavement Care
Cruse House
126 Sheen Road
Richmond
Surrey
TW9 1UR
Helpline 0181 332 7227
Fax 0181 940 7638

Child Death Helpline
Great Ormond Street Hospital for Children NHS Trust
London
WC1N 3JH
Helpline 0800 282 986
Fax 0171 813 8516
A confidential helpline staffed by bereaved parents offering support
to anyone affected by the death of a child.

Sudden Death Support Association
Chapel Green House
Chapel Green
Wokingham
Berks
RG40 3ER
Helpline 01734 790790
Fax 01734 790790

Stillbirth and Neonatal Death Society
(SANDS)
28 Portland Place
London
W1N 4DE
Helpline 0171 436 5881
Fax 0171 436 3715

Cancer

Breast Cancer Care
Kiln House
210 New Kings Road
London
SW6 4NZ
Helplines 0500 245 345; 0171 384 2344

British Association of Cancer United Patients
(BACUP)
3 Bath Place
Rivington Street
London
EC2A 3JR
Information helpline 0800 181199
Counselling helpline 0171 696 9000
Fax 0171 696 9002

**Cancer and Leukaemia in Childhood
(CLIC)**
12–13 King Square
Bristol
BS2 8JH
Helpline 0117 924 8844
Fax 0117 924 4505
Supports young people under 21 who have any form of cancer or
leukaemia and their families.

Cancerlink
17 Britannia Street
London
WC1X 9JN
Helplines 0800 132905; 0800 591028 (for young people affected by
cancer); 0800 590415 (Asian helpline)
Fax 0171 833 4968

National Cancer Alliance
PO Box 579
Oxford
OX4 1LB
Helpline 01865 793566
Fax 01865 251050
For patients and professionals.

Carers

Association of Crossroads Care Attendant Schemes
10 Regent Place
Rugby
Warwickshire
CV21 2PN
Helpline 01788 573 653
Fax 01788 565 498

Carers National Association
Head Office
2025 Glasshouse Yard
London
EC1A 4JS
Helplines 0345 573369; 0171 490 8898

Children

NSPCC
42 Curtain Road
London
EC2A 3NH
Helpline 0800 800 500
Fax 0171 825 2763

Childline
2nd Floor Royal Mail Building
Studd Street
London
N1 0QW
Helpline 0800 1111
Fax 0171 230 1001

Cystic Fibrosis Trust
Alexandra House
5 Blyth Road
Bromley
Kent
BR1 3RS
Helpline 0800 454482
Fax 0181 313 0472

National Autistic Society
276 Willesden Lane
London
NW2 5RB
Helpline 0181 830 0999
Fax 0181 451 5865

National Deaf Children's Society
15 Dufferin Street
London
EC1Y 8PD
Helpline 0800 252380
Fax 0171 251 5020

National Meningitis Trust
Fern House
Bath Road
Stroud
Glos
GL5 3TJ
Helpline 0345 538118
Fax 01453 753588

Disability

Disability Alliance
89–94 Wentworth Street
London
E1 7SA
Helpline 0171 247 8763
Fax 0171 247 8765

**Down's Syndrome
Association**
155 Mitcham Road
London
SW17 9PG
Helpline 0181 682 4001
Fax 0181 682 4012

Dial UK
Park Lodge
St Catherine's Hospital
Tickhill Road
Doncaster
DN4 8QN
Helpline 01302 310123
Fax 01302 310404
A disability helpline.

**Information Service
on Disability**
Oak Tree Lane Centre
Oak Tree Lane
Selly Oak
Birmingham
B29 6JA
Helpline 0121 414 1495
Fax 0121 627 8210

**Mencap (Royal Society for
Mentally Handicapped
Children and Adults)**
117–23 Golden Lane
London
EC1Y 0RT
Helplines 0171 454 0454; 0171 696 5593
Fax 0171 608 3254

Royal National Institute for the Blind (RNIB)
224 Great Portland Street
London
W1N 6AA
Helpline 0171 388 1266
Fax 0171 388 2034

Royal National Institute for Deaf People (RNID)
19–23 Featherstone Street
London
EC1Y 8SL
Helpline 0870 605 0123
Fax 0171 296 8199

Scope (Cerebral Palsy)
12 Park Crescent
London
W1N 4EQ
Helpline 0800 626 216
Fax 0171 436 2601

Health advice and support

Arthritis Care
18 Stephenson Way
London
NW1 2HD
Helpline 0800 289 170
Fax 0171 916 1505

Continence Foundation Helpline
The Dene Centre
Castle Farm Road
Newcastle upon Tyne
NE3 1PH
Helpline 0191 213 0050
Fax 0191 404 6876

Motor Neurone Disease Association
PO Box 246
Northampton
NN1 2PR
Helpline 0345 626262
Fax 01604 624726

Multiple Sclerosis Society
25 Effie Road
Fulham
London
SW6 1EE
Helpline 0171 371 8000
Fax 0171 736 9861

Muscular Dystrophy Group
7–11 Prescott Place
Clapham
London
SW4 6BS
Helpline 0171 720 8055
Fax 0171 498 0670

**National Association for Colitis
and Crohn's Disease (NACC)**
4 Beaumont House
Sutton Road
St Albans
Herts
AL1 5HH
Helpline 01727 844296
Fax 01727 844296
Information and support for those affected by inflammatory bowel
diseases.

National Asthma Campaign
Providence House
Providence Place
London
N1 0NT
Helpline 0345 010203
Fax 0171 704 0740

National Eczema Society
163 Eversholt Street
London
NW1 1BU
Helpline 0171 388 4800
Fax 0171 388 5882

National Endometriosis Society
Suite 50
Westminster Palace Gardens
1–7 Artillery Row
London
SW1P 1RL
Helpline 0171 222 2776
Fax 0171 222 2781

National Kidney Federation
6 Stanley Street
Worksop
Notts
S81 7HX
Helpline 01909 487795
Fax 01909 481723

National Osteoporosis Society
PO Box 10
Radstock
Bath
BA3 3YB
Helpline 01761 472721
Fax 01761 471104

National Society for Epilepsy
Information Department
Chalfont St Peter
Gerrards Cross
Bucks
SL9 0RJ
Helpline 01494 601400
Fax 01494 871927

Pain Concern (UK)
PO Box 318
Canterbury
Kent
CT2 0GD
Helpline 01227 264677

Spinal Injuries Association
76 St James's Lane
London
N10 3DF
Helpline 0181 883 4296
Fax 0181 444 3761

Stroke Association
CHSA House
123–127 Whitecross Street
London
EC1Y 8JJ
Helpline 0171 490 7999
Fax 0171 490 2686

UK Thalassaemia Society
107 Nightingale Lane
London
N8 7QY
Helpline 0181 348 0437
Fax 0181 348 2553

Victim Support
National Office
Cranmer House
39 Brixton Road
London
SW9 6DZ
Tel 0171 735 9166
Fax 0171 582 5712

Mental health

Alzheimer's Disease Society
Gordon House
10 Greencoat Place
London
SW1P 9PH
Helpline 0171 306 0606
Fax 0171 306 0808

Depression Alliance
35 Westminster Bridge Road
London
SE1 7QB
Helpline 0171 633 9929
Fax 0171 633 0559

Manic Depression Fellowship
8–10 High Street
Kingston upon Thames
Surrey
KT1 1EY
Tel 0181 974 6550
Fax 0181 974 6600

Mind
(The Mental Health Charity)
15–19 Broadway
London
E5 4BQ
Helpline 0345 660163
Fax 0181 522 1725

National Schizophrenia Fellowship
(NSF)
28 Castle Street
Kingston upon Thames
Surrey
KT1 1SS
Helpline 0181 974 6814
Fax 0181 547 3862

The Samaritans
10 The Grove
Slough
SL1 1QP
Helpline 0345 909090
Fax 01753 819004

Older people

Age Concern England
Astral house
1268 London Road
London
SW16 4ER
Tel 0181 679 8000
Fax 0181 679 6069

Counsel and Care
Twyman House
16 Bonny Street
London
NW1 9PG
Helplines 0800 300 7585; 0171 485 1566
Fax 0171 267 6877
Information and advice for people over 60.

Help the Aged
61–8 St James's Walk
London
EC1R 0BE
Helpline 0800 650065
Fax 0171 250 4474

Sexual health, contraception, pregnancy and childbirth

Body Positive
51b Philbeach Gardens
London
SW5 9EB
Helpline 0171 373 9124
Fax 0171 373 5237
Information and support for people with HIV/AIDS.

British Pregnancy Advisory Service
Austy Manor
Wootton Wawen
Solihull
West Midlands
B95 6BX
Helpline 0345 304030
Fax 01564 794935

**Brook Advisory
Centres**
165 Grays Inn Road
London
WC1X 8VD
Helplines 0171 713 9000; 0171 713 8000
Fax 0171 833 8182

Child
Charter House
42 St Leonards Road
Bexhill on Sea
East Sussex
TN40 1JA
Helpline 01424 732361
Fax 01424 731858
Support, counselling and information for people suffering effects of infertility.

**Family Planning
Association**
2–12 Pentonville Road
London
N1 9FP
Helpline 0171 837 4044
Fax 0171 837 3042

**Issue
(The National Fertility Association)**
509 Aldridge Road
Great Barr
Birmingham
B44 8NA
Helpline 0121 344 4414
Fax 0121 344 4336

Miscarriage Association
c/o Clayton Hospital
Northgate
Wakefield
West Yorks
WF1 3JS
Helpline 01924 200799
Fax 01924 298834

National AIDS Helpline
PO Box 5000
Glasgow
G12 9BL
Helpline 0800 567123

Terrence Higgins Trust
52–4 Grays Inn Road
London
WC1X 8JU
Helpline 0171 242 1010
Legal helpline 0171 405 2381
Fax 0171 242 0121

**National Childbirth Trust
(NCT)**
Alexandra House
Oldham Terrace
Acton
London
W3 6NH
Helpline 0181 992 8637
Fax 0181 992 5929

Single parents

Gingerbread
16–17 Clerkenwell Close
London
EC1R 0AA
Helpline 0171 336 8184
Fax 0171 336 8185

GLOSSARY

Acute Health care that deals with short-term injury or illness, which is often known as an 'episode' of care, so *acute* hospitals, or *acute* care.

Allopathic Western medicine, which emphasises the scientific, biomedical method of treating particular symptoms.

Alternative medicine/therapy Treatments which use approaches to health care which are unconventional according to established western medical practices, e.g. acupuncture or reflexology, also known as *complementary* medicine/therapy.

Assessment A judgement about a person's capability (mental or physical state), or their financial circumstances, in order to provide services according to individual needs, so *needs assessment*.

Capitation Usually referring to money, this is the amount allowed 'per head', i.e. for each individual. A GP gets a capitation fee for every person on the list.

Charter A written statement of the rights of people and the standards of service they can expect. This can be a national charter or a local pledge from a hospital or GP.

Chronic Long-term health condition which will not be sorted out in the short term. Asthma and diabetes are two chronic conditions. See *acute*.

Clinician General name for someone who is professionally trained for clinical work, so usually means a doctor or nurse or a paramedical therapist, e.g. physiotherapist.

Community care Used broadly this just means any professional health care which takes place outside a formal health setting, such as a hospital or clinic. But also used to mean the change from treating long-term health problems (mental illness, learning difficulties) in institutions to supporting people in their homes.

Community health council (CHC) Parts of the NHS which monitor the health services in a particular part of the country and represent patients, either individually (e.g. with a complaint) or collectively (e.g. over closures).

Complementary medicine/therapy See *alternative medicine/therapy.*

Care programme approach A way of providing health services which put the individual patient in the centre and develops a team of different workers to support the individual. Used most frequently as an approach to patients with mental health problems.

Day case Hospital health care which is provided the day the patient comes into hospital, allowing them to leave the same day, without an overnight stay.

Department of Health That part of government which is responsible to parliament for health and personal social services, headed by the Secretary of State for Health, who is a government cabinet minister.

Discharge The act of leaving hospital, and so leaving the formal care of the doctor who is treating you. Can be done either by the doctor or by you, providing you are a voluntary patient.

General Medical Council (GMC) Statutory body which registers and regulates (including disciplining) all doctors who are allowed to practise medicine in the UK.

Health authority NHS organisations which are responsible for the health of a geographical population and the health care that population receives. They do this by commissioning services from hospitals, community health services and GPs.

Health centre A building from which primary care and community health services are available, including GP surgeries, maternity, mother and child care, day care services for particular groups of people, and a range of clinics and health groups.

Health check Sometimes called 'human MOT' , these can be general checks on your state of health (blood pressure, weight, activity) or specific to age (over 75s) or for child development. May also be carried out for personal insurance purposes.

Health Services Commissioner Also called the health ombudsman. Investigates and passes judgement on serious complaints about health services (but not about individual doctors or nurses).

Informed consent Permission for treatment given by a patient to a doctor (often in writing). The patient must understand what the treatment is, including the possible outcomes of the treatment and any alternatives to the treatment, before the consent can be said to be informed.

Inpatient Someone who has been admitted to a hospital and is under the care of a doctor.

Locum A doctor who is temping, i.e. filling in for another.

Means testing Assessing the financial state of someone, usually with the intention of finding whether they qualify for particular service.

Minor injuries unit A walk-in service staffed by nurses and doctors to treat non-serious accidents and injuries which do not require the back-up of a fully staffed general hospital.

Needs assessment See *assessment*.

NHS Executive The most senior management level of the NHS, run by civil servants who are directly responsible to health ministers for the day-to-day running of the health service.

NHS trust An organisation within the health service responsible for running a particular set of services, such as a hospital, mental health services, or (shortly) primary care services.

Non-executive director A person who sits on the management board of an NHS trust, health authority or a primary care group, to support the running of the organisation, but who is not employed by that organisation.

Outpatient Someone who comes to consult a specialist doctor without being admitted to hospital.

Palliative care Care which is given to relieve symptoms, such as pain, rather than to cure an illness. Often associated with the care of people who are dying.

Paramedic Someone trained to provide health care who is not a doctor, e.g. providing emergency care to stabilise someone whose life is threatened, before medical care can be given.

Primary care The first point of contact with the health care system, provided by general practitioners and other health professionals, such as nurses, health visitors, dentists, community pharmacists and opticians.

Primary care group New way of arranging general practitioner services into groups of around 50 GPs who are responsible for organising the overall care of their patients.

Primary care team The group of health professionals, including GPs, nurses, health visitors, counsellors, physiotherapists, social workers, etc., who provide primary care services.

Rationing Decision taken by the NHS to limit particular treatments, or even exclude particular services, primarily because the demand for services exceeds what the health service can afford.

Screening Testing to reveal health problem which is not evident to the individual. This may be done as part of a national programme (for cancer of the breast or cervix) or because a person may be particularly prone to disease because of family history. The purpose is to pick up early signs of health problems to prevent more serious illness.

Specialist A clinical professional who has trained in a particular branch of health care and has been 'accredited' as an expert in that branch by the profession.

Secondary care Specialist care, usually given in hospitals, and usually after the person has been seen by a GP.

Statutory A service which is provided as a result of an act of parliament and which is answerable to parliament.

Tele-medicine Medical care which involves pictures of the patient being 'broadcast' to a remote site to be used by a clinician who is providing clinical advice or treatment, sometimes as part of a team, but at a distance from the patient.

Terminal care Care of people who are dying. See *palliative care*.

Tertiary care Referral from a specialist doctor to another specialist who has a particular expertise which is not available locally, such as at a regional or national cancer centre.

United Kingdom Central Council (UKCC) The registration and regulatory body (including discipline) for nurses.

Voluntary A misleading term, as many voluntary services do not use volunteers and may be providing essential services. Voluntary organisations are not public services and their services are not part of the state, although they may work very closely with public services and be governed by statutory regulations.

Waiting list/time The number of people waiting for a particular service after having been seen by and accepted for treatment by the specialist. The waiting time is the length of the wait, after acceptance.

INDEX

Note: Page numbers in **bold** numbers indicate Glossary entries and in *italics* indicate addresses and/or telephone numbers.